WOMEN AND MORAL IDENTITY

Elisabeth J. Porter

ALLEN & UNWIN

The book is dedicated to Norman and to
Shantala, Simon and Luke—with my love.

First published in 1991
Allen & Unwin Pty Ltd
8 Napier Street, North Sydney, NSW 2059

National Library of Australia
Cataloguing-in-Publication entry:

Porter, Elisabeth J.
  Women and moral identity.

    Bibliography.
    Includes index.
    ISBN 0 04 442332 2.

    1. Feminism—Philosophy. 2. Ethics. I. Title.

305.4201

Set in 10/11pt Sabon by Graphicraft Typesetters Ltd, Hong Kong
Printed by SRM Production Services Sdn Bhd, Malaysia

WOMEN AND MORAL IDENTITY

Community, Identity and Difference: *Racism, Sexism and Feminism in Australia*
Jan Pettman

Contemporary Western European Feminism 1968–1988
Gisela Kaplan

Dissenting Opinions: *Feminist explorations in law and society*
Regina Graycar (editor)

Female Crime: *The Construction of Women in Criminology*
Ngaire Naffine

Feminine/Masculine and Representation
Edited by Terry Threadgold and Anne Cranny-Francis

Gender Shock: *Practising feminism on two continents*
Hester Eisenstein

The Gifthorse: *A Critical Look at Equal Employment Opportunity in Australia*
Gretchen Poiner and Sue Wills

Intersexions: *Gender/Class/Culture/Ethnicity*
Edited by Gill Bottomley, Marie de Lepervanche and Jeannie Martin

Law and the Sexes: *Explorations in Feminist Jurisprudence*
Ngaire Naffine

Male Violence: Female Target
Jan Horsfall

Populate and Perish: *Australian Women's Fight for Birth Control*
Stefania Siedlecky and Diana Wyndham

The Promise and the Price: *The struggle for equal opportunity in women's employment*
Clare Burton

Same Difference: *Feminism and Sexual Difference*
Carol Bacchi

Sexual Subversions: *Three French Feminists*
Elizabeth Grosz

Contents

Acknowledgements

My doctoral dissertation forms the basis for this book. Bill Brugger has actively encouraged the progress of ideas and offered useful advice. I appreciate immensely the constructive critical comments made by Lorraine Code, Carol Gould, Genevieve Lloyd and Denise Russell. Angela McKay has been an excellent typist. Deborah Conyngham has given sound editorial advice. My parents, Harrold and Gwenda Steward, have consistently encouraged me. I am extremely grateful to Norman—as my most astute critic and best friend, his sensitivity is indispensable. Finally, Shantala, Simon and Luke have waited enthusiastically for the completion of this book.

Introduction

In Chapter One, I establish the relationship between feminism and philosophy. A factor inhibiting this relationship is the tendency of traditional philosophy to value what is abstract and universal over the concrete and particular concerns important to feminism. I resolve this dilemma by outlining a concrete universality that stresses the common attributes humans share and the range of differences that make each individual unique. I then review the current debates on feminist philosophy and gender difference, establishing the importance of the sex–gender relation in our evolving identities. In outlining the feminist debate on epistemology and ontology, I also explain the reciprocal relationship between knowing and being. While acknowledging that differences add to the rich complexity of multiple notions of moral identity, I diffuse certain feminist and philosophical notions of the subject. I hint at the limitations of ethical relativism in failing to address the specific articulation of modern selfhood.

Thus, I suggest four central themes that avoid such relativism and help formulate adequate alternative notions of moral identity. These themes recur in all of the following chapters in various forms. They are that of the *narrative unity* of subjects, the development of this unity through the growth of a *self-in-relations*, which occur within a context of the *reciprocity of knowing and being*, and affirm the importance of *character models*. While the integration of these themes into a developmental idea of the self has particular appeal to women in that its theoretical formulation emerges largely from women's practical experiences, it is, in principle, applicable also to men.

In Chapter Two, I argue that *moral dualism* lies at the basis of four major concepts—*nature, reason, individualism*, and *moral development*—and, as conventionally used, acts against women being acknowledged as fully fledged moral identities. Having established the gender basis of moral dualism, I note how each side of the polarity is valued hierarchically within traditional philosophy. Historically, the side of the polarity attributed to typical masculine ideals is prized over its opposite. Typical ideals of the feminine are defined as residual to such prized traits, as opposite to philosophical ideals. In these terms, women are seen as incomplete, inferior subjects.

Dualistic ideals are not incidental to personhood but strongly affect the formation of self-identity. I examine a gynocentric account of identity that stresses the uniqueness of female experience and yet which claims to transcend dualism. I expose the limitations of this extreme gynocentric view, not only for its rejection of men and negative forms of masculinity, but also for its female exclusivity and reversion to naturalistic tendencies. The gynocentric account fails to fulfil the task it set itself, namely, to transcend dualism.

In response, I propose a philosophy of synthesis. I question the inevitability of polar opposites which rely on a monism or a dualism, or any separatism between the sexes. I suggest, rather, that we reformulate such seeming opposites as pairs, albeit pairs that often stand in tension. I argue that a balanced idea of identity requires men and women to incorporate elements of these pairs into their lives. Subsequent chapters repeatedly extend this philosophy of synthesis.

In Chapter Three, I trace the association of women with nature. I compare varying philosophical definitions of personhood with certain feminist definitions. The biological component of 'nature', particularly in the lives of women, is often problematic. Dominant responses to this issue deny biology's relevance to moral status, impute a notion of biological destiny, or see women's traditional association with nature as something that should be embraced. As a result of the deficiencies in such responses, I affirm the importance of viewing the relationship between nature, women and morality in terms of a combination of various factors: nature, culture, reproductive potential and individuality. These factors intermesh to influence what we recognise as 'women's nature', which is not a static, purely biological phenomenon, but one that has some components women share, some components affected by culture, race, age or life-style, and some that may only be described as 'individual differences'.

The point of trying to articulate moral nature is practical, rather than theoretical: that is, to determine what conditions might allow it to flourish. I suggest that, while moral subjects need a sense of purpose to provide direction for moral pursuits and to provide meaning for the overall narrative of their life, 'purpose' has in the past been conveniently tied to biological nature and reproductive functions. The integration of purpose and human growth with potential lessens the likelihood of static notions of nature and provides open-ended possibilities for the development of human nature.

In Chapter Four, I examine the association of reason and objectivity with masculine ideals, and passion and subjectivity with feminine ideals. I distinguish between deliberate, explicit sexist categorisations and genderist categorisations, which are more elusive and built into gender character ideals. For example, the philosophical ideal of reason is seen not only as a public ideal of the citizen and the full moral subject, but as a masculine ideal. The association of women with passion is viewed frequently in philosophy as a disorder that prevents the ultimate realisation of reason. Women's confinement (voluntary or otherwise) to the sphere of particularity does encourage the development of love, affection, intimacy and intuition, emotions which may seem technically non-rational, but are certainly not irrational. The re-evaluation of such passionate expressions, and the sphere in which they flourish, is an important achievement of contemporary feminist philosophy.

Intrinsic to this re-evaluation is the assessment of the influence of early rigid gender socialisation. I contrast the way girls frequently are encouraged to develop a relational identity based on their connections with others, with the way boys often are encouraged to develop a strong sense of masculine autonomy. This autonomy reinforces emotional distancing and self-sufficiency, and parallels the modern notion of the successful, rational public being, who can retreat to the private sphere for emotional refurbishing. Again, in maintaining an emphasis on balance, integration and synthesis, I suggest that many of the problems involved in typical notions of reason and passion may be resolved through a concept of 'rational, passionate personhood'. This concept seeks to remove the association of reason with maleness, and passion with femaleness. The possibility of synthesis creates a liberating potential.

Chapter Five shows how many of the tenets relating to the successful public person come to the fore within the liberal individualistic tradition. Despite the progressiveness of many liberal characteristics, the association with individualism works contrary to its being a satisfactory theory of social subjects. Indeed, with its stress on the individual as prior to the community, on autonomy and the individual rights of self-sufficient being, liberal individualism tends to reduce rational choice to subjective preference, or to instrumental bargaining.

Liberal feminism is unavoidably tarred with the same brush. Its emphasis is on equality and the provision of equal rights, an emphasis indispensable in changing legislation and procuring substantial formal equality and rights. Yet, the political changes are fraught with difficulties because women simultaneously claim equality with men and clear differences from them. The conjunction of equality with difference must be carefully articulated. I look, thus, at equal rights to civic and contractual relations. I contend that problems of instrumentality intrinsic to such relations work, at a general level, contrary to the flourishing of social subjects and, at a specific level, contrary to the intimate ways of relating that many women operate in and wish to continue developing. I explore the possibility that some injection by women of a strong relational orientation into the public sphere may act as a counter to the negative dimensions of contractual relations and that this may be a positive ramification of liberal feminism.

Chapter Six explores the influences of moral development on

the idea of women and moral identity. Kohlberg's influential views on moral stages are summarised, and criticised for being too concerned with formalism at the expense of the content of moral dilemmas. I then explore the idea of a differential morality between women and men, as presented particularly by Gilligan. To focus this discussion, I offer explanations as to why people who spend a lot of time nurturing others tend to develop a high degree of moral responsibility. I examine an attitude of 'maternalism' that emerges through forms of living that are intensely contextual-based and that invite a focus on the consequences of dilemmas for others. While this attitude is commendable, and preferable to an individualistic concern with rights, I show how, when women concentrate on moral responsibility and relations at the expense of their own individual rights, then not only do they 'lose' by not claiming their legitimate place in the moral world, but the 'morality' of their actions is in itself questionable. This is because a balanced view of the moral subject is one which considers the needs and the rights of both self and others.

To support this argument, I contrast Gilligan's vision of moral maturity with the concept of the self-in-relations I progressively develop. While Gilligan's vision aims at an integration of traditional feminine and traditional masculine moral concerns, I suggest that her conclusions lack a critical questioning of the relationship between these concerns and so I examine some of these important internal relations. The chapter weighs the possible advantages and disadvantages of combining an autonomous self with a caring self, and vice-versa. I conclude that the concept 'self-in-relations' opens enormous possibilities in being applicable to both men and women.

Chapter Seven is based on the positive affirmation by certain groups of women of their claims to moral differences. In surveying women's motivations for activity in the peace movement, it seems clear that they are offering an analysis of their selves distinct from men. While this analysis aids our understanding of why some women believe they think and act in particular ways, it leaves women practicing roles and ideals of the feminine that have been part of women's confinement to the private sphere. The involvement of women in the eco-feminist movement is quite different. While this movement is based on traditional notions of women being peaceful nurturers in harmony with nature, it is explicitly feminist and self-critical. It does not unreflectively practice traditional traits, but merges such traits with the specific feminist attempt to eliminate the domination of nature and hence, tangentially, the domination of women as nature. I use this analysis as a springboard to discuss the broader issue of military domination. I show the intrinsic connections between military pursuits, aggressive masculinity and ideals of citizenship. In this context, the moral worthiness of women's involvement in combat is assessed. I concede that, if the right to combat is an essential dimension of citizenship, then it is a right women should possess, even if it is not claimed.

My argument explores the possibility of developing a positive conception of women and moral identity. I set three tasks to establish this possibility: criticism, conservation and construction. I argue that standard interpretations of five concepts—moral dualism, nature, reason, individualism and moral development—work against women being accepted as full moral subjects. Women's claims to their equality with men, and their simultaneous affirmation of their differences, provide many useful examples of this. I criticise both 'femininity' and 'masculinity' and develop a concept of moral identity that, in encouraging particular differences, can include both women and men.

1 An approach to feminism and philosophy

In order to examine the issue of *women and moral identity*, this study undertakes two major tasks. First, it looks at the way traditional philosophical ideals of moral identity are biased against women, that is, how these ideals deny women equal moral status with men, and how they attribute moral significance to traits customarily associated with maleness and underplay the moral importance of traits customarily associated with femaleness. Second, this study proposes alternative conceptions of moral identity that explicitly incorporate the 'female' traits given minimal attention in traditional philosophical theories. This alternative celebrates women as moral identities, but also entails a moral vision that reflects a synthesis of traits previously ascribed, mistakenly, to one or the other gender.

Before proceeding to these tasks, however, it is worth preparing the ground by showing how the position to be developed here relates to recent work in feminist philosophy. Although there are gestures in its direction, the theme of women and moral identity has not yet received the full treatment it is due. Nevertheless, my position derives in part from a certain understanding of the relationship between feminism and philosophy, is clearly indebted to a variety of insights contained in feminist philosophical literature, and yet is also at odds with certain recent trends in this literature.

In order to clarify the relation of my study to recent feminist philosophical literature, I start with a general discussion of the relationship between feminism and philosophy, and reveal some disputes in their perceived purposes. Secondly, I explain how these disputes have emerged within contemporary feminist philosophical debates on the question of sexual differentiation. Thirdly, I explain how these disputes over sexual differentiation contrast with the concept of moral identity I develop throughout the book. I explore the question that others raise also, namely, when do arguments of moral difference serve progressive ends, and when are they counter-progressive, if not reactionary?

Concerted philosophical research on feminist issues emerged in the early 1970s. The issues included sexual justice, equality, reproduction, abortion, child-care, pornography, rape, domestic violence, domestic labour and work opportunities. The early aim of this research was to criticise, from a feminist perspective, conventional scholarship in the history of ideas and contemporary political and moral philosophy.[1] The strategy was to correct the historical record, and to challenge the universality of many philosophical claims that systematically conflate human nature with male nature. In order to reinforce the philosophical foundations of feminist theory, feminist philosophers sought to expose the explicitly moral dimension of questions feminists posed. This was important, for issues such as those outlined above were previously considered in traditional philosophy as domestic, and hence not crucial to philosophical discussion.

Two significant problems emerged in early attempts to integrate philosophy and feminism. First, there was an initial difficulty in relating moral-philosophical considerations to women's sense of uniqueness. Hence, there was a tendency for discussions on the issue of women and morality to orientate towards two extremes, one emphasising the 'woman' side of the issue (Firestone, 1970; Morgan, 1970)[2] and the other the 'conceptual moral-philosophical' side (Richards, 1982). For example, those supporting the woman's side emphatically stressed women's right to choose on such matters as abortion, sexual preference, children and jobs, but had little to say about the moral basis on which their choices should rest. The typical emphases here lay in affirming the value of women's experiences, in stressing the need for self-determination, and in advocating the implementation of socio-political programmes that secured women's rights. These emphases gave prominence to moral concerns of the utmost importance to women, but were rarely informed by a clear grasp of the grounds of moral evaluation. On the other hand, where attempts were made to clarify such grounds, namely, when philosophical debates started to focus on feminist concerns, they were inclined to bypass the experiences from which the concerns derived. Initial philosophical emphases here were largely on conceptual analyses of moral problems such as choice, judgement, justice, equality and freedom. These conceptual analyses were often conducted with minimal reference to the experiential level which is important to feminism.

The first difficulty, then, was in many ways acute: some people highlighted women's experiences without the aid of philosophically articulated moral concepts, and others endeavoured to provide such concepts independently of the experiences they were intended to illuminate. This created an imbalance overcome only as equal weight is granted to both emphases so that, for example, abortion can be viewed as both a moral and a women's issue. A more balanced position stresses the interrelation of the two emphases (Vetterling-Braggin et al., 1981), as is recognised in a good deal of current feminist philosophy.

A second problem evident in early attempts to integrate moral philosophy and feminism concerned perceptions of their respective purposes. What seemed essential to the one seemed rather less so to the other. For instance, the purpose of challenging and rectifying the systematic philosophical devaluation of women's experience—characteristic of a feminism that was becoming more intellectually astute—was difficult to accommodate within the terms of mainstream moral philosophy, which did not recognise itself as inculpated by the charge of devaluation, but, rather, defined its purpose as that of understanding humans as humans. Accordingly, certain difficulties lay in the path of feminists trying to use moral philosophy. These centred on the presumption that philosophy was embarked upon a universal mission. In the hands of the most celebrated exponents this presumption received such varied influential construals as the following: the 'universal' interest of philosophy applies chiefly to males because female nature is seriously deficient; questions of sexual differentiation are of no consequence to philosophy because the main concern is with universal attributes of personhood, not particular ones; philosophy expresses its universal preoccupation through the image of a disembodied subject, unanchored in history and undistracted by particularities; typical feminine traits—piety, self-sacrifice, empathy—are not constitutive of definitions of a 'good person' or a full 'moral subject' (Allen, 1979).

The question, then, is whether these sorts of difficulties, which threaten to frustrate the purposes of feminism, can be overcome, so that the tension between philosophy and feminism can be reconciled, or whether they point to an unbridgeable chasm between the two.

Current feminist theory

The problems of merging philosophy and feminism meet with positive responses within current feminist theory. The common thread in these responses is a total opposition to philosophical mores that disregard the question of sexual differentiation. Yet, not only is this enterprise still viewed with scepticism by many academics, but there is no feminist consensus on how the question should be dealt with, or how the problems mentioned above should be resolved. There are three major approaches to these issues (Gatens, 1986a). (Specific references to advocates of these approaches appear later in the text.) The first position incorporates branches of radical feminism that adopt a theoretical separatism along sex–gender lines. Those who subscribe to this position identify the activity of traditional theorising with maleness and assume a necessarily oppressive relationship between feminism and philosophy. They accept that effective feminist political action therefore demands a dissociation from traditional theory. I consider this position to be largely negative since, in rejecting all theory as necessarily male-defined, and thus oppressive, it diminishes the possibility of constructing new theoretical approaches. This works counter to my specific goal of combining a critique of mainstream ideals of moral identity with the formulation of alternative approaches to identity.

Feminists in a second category accept a philosophical framework, but challenge the misogyny or omission of women within conventional philosophical scholarship. One response to this is to fill in the gaps or rectify the mistakes in this theory. People within this category see the addition of women's experience as transforming theory from a male-dominated enterprise into a human one. Its specifically feminist contribution is not always clear. Again, this approach is inadequate for my concerns, for the following reasons.

If it is the case that philosophy's problem lies solely in an inadequate content rather than framework, a project of inclusion and extension appears viable. Yet, if it can be shown that the basic philosophical capacities deemed crucial to selfhood have been constructed with typically masculine imagery, then the case becomes different. The attempt at equal inclusion has meant that women's sameness to men, that is, their humanity, is discussed but not their womanliness (Gross, 1986b). Elucidating the nature of 'womanliness' is a major task of this study. It is important because equality with men is valid only when the opportunities open to men and resultant practices can be endorsed. Close scrutiny reveals that until recent policy changes, 'equality of opportunity' has meant 'opportunity just like men's opportunities', (Code, 1986: 49). But it might be the case that such equality should not be wholeheartedly endorsed; that it involves distortions of one sort or another.

Accordingly, I question the validity of the hypothetical inclusion of women as equals into most traditional philosophers' positions, for this alters basic tenets of their ideas, and leaves their philosophy disjointed and historically inaccurate.[3] Many theorists have not accepted that women are equal, free, active citizens in the same sense as men. In not fitting neatly into familiar categories, women are often characterised as defying theorisation, thus forcing onto the agenda 'the woman question' (Gould, 1976: 39). I believe that a critical philosophy *can* adequately deal with issues like women's social role, their oppression and liberation, and that a more useful third approach to feminism and philosophy is to confront the conceptual biases within the mainstream philosophical tradition, so that the terrain of contest is theory, rather than 'woman' (Gross, 1986: 195).

Feminist philosophy

Thus, there is a shift of emphasis with feminists who now concentrate on the problems *within theory*, rather than within women's issues. This emphasis enables a broadening of the definition both of feminism and of what is philosophically relevant.

Regarding the first definition, I adopt a general notion of feminism as a perspective that seeks to eliminate the subordination, oppression, inequalities and injustices women suffer because of their sex. My emphasis is on the consequences of this for the self and for all relationships. I place feminism firmly within the context of male–female interaction.[4] Both men and women have been engaged in oppressive and distorted relations with each other, and both can benefit from, and contribute to, constructing creative alternatives. My understanding of feminism is equally concerned with the rearing of sons as with the rearing of daughters, and is concerned with relationships between men and women, as well as between women and between men. My objective is to formulate through this feminist understanding a developmental concept of personhood that emphasises human mutuality. This concept is an alternative to distorted relationships and permits an evaluation of actual relations between actual human beings (Held, 1987: 118).

I adopt as philosophically relevant that which is clear, logical, rational, objective, abstract, evident in principle as well as that which is intuitively persuasive, reliant on lived experience, subjectively known, or is particular or contingent. With those who accept such a definition, there is a consensus that feminist philosophy is a vital aspect of moral and political philosophy. What this actually means within feminist scholarship is that traditional tight distinctions between philosophy, political theory, politics, moral philosophy and ethics are loosened. While this does not encourage an undisciplined sliding between categories, it does permit overlaps and an acceptance of close interrelations between categories. Indeed, it enlarges the object domain of moral theory, so that there is 'no privileged subject matter of moral disputation' (Benhabib, 1987: 170). This permits links to be drawn between conceptual and practical connections associated with contemporary feminist projects and between traditional political and moral philosophical concepts such as justice, freedom, equality, human nature, rights, needs, rationality, expressivism, the good life, friendship, moral agency and identity.

My concern is to expose what is excluded from traditional philosophy, to ask why it has been excluded, what precisely is said, what is not said and what cannot be said. 'When intellectual critique is reflexive and self-critical, that is, when it both questions and questions how its questions have been and are being posed, then intellectual critique is truly philosophical' (Young-Bruehl, 1987: 209).

My questions relate to how and why the tradition of patriarchal discourse has been shaped and interpreted against women. A key structuring principle within patriarchy is *exclusion*, which prevents women from shaping and interpreting the tradition from their own unique, although not monolithic, experience. This is an exclusion of women as self-knowing persons. My project inserts the historical reality of women's lives into the philosophical tradition, not by discarding that tradition, or by rewriting it, but by confronting it with hitherto neglected experience, forcing it to become self-reflective and self-critical. The critical dimension of my approach attempts to unmask injustices and alienating experiences that negate or trivialise women. It recognises overt and covert forms of misogyny. It notes the absence of certain questions relating to women and reveals the role these silences play in suppressing ideals and practices of active female being.

Mine is a critical philosophical approach, intent on interpretation, and suggesting radical changes. In general terms, I examine the assumptions, basic premises, underlying logic and conclusions of philosophical and feminist literature. Rather than highlighting the entire works of specific theorists, or texts as the basis of debate, particular philosophers are examined where their writings relate to the themes with which I deal. My methodology involves interweaving three emphases—conservation, critique and construction. That is, I conserve what I view as valuable and explain why, criticise what appears inconsistent, inadequate, biased, or rooted in male experience alone, and then offer constructive alternatives. There are anticipatory, normative alternatives of moral identity and relationships. I express this methodology as both a 'practical theory' and a 'theoretical practice', an 'interweaving of strands that are simultaneously theoretical and practical' (Gross, 1986b: 202). My intent is to diagnose, to interpret, to understand and to invite changes.

I want to stress two aspects of this intention. First, any uniqueness in these changes lies not in merely affirming a principle of 'full humanity', but in women claiming this principle for themselves. In being freed of inhibition and self-deprecating tendencies of subservience, women can name themselves as authentic subjects. Second, what is novel about a feminist hermeneutical approach to critical philosophy 'is not the category of experience as a context of interpretation but rather the appeal to women's experience' (Ruether, 1985: 112). The idea of reinterpreting evidence from personally defined criteria is both promising in that it allows people to personally represent their particular lives, especially when it contradicts status quo, and dangerous in that it might not adequately record and analyse subjective dimensions of experience. While any discussion of a socially constructed subject must remain critical of a theory grounded in women's identities as gendered subjects, we need to represent women's activities as accurately as possible in the attempt to genuinely interpret underlying symbolic meaning. To use O'Brien's strong imagery, this involves 'labouring to give birth to a new philosophy of birth' (1983: 13). These images celebrate the fact that women bring certain female experiences related to nurture to the interpretive task. While this approach searches for a space where women can define their *selves*, there is no implication of uniform experiences, but a plurality of perspectives.

Clearly, the amount of moral experience open to all humans is vast but 'the contexts in which experience is obtained may make a difference' (Held, 1987: 113). I agree with those who argue that, while we currently need feminist moral theory to deal with significant differences of which we are now aware, the aim is that such theories will contribute to the development of non-sexist societies, new modes of togetherness and of relating to ourselves so that the need for such a distinctively feminist moral theory is rendered obsolete (Held, 1987: 113; Benhabib, 1987: 158). What emerges is not the philosophical categories of the past, nor a utopian blueprint, but an exploration into expanding possibilities for contemporary ideas of moral identity.

THE DEBATE: GENDER DIFFERENCE, PHILOSOPHY AND A FEMINIST PERSPECTIVE

Let us explore further the broadly construed on-going debate on sexual differentiation, within which my argument is situated. I want to clarify my position regarding three points within this debate, namely, the significance of gender, the relationship between knowing and being and the importance of affirming moral difference, with emphasis on how these points bear on moral agency.

Sex and gender as constitutive categories

Terms such as 'sex' and 'gender', 'femaleness' and 'femininity' are rarely without evaluative interpretation. These interpretations *affect* as well as *reflect* experience. Thus 'being a woman' affects notions of 'being' and, similarly, notions of 'female being' influence women's experience. In confronting the evidence of sex-role systems, feminist researchers sought to discover why 'being a woman' often appeared empirically and conceptually different from 'being a man'. Such researchers grew aware of the need to avoid a reductionist conclusion that might explain the difference in terms of a single causal factor, like biology or economics. What became clear, particularly in consciousness-raising groups at a grass roots level, is that the shared effects and consequences that may stem from being biologically female and treated 'as a woman' lie within a social construction of gender.

After these initial general tendencies were established in feminist research, sophisticated analysis of the sex–gender system escalated.

This system denotes the arrangements by which sex and procreation are shaped by human social intervention (Rubin, 1976: 165; Eisenstein ed., 1979), as a system of 'dominance made possible by men's control of women's productive and reproductive labour' (Harding, 1983: 311). The particular form of the system affects the type of asymmetrical or exploitative exchange relations that occur, which differ according to modes of production. The outstanding feature of the sex–gender system emanates from an underlying dynamic in all historically documented cultures, relating to the organisation of collective life and to cross-cultural similarities linked to nurturing (Chodorow, 1971; 1978). Despite variations in kinship patterns, there is a universal sexual division of labour where the domain of young children and most housework is the exclusive or major province of women. These common features are sufficiently conspicuous to constitute a sex-gender system which most women would recognise and, to some extent, identify with. This does not imply a common viewpoint but a shared organisation of social relations which has accomplished women's exclusion (Smith, 1979: 163) from much of what is socially valued.

Yet, while feminists have been keen to delineate demarcations between sex and gender, the relationship is more accurately perceived as dialectical, each creating the other, as 'an organic social variable' (Harding, 1983: 312), affecting the way in which social reality is organised, symbolically divided and experienced (Benhabib, 1987). Ideals of femaleness fundamental to social feminine practices evolve historically and interact with other variables. These ideals have formulated our perceptions of conventional feminine behaviour and appropriate attitudes towards female bodies. While in most cases 'biological woman' is circumscribed fairly clearly, the social and moral entity 'woman' is more complex. The same complexity occurs in trying to understand what is entailed in being a 'man'. When the relationship between sex and gender is viewed as a dynamic interaction, processes of oppression are uncovered and space is created for change.

To speak of women and moral identity is not to see women as a 'sex-class', or to invite a false universalism. The term 'sex-class' is used by certain radical feminists to delineate a sex dichotomy based in the biological reality of being potential child-bearers, and thus, in their terms, subjugated and dependent (Firestone, 1970; Mitchell, 1973). A discussion of sex-gender is analytically different from sex-class in being concerned with dialectical relations rather than single-cause theories. The nature of patriarchy ensures enough common experiences for it to be reasonable to talk of 'women' as a group in this way (Williams and Giles, 1978; Breakwell, 1979: 15). I refer particularly to the experiences that relate to reproduction, nurture, subordination and social marginality. I avoid, however, a 'metaphysical feminism' where women are seen to have an eternal, biological, historical oneness. This is because such a 'metaphysical feminism' states that all women posses an essential femininity (Morgan, 1977). In my understanding, this draws on a false universalism (Clavir, 1979).

Feminist debates on epistemology and ontology

The task now is to clarify the major debates among feminists concerning differences between a feminist perspective and a feminist standpoint, and then to clarify different views of the relationship between knowing and being. I contrast these views with my own position which argues for the coincidence of epistemological, ontological and ethical concerns.

Feminist perspective versus feminist standpoint

Within the literature a feminist perspective and a feminist standpoint share certain beliefs, yet also differ. Both view feminist approaches as a basis to move beyond oppressive relationships to new versions of human activity. Major differences affect the extent to which feminism is seen as a perspective to explain dimensions of relationships, or is seen in the case of a standpoint to embrace a comprehensive world-view.

For example, the feminist perspective I seek to develop draws directly on women's interpretations of their experience, but adopts a self-conscious recognition of the historical effects of subjugation. Furthermore, while I do not disregard substantive variables that do distinguish women, such as class, race, generation or religion, I do not deal in detail with these specific factors. To do so adequately would involve a detailed application of my analysis, which is not my primary purpose here. Rather, I explore the tensions invoked in de Beauvoir's (1975: 737) premise that the commonality of our humanity is more important than the peculiarities that distinguish human beings from one another. Nevertheless, it is crucial to try to understand the nature of our 'peculiarities'. In this context it requires exploring differences between 'female human being' and 'male human being'. Sexual being involves for some people a unity, for others a discordance, for others an acceptance of tensions.

This general understanding of a feminist perspective differs from a more specific feminist standpoint, which aims to develop 'a morally and scientifically preferable grounding for our interpretations and explanations of nature and social life' (Harding, 1986: 26). This grounding is regarded by feminist standpoint theorists as necessarily less perverse and distorting than knowledge constructed in alliance with masculine activity, and is supported by a variety of arguments, particularly in anthropology, biology, psychoanalysis, political economy, sociology of knowledge, and more recently in epistemology and moral philosophy.

9

The major feature of a feminist standpoint is its *engaged position*. We are familiar with a scientific approach or a liberal epistemology that perceives the correct standpoint to be the neutral, disinterested observer. This stands in stark contrast to a feminist standpoint which is explicitly and unashamedly engaged (Hartsock, 1983b: 285). Women, or feminists, (depending on the theorist), are seen in this literature to be in an epistemically privileged position in terms of addressing central issues that affect them. For example, a personal understanding of oppression is thought to be more perceptive than an 'expert' view.[5] This is relevant for any oppressed group, class, race or gender, in explaining, interpreting and critically examining their *own* condition, despite an accumulated heritage of disadvantages, powerlessness and crises of self-identity within such groups. In this context, the authority of the inquirer and the authority of the subjects of inquiry are on the same epistemological plane (Smith, 1974). Here the *knowing subject* and the *knowable object* are one and the same person. While a 'detached position' may accurately reflect certain lived experiences, it is qualitatively different from those experienced through engagement.

I see strengths and weaknesses in a standpoint approach. Scholars using this approach place immense significance on the possibility of comprehending one's own life as a unity. This unity is not the seamless, integrated concept of self that obscured female specificity, but is a first-hand knowledge of the diverse nature of female being, whereby the combined discrete elements contribute to overall moral identity. For example, Rose (1983: 142) argues that, in the case of many women, the knower, the world to be known, and the processes of knowing, reflect the unification of the general manual, mental and emotional activities characteristic of women's work. What Rose advocates is the understanding of women in a way that unites personal, social and biological factors. The specific unity Rose refers to can be explained in terms of the division of labour by gender, in that the daily maintenance and child-rearing in which many women engage for a significant part of their lives ensures a concrete and sensuous position. Women familiar with the processes of this position prize species reproduction as a paradigmatically human, moral act. De Beauvoir (1975) affirm's men's uniqueness in risking life, rather than women's in giving life. In the above debate, this signifies the reverse order of priorities. In my reckoning, the most valuable dimension to a standpoint is its stress on a *reciprocity between knowing and being*, a theme integral to my purposes.

While I am sympathetic to this emphasis, I see problems with other claims presented by feminist standpoint theorists. It may be argued that, to avoid romanticisation, the racial, ethnic, class, geographic and religious factors that distinguish women from each other must be considered within a standpoint and, in exposing such differences, 'the standpoint of women' is revealed as a meaningless concept (Soble,

1983). As will become evident, I see this problem occurring with the extreme women-centred perspectives. To speak 'in the women's voice' unavoidably assumes traditional notions of the feminine, however radical they appear on the surface. This does not permit the incorporation of differences.

I agree with Gadamer (1975: 269) that a situated standpoint may limit the possibility of vision. That is, it restricts a person's 'horizon', or the range of vision from a particular vantage point. A horizon incorporates simultaneously a perspective, a world-view, an orientation, a framework, a frame of reference and self-understanding. Gadamer's horizon implies a wider vision than has already been grasped by a standpoint, in that the horizon is being continually formed in an on-going dynamic. This involves the unified process of understanding, interpretation and application.

While there are conspicuous advantages with engaged positions, I see narrow feminist standpoints tending toward closed vision, understood as the opposite to Gadamer's 'horizon'. Such narrowness precludes the possible expansion of horizon or the opening of new horizons. On the other hand, when feminist theory takes different horizons seriously and engages in dialogue, a dynamic relationship of learning and developing occurs: the feminist interpreter allows the message of distant texts and ideas to question the validity of her personal horizons. Pre-understanding is scrutinised and prejudgements are displayed and assessed. What emerges is genuine dialogue with ideas, texts and other writers, and what Gadamer calls a 'fusion of horizons' occurs. While interpretation and understanding constitute the dynamic movement of this fusion, its application is manifest when, through texts, theories or practices, the interpreter's own broadened horizon creates a new expression.

In conclusion, I prefer to retain a critical stance on the question of whether the feminist standpoint is excessively rooted in a problematic politics of essentialised identities (Harding, 1986: 27). Clearly, the celebration of a feminine standpoint that embraces traditional versions of womanhood is distinct from a feminist standpoint that incorporates a critical stance on questions of identity. I hope to demonstrate that it is possible to construct a concept of moral identity that is open to a vast range of human 'horizons'.

Knowing, being and feminist trends

It would be misleading to give the impression that all strands of feminism incorporate similar ideas on knowing and being. Because they do not, it is germane to mention four significant variations, with greater attention given to the fourth position, which I support.[6] Undoubtedly, as Jaggar (1983) has systematically outlined, a commitment to a theory of human nature carries with it a commitment to a certain epistemology.

First, liberal feminist theories rest on an individualistic conception

11

of the subject where the human is seen to be a separate rational agent. This agent operates with a notion of 'objectivity' which is seen as lack of bias and defined by the inquiry's supposed independence from subjective interests. Devices to handle this include the postulation of rational spectators, veils of ignorance and neutral dialogues. The liberal feminist's concern with equal rights and equal opportunities means that she is obliged to adopt an impartial perspective as a rational, detached observer. In Chapter Five, I provide examples of advocates of this position and explain how it cannot easily adapt to differences among women.

Secondly, Marxist feminism differs drastically from a liberal conception. Humans are conceived as existing in dialectical interrelation with each other and with nature. The essential human activity is praxis, of which the development of human knowledge is just one aspect. That is, knowledge is not the abstract construct of a detached spectator, but emerges through practical, purposive activity. In orthodox Marxism, one's world-view, as well as one's material position, is seen to depend on one's class location. The adequacy of competing theories, or personal views, is measured according to how their contribution strengthens the power of the working class to undermine capitalist exploitation. Socialist feminists, aware that neither the activity of exchange nor productive activity allows an understanding of the domination of women, inject an emphasis on reproduction into their analysis as a more viable challenge to patriarchal concepts of knowledge and practice.

For radical feminism, a third variant of feminist analysis, the oppression of women is fundamental, requiring a self-conscious elaboration of a specifically feminist view of reality. Its methods include consciousness raising and activities which are collective, non-judgemental, supportive and personal. The emphases here include intuition, spiritual connection with others and special modes of knowing that either cause or are the effect of sensitivity and empathy to others. Opposing hierarchy and dualism, connections between the observer and the observed, the knower and the known, the subject and the object are valued. While this theory is guided by practical interests and informed by the entire range of emotions, the postulation of conventionally unrecognised modes of knowing increase exclusivist tendencies, and thus, reduce radical feminism's scholarly credibility.

A fourth category, with which my position identifies, asserts that the possibilities of understanding an integrated moral identity are more evident when epistemology and ontology coincide. Clearly, how people know themselves and are known by others, affects significantly their mode of being which, in turn, creates further possibilities for various modes of knowing. The full development of this argument involves both a critical exposure of the debilitating effects on women of imposed masculine ideals of the moral subject, and the articulation of a specifically feminist epistemology and ontology.

The background to my argument is as follows. In standard moral philosophy, the moral self is viewed as a disembedded and disembodied being. The tension is between universal selves and particular individuals. Feminist moral theory, on the other hand, views the self as closely entwined with significant others and thus emphasises the 'domain of particular others in relations with one another' (Held, 1987: 117). These 'others' are not abstract concerns, rational constructs or universal principles but other people whom we experience feelings for and perceptions of. At the core of the feminist epistemology and ontology I elaborate is a conception of the self–other *relationship* in contradistinction to a self–other opposition or abstraction. This core originates in women's experience with others, not in female nature. Mothering, in particular, is one of the best contexts in which to make explicit why familiar moral theories are so deficient in guiding action (Held, 1987: 118). That is, when a self-identity emerges predominantly from relational activity, where the demands require weighing claims, considering context and diverse actions in order to maximise harmony, it is not difficult to understand why reciprocity is central to this self-identity, and why this identity views an abstract, oppositional, dualistic conception of the person and ethics as inappropriate, if not perverse. With a distorted concept of identity, the recognition of others assumes an oppositional thrust, taking forms like antagonism, egotistic competition, conflict or violence. Women who attempt to succeed on masculine terms may also adopt similar stances.

Gender difference—particularity and multiplicity

The significance of 'difference' is another dimension in the current feminist debate. What is the place of particularity within a concept of interconnected selves? My concern is for accurate representation of the different, particular qualities that distinguish our unique individuality. Let us compare one particular feminist argument on multiplicity and fragmented identity with my own position, where I argue that a celebration of difference is part of accepting the multi-faceted nature of selfhood.

At a general level, feminist philosophy considers whether gender difference is to be celebrated, rejected, or simply understood. A prior concern is to determine whether there are significant gender differences and whether these might be integrally or contingently connected to notions of the self. One major impediment to this lies with the complex historical legacy surrounding the philosophical construction of the 'universal individual'. This construction ignores particularities and generally represents male, public citizens. Yet individuality is not a unitary abstraction but an embodied and sexually

13

differentiated expression (Pateman, 1986: 9). The feminist assertion of women's self as a subject of knowledge with particular perspectives, sometimes systematically different from men's, demands a redefinition of the nature and status of 'difference' itself. At this stage, I merely raise the importance of these questions to avoid being accused of idiosyncrasy in exploring women as moral subjects.

Nevertheless, this specific exploration does not imply uniformity, but involves open-ended multiple quests for difference (Braidotti, 1986: 60). This idea of multiplicity means more than non-uniformity, or even diversity. It implies interactive processes between individual concepts of selfhood, others' evaluations of differences, and social and moral valuations. Plural ideas of the self differ from relativist ideas in being subject to reference points outside of one's own self-expression and desires. That is, while acknowledging plural modes of being and actual differences among humans, my position does not necessarily support all of these pluralities and differences as morally and politically valid (Benhabib, 1987: 158). For example, it does not support modes of being which suppress, oppress or exploit others' self-expression. While I endorse the enormous range of possibilities which this quest for differences encourages, I have three reservations concerning possible inconsistencies in the basic premises and implications of the quest for multiplicity.

First, terms like 'proliferation of voices', 'plurality of perspectives', 'new positions of enunciation' and 'a new discursive space' abound in this literature. These are seen to apply to spaces wherein 'women can write, read and think *as women*' (Gross, 1986: 204). I support the struggle to find and articulate this 'space'. Yet it is inconsistent to argue for the desirability of difference, multiplicity and plurality, and then to restrict this exclusively to women as do theorists who strongly advocate this position.[7] Admittedly, it is consistent with a quest that concerns itself exclusively with the fate and future of women. But it is inconsistent with a presumption that a celebration of difference is based on accepting the existence and desirability of differences among *all* people.

This first reservation resembles my earlier criticism of exclusivity in extreme standpoint positions, including the tendency of some feminist ideologies to reject masculine ideas and achievement solely on the basis of the sex of the originators.[8] Surely, a critical evaluation of the male world can coincide with acknowledgement and appropriation of those things from the male world that have proved beneficial (Code, 1986: 64). What is required is the means to evaluate what is worthy of appropriating as humanly best. Later, I suggest some criteria we can use to assess what it might mean to create identities in which the best human qualities flourish. This resolution requires a rethinking of what it means to be a human being as well as what it means to assert a sex-specific identity.

My second reservation concerns the premise on which 'multiplicity' is often based, namely, that there can be no notion of female subjectivity, only a host of females. The phenomenon of 'feminist postmodernism' best illustrates the premise against which I am arguing. Along with other intellectual movements such as semiotics, deconstruction, structuralism, nihilism and branches of psychoanalysis, postmodernism shares a scepticism regarding universal claims of reason, progress, science, language and, in particular, the subject itself. Its starting point is the proposition that there is no external reference point in a material and discursive system. An offshoot of this proposition is the acceptance of the 'death of the subject', or at least a rejection of any strong sense of the subject. I too am critical of the static view of the subject, advocating, instead, a degree of commonalities and a host of pluralities. Postmodernists reject a concept of 'uniquely human consciousness' such as I am presenting, as fiction. In its place they assert identity as a game of interchangeable masks (Braidotti, 1986: 54), as partial and fragmentary. Postmodernist politics aspires to strategies, as the constant, dispersed quests for critical standpoints and points of resistance (Briadotti, 1986: 54) that 'cannot help but liberate and enslave' (Foucault, 1977: 5).

This approach, strong in French feminist theory and linguistics, embraces the specific fractured identities thrown up by modern life, including shifting configurations of class, race and gender. A woman who identifies herself as a black-feminist, a socialist-activist, and a single-welfare-mother absorbs these modern identities as paradoxical tendencies intrinsic to her self, which postmodernist positions maintain cannot be identified as a unity. The postmodernist sees the notion of a 'unity' as a delusion, and thus prefers 'permanent partiality' (Harding, 1986: 193) and 'oppositional consciousness' (Haraway, 1987).

Advocates of 'permanent partiality', propose that we accept a reality and an identity that constantly shifts, wavers, and maybe, but not necessarily, recombines (Wyatt, 1986: 125). They rely on the symbolic components of identity. With regard to this point, Gross, interpreting Kristeva, claims that the West does not accept that such 'a symbolic emphasis depends on a fragmented, chaotic, bodily libidinal, feminine energy' (1986a: 128). When the symbolic is combined with an 'oppositional consciousness', internal disputes or disagreements with others are not seen as issues to be resolved, but an indication of the need to come up with alternative questions. In this context, conceptual choices regarding revision of ideas, 'create no-win dilemmas' for 'there is no "we" of feminist theorising' (Harding, 1986: 244), hence no consensual answers.

My third reservation concerns the implications of the quest for multiplicity. While I endorse wholeheartedly the need to respect and to rejoice in differences, I have difficulty in agreeing that the postmodernist celebration of fracture, discontinuity, partiality, dissonance, oppositional consciousness, destabilised thoughts and fragmented identities should be seen as primary. I contend that discontinuity is frequently a negative, traumatic component of our lives, in instances such as disruption of studies or work, changes in homes or sexual partners or concepts of self. Destabilisation of thought, even if trying and confusing, has benefits when positive changes in attitudes and practices occur, but the benefits surely lie in the changes produced not in dissonance as such.

I find it difficult to envisage connectedness with others where there is an emphasis on the value of opposition. Under the auspices of opposing philosophical dichtomy, the postmodernist position appears to be celebrating another form of dichotomy. Many women have fought angrily against the confusion disjunction brings in being simultaneously mothers, students, writers, workers and political activists. To say the choice lies between a fictional unity or a fragmented conceptualisation of the self fails to arrive at alternatives that incorporate the full complexity of being a moral identity. Furthermore, the advocation of multiple subjectivity is a theory of self, not just a theoretical perspective. In claiming the self cannot be articulated, a notion of the subject is being defined, albeit minimally.

Yet a problem arises in fairly evaluating positions that reject normative discourse. Without normative guidelines, however, it is difficult to evaluate feminist experiments with identity. If sexism is bad, then we prescribe without controversy, 'Do not be sexist'. In order to answer intelligibly the questions, 'Why not?' or 'How do we know we're sexist?' or 'How do we determine what is non-sexist behaviour?', moral guidelines are necessary. I maintain that a rejection of the need for such guidelines accompanies the inability to cater adequately for the relationship between 'knowing and being'. Postmodernist feminism, in debunking the subject, cannot offer more than an acceptance of fractured identities.

In summary, I am advocating a quest for an evaluative, open-ended self-determination. Unity is fictional when it is a closed, essentialised view. While it is debatable whether having a unified personality is a moral goal, it does seem a morally worthy goal to face our important decisions with minimal self-fracturing obstacles (Hill, 1987: 136–137). A concept of an integrated life incorporates the variegated nature of fragmented selves, without the exaltation of discontinuity. This is quite different from a position that begins with the primacy of fragmented identities constructed against cultural hegemony. Indeed, I am not just discussing 'the ideal consensus of fictitiously defined selves' (Benhabib, 1987: 158–159), rather I am looking to explicate the contextual processes in practical morality and politics of the struggle of concrete, embodied selves. This necessitates a concerted effort in understanding what human *be-ing* is.

THE ARGUMENT: WHAT IS A MORAL IDENTITY?

What is meant by 'being a moral identity' and 'treating one as a moral identity'? First, we all possess a common humanity, or the significant defining features that distinguish humans. These features include rationality, articulate speech, deliberation, intention, agency, evaluation, responsibility, sociability, and the emotional capacity.[9] These features are constitutive of one's self-dignity, and should ensure that one is not the instrument of another's will, but is free to realise self-purposive activity.[10] My second point builds on this and addresses the need to discern what potential such capacities have to distinguish us from each other, beyond this basic shared humanity.

The context in which a discussion of the moral identity takes place is one in which the theoretical and practical basis of morality is confused. Typical modes of moral argument often pivot around squabbles about the logical validity of a debate. In a climate that explicitly links morality with subjective feelings, the validity of systematic justification of an individual's beliefs is undermined, for a pretense of principles often masks the expression of mere personal preference. This is exacerbated by the dominance of a philosophy of individualism, where the individual as moral agent is seen to be sovereign, and with utilitarianism, where individual desire is seen to be primary. In these situations, a paradox emerges. Each autonomous agent seeks to protect personal autonomy by not manipulating others, yet in asserting individual will, often cannot avoid the coercion of others (Yeatman, 1984). Both individualism and utilitarianism manifest themselves sociologically.

The issue of moral choice provides us with an appropriate example. Individualists, utilitarians and existentialists view the project of engaging in choice as paramount. I contend that this misinterprets moral choice as really no more than a *de facto* individual preference. In the absence of widespread consensus on ideals and the community good, there are few widely accepted justifications for 'good choices'. Even a language of morality dealing with honour, honesty, courage, consistency and fidelity is no longer common (MacIntyre, 1982), hence the priority placed by many on individual choice (e.g. Sartre, 1973). The central conflict here is that ethics presents itself as a body of principles having authority, independently of personal attitudes or preferences. How one feels should be irrelevant to the question of how one should live. This is not to understate the significance of emotions. On the contrary, ethics must address both our rational and our passionate capacities.

In affirming moral identity as the key to understanding our selves and our relationships with others, identity cannot be defined by reference to choice alone. Choice is one dimension of affirming identity. Our actions simultaneously express the commonality among people and the uniqueness and differences between them (Benhabib, 1987: 170). How can we comprehend this uniqueness? Benhabib defines identity as 'how I, as a finite, concrete embodied individual, shape and fashion the circumstances of my birth and family, linguistic, cultural and gender identity into a coherent narrative that stands as my life's story' (1987: 166). Her argument, which I expand in my own way, is that it is our moral identity as concrete selves that distinguishes us from each other. Identity embraces our *subjectivity*, the personal particularities that constitute our selfhood, and our *agency*, the way we choose to express our selfhood. My goal is to develop a theory that allows for an adequate conception of women as active moral identities.

Self-respect and self-reflective evaluation

Such a theory involves a commitment to respecting persons and enhancing their self-development. While some conceptual abstraction is necessary to determine this, it does not imply the 'abstract conception of the individual' (Lukes, 1984: 146). Yet, the standard form of the knowing subject has been a disembodied, non-historical, non-sexual subject. I am arguing that to reinstate the concept of a person as a particular *knowing* subject is to imply a self-determinative *principled* subject. Personhood is a moral category, not primarily a psychological category (Massey, 1983: 247). As a moral construct, as Kant (1964) reminds us, one shows self-respect by treating oneself and others as ends not means. The typical extension of this associates self-respect with the proper valuation of equal rights (Bedau, 1968: 571; Feinberg, 1970; Held, 1973; Hill, 1977). There is a tendency, then, for self-respect to be derived from the priority of rights. This understates the intersubjective nature of morality.

What, then, is self-respect linked with? I am proposing its link with values, beliefs and ethical orientations that are not merely subjective value judgements, but elements of *Weltanschauungen*, a world-view endowing life with meaning and suggesting paths of action. To be devoid of a value-orientation is to be devoid of character. Such orientations shape and guide action, endowing life with meaning and dignity (Brubaker, 1984: 63). This personal stamp of meaning is an essential property of human agency, endowing the concept of personhood with moral significance and linking personal interpretation with overall narrative understanding. This approach involves shifts from determinate rules to models of 'practical rationality' that emphasise the role of exemplars and judgement.

The keys to finding appropriate models lie in self-reflection and moral evaluation. In being self-determining, we affirm the modern individual's project, the significant difference being the stress on qualitative reflection and assessment. Practically, this invokes moral hierarchies of goodness. To make meaningful evaluations as self-respecting persons, we need reliable concepts of the good,[11] and of human potential.[12] A continual re-evaluation of these concepts places the self in a dynamic questioning mode in that 'to acquire a strongly evaluative language is to become (more) articulate about one's preferences' (Taylor, 1976: 288). Furthermore, the individuated nature of moral situations, emotions and attitudes, only comes to light when they are evaluated in terms of our knowledge of the history of the agents involved in them (Benhabib, 1987: 167).

Part of this process of individuated articulation, intrinsic to a notion of agent-morality, is the statement of the conditions required to 'live well'. Living the 'good life', commonly understood in material or hedonistic terms, is different to 'living well' in moral terms. By this I mean it is necessary to ascertain what practices encourage humans to flourish as moral identities. For Aristotle (1977: Books One and Two), the starting point of ethical enquiry lies in explaining the relationship of what it means to be 'human' to 'living well', suggesting it is analogous to understanding 'harpist' as 'playing the harp well'. To call something 'good' is to make a factual statement and an evaluative statement. To declare a wine for guests to be 'good' implies not only that it is tasteful, but that there are standards to measure it. If the guests suddenly decline, the purpose for wanting a 'good' wine becomes blurred. New reasons may emerge. Both purpose and potential are key issues when defining the *good* of something. Yet, as I shall demonstrate, in the case of women, purpose has too frequently been associated with reproductive function, limiting self-reflective interpretation of good moral identity. When purpose is tied to open possibilities of potential, such limitations are undermined. To define purpose and potential, we can include knowledge and assessment of past experience, context, changed circumstances and new adaptations.

A moral weighting of activities required to live well thus demands the determination of priorities, such that the greater the intrinsic good of an activity, the more basic is this activity. For example, beyond physical welfare, these 'basic goods' include needs like, 'love, respect, honour, dignity, solidarity with others' (Ignatieff, 1984: 15). On this line of reasoning, these have higher priority than, say, excitement, material luxury or aesthetic satisfaction. The idea of interpreting needs as a basis for the good life, rather than rights or principles of justice, is to enlarge the domain of moral theory and formulate an alternative framework 'within which moral and political agents can define their own concrete identities on the basis of recognising each other's dignity' (Benhabib, 1987: 169).

Furthermore, I am suggesting that clear, but open moral direction is more likely to emerge from considering the relationship between intention, purpose and reason for action, when these are attached to notions of moral good and civic virtue. Statements pertaining to agent-morality then incorporate a generalisable notion of what is

19

valuable to humans, with scope for particular differences. As indicated, modernity prides itself on freeing the individual to decide privately on what is valuable or preferred. I am arguing that moral judgement requires we sift out the virtues conducive to being a *good person*. Good reasoning thus is adjusted to the exigencies of the practical sphere which recognises that because people differ, different virtues may be more appropriate (Stocker, 1987: 57) in different situations, reaffirming the importance of an individuated 'needs' interpretation.

Character–narratives

I am advocating a virtue-based morality, where moral goodness is visible in practical, concrete examples, developed through habit. This is where the concept of character models that might shape conceptions of human possibilities, as 'living instances of possible ways of being' (Code, 1986: 58), is crucial. This notion of character does not imply eccentricity or glamour, but the propensity to act, as 'moral representatives' (MacIntyre, 1982: 191). My specific motivation is an attempt to rectify the long history of female invisibility by recognising woman as what code calls an 'authoritative being' (1986), or a character who by her example, commands respect.

In developing the specific nature of this character progressively throughout the book, I adopt a narrative approach to moral identity, which is, as MacIntyre puts it, 'a concept of a self whose unity resides in the unity of a narrative which links birth and life to death as narrative beginning to middle to end' (1982: 191). A narrative approach has two inseparable components. That is, *I am the subject of a history* with particular personal meaning, and *I am part of others' stories* (see Steedman, 1986). As MacIntyre explains, 'the narrative of any one life is part of an interlocking set of narratives' (1982: 203). Moral identity is built on the basis of recognising the mutual dignity of self-reflective others.

The idea of a narrative has two inseparable purposes—it has value as a conversational approach and as a mode of understanding the subject. First, to extend the literal idea of 'conversation', a narrative 'is a constant interconnecting of all sorts of representations of our experience and also potentially an extension of our experience as we hear ourselves and others and reflexively interpret ourselves, in and through...conversational moments' (Young-Bruehl, 1987: 216). Our mind is made up of interacting structures: the unconscious, the preconceptual and the conscious.[13] A conversational approach permits active dialogue with these structures and with other voices. The demand is thus triggered not only to hear, but to understand and to comprehend the parts in the whole.

To comprehend numerous meaningful actions within a narrative provides a partial self-understanding, but to comprehend relationships which link all the parts provides a more complete under-standing of identity (Dilthey, 1976: 185). The detail and the whole interact. What I am stressing is that the significance of particular events is grasped only when specific impressions of lived experience are related to the whole of one's narrative. In addition to making sense of life, this affirms us as subjects of significance. This process is 'not just a performance criterion for agency' (Taylor, 1985b: 109), but defines our moral status. This criterion cannot be precisely measured, as it is necessarily tentative and exploratory. The narrative approach is vastly different from the emphasis on fracture and discontinuity prominent in the postmodernist positions discussed earlier.

Social subjects

An appreciation of the possibilities surrounding moral character emerges through grasping the social basis of selfhood. The idea that the self identifies with and is identified through membership of various groups has diminished. Statements like, 'I am a daughter, a sister, an aunt, a mother, a spouse, a member of this community and of this nation' have lost their significance for many. In modern society, the individual is supposedly 'freed' from 'natural' bonds. The loss is ours, for the notion that common ends sustain individuals within community has diminished with it. Corresponding to this loss is a comprehensive segmentation of life, in terms of both social and philosophical divisions, which are the focus of the following chapter. All these factors hinder the attempt to grasp and evaluate our lives as a unity.

Hence it is necessary to posit some compelling 'notion of human sociality as a constituent feature of human nature' (Elshtain, 1978: 47). This notion seeks the realisation of selves intrinsically tied to other beings. The mere holding of superficial common interests, or mutual instrumental ties, cannot bond individuals together. Modernity alienates us from fully understanding civic belonging. What I am advocating is *human interdependence* as the basis for creative interaction. There is a qualitative difference in this sense of belonging, in that it enables us to identify the nexus with others, a powerful and dynamic link, a 'glue' that underlies any 'community of feeling' and without which social life becomes 'impoverished and oppressive' (Elshtain, 1978: 51). In adult friendship, the moral nature of this belonging can be evaluated by the levels of care, concern and well-being between friends (Stocker, 1987: 63).

Moral experience is personal and also deeply embedded in a wider social coherence. The link I make is between the particular self and common experiences. The evaluation of moral identity and experi-ence is thus linked to relationships in that the *good, for me*, can be seen as the *good I share* with those I am connected with in human community. Stories told through literature, mythology and the oral tradition have always played a key part in educating us in the virtues associated with these connections. The search for a life lived well, where humans flourish, necessitates the search for new modes of relationship.

Integral to this search is the attempt to make sense of our own experiences, and the accompanying accountability for our actions. Mutual accountability is more likely to occur when dialogue is in the context of equality and nondependence. The purpose of this sort of dialogue is less that of self-identification, than of 'intersubjectively recognised self-identification' (Habermas, 1979: 107). A communicative form of life creates 'the possibility of conversational reconciling, both in ourselves and with others', (Young-Bruehl, 1987: 219), a development of the narrative mode outlined earlier. This stresses the dialectical nature of relationships and the impact of particularity on such relationships. We are moral identities whose history, integrity and creativity is realised through relationships.

The social subject is best understood as *self-in-relations* (Gould, 1978, 1983, 1988).[14] This concept acknowledges that 'relationships, past and present, realised and sought, are constitutive of the self, and so the actions of a person reflect the more or less successful attempt to respond to the whole configuration of relationships' (Whitbeck, 1984: 76). The feature of this response is that relationships between people are understood not as attempts to dominate, suppress, deny or annihilate the other, but as developing through differentiation, identification, speaking and listening, with each other. This generates a 'multifactorial interactive model' (Whitbeck, 1984) where reality is comprised of groups of relations that intersect, interact, and change in the process but are not in essential opposition. Practices like co-operative activity, joint decision-making and mutuality create certain ways of living and develop specific virtues appropriate to the mutual realisation of moral identities. Moral particularity is again affirmed in the idea of self-in-relations. It concretises both the self and others by affirming historical and emergent identities.

This demands we treat persons as moral subjects (Spelman, 1977–78) and respond to the person as a specific identity.[15] If we are all moral agents, then respect is owed to all equally. This is not an abstract concept, because content can be attached to it. In treating 'each as an end', a clear distinction emerges between regarding a person's character, actions and stated purposes from an instrumental viewpoint, and being concerned primarily with what it means for a specific moral identity to have a particular character, actions and purposes. It means that everybody is owed an effort at genuine identification rather than a superficial application of a label, be it prostitute, housewife or mother. Labels may provide an uncomplicated factual explanation, but the presumption that one is essentially, for example, a wife, fails to recognise and respond to a woman as the person she really is, that is, a full moral identity. To hold a person responsible for self-determination within a network of narratives is the pivotal concern in treating a person as a moral subject. It is this respect which has so frequently been denied to children and to women, when men have acted 'on their behalf'.

Finally, I aim to posit what Code (1986: 63) describes as 'authoritative being, knowing and doing' as exemplars of moral character. A scarcity of female models for these exemplars means that imaginative effort is required to envisage widespread examples. An understanding of the contribution of past thought to female and male consciousness, helps make available a diversity of intellectual styles and character ideals. Differences within social subjects can be seen as a 'source of richness and diversity in a human life whose full range of possibilities and experiences is freely accessible to both men and women' (Lloyd, 1984a: 107). In the following chapters, I analyse why this richness has not occurred and what processes best facilitate its evolution.

NOTES

1   Much of the influential literature is listed in the bibliographical essay at the end of Lloyd, 1984a.
2   Works cited in my text by author and year of publication receive full citation in the bibliography.
3   Okin (1979) admirably tries to hypothesise the inclusion of women as complete equals. Her work is a valuable contribution. To examine the applicability of theorists' presuppositions to women, when women are not even accepted as active subjects in most original texts, may not only lead to ambiguity, but to an absurdity not evident in Okin's work.
4   This does not exclude homosexual relations. My point is simply that the eradication of sexism concerns both sexes, and my analysis is concerned with principles affecting all types of relationships.
5   Jaggar (1983: 370–371) argues that from the standpoint of the oppressed, there is some epistemological advantage in terms of being able to provide a more comprehensive view of their reality than the ruling class or patriarchal powers. I agree with her. Radcliffe Richards (1982: 59) argues, in a counter view, that 'women are hardly in a better position than men to know about the nature of women.' The equivalent of Jaggar's 'standpoint', is in Radcliffe Richards' terms, a 'position of ignorance'. I contend that Radcliffe Richards' view undermines the self-determinative potential of individuals within the groups in question, and permits elitist and paternalistic analyses.
6   Owing to the brevity of this outline, I have kept my remarks to a general level, and do not refer to specific theorists within the particular positions. References to such theorists will be provided in forthcoming chapters. Some indication of proponents of these views can be found in Jaggar, (1983). Liberal feminism, chapters 3 and 7, traditional Marxism, chapters 4 and 8, radical feminism, chapters 5 and 9, and feminism as political philosophy, chapters 1 and 2.

7   Kristeva in her 'Woman Can Never Be Defined', (1984: 138) argues against what she sees to be a 'naive romanticism, a belief in identity'. In response to being asked to define what she means by the 'work of a woman', Kristeva calls this absurd and obscurantist, but advises that strategically the statement 'we are women' should be used as a slogan for demands.

8   Consistency would demand an outright rejection of most theory, literature, music, art, science and medical inventions, simply because of the sex of the originators.

9   Natural ability, opportunities in life, fortune, and initiative influence the degree to which humans can actualise potential. Considerations of potential should be sensitive to the intellectually impaired who attempt to fulfil their potential, and to those who have physical handicaps and use alternative means of communication.

10   The notion of willingly being an instrument, is fraught with complexities, particularly in the case of women who are obliged or coerced to yield to others, and through dependency, become victims.

11   This contrasts with Rawls' (1971) 'thin theory' of the good. He maintains that there is no rational criterion for assigning preference between values. See particularly the section on 'Intuitionism' (34–40). Rawls' argument is that rational agreement on the nature of the good life is impossible, and impedes individual freedom to choose. Moral neutrality thus is appropriate, concentrating rather on agreement on roles. It is difficult to answer then, what makes it just for one good to take precedence over another.

12   Against Aristotle, I reject any natural, immutable elitism where the achievement of penultimate moral activity depends on natural, unequal, fortuitously distributed capacities. Nevertheless, his practical ethics presuppose an account of potentiality that seeks to instruct and instigate change. To suggest why someone ought to do something, is to state what action should lead to their fulfilled end.

13   With the unconscious, we are not completely aware of the processes. The preconceptual stage is difficult to define. It probably covers everyday activities we do 'without really thinking' like showering or habitual skills like driving a car, or natural occurrences like children racing about. It also covers grappling with deeper issues like 'falling in love' or coping with death, which, by their nature, are complex, mysterious and cannot be fully comprehended. Increased understanding may alter the preconception. At the conscious level, our mental faculties are aware of active processes, such as deliberate, self-reflective choice.

14   Gould develops this concept of social individuality both ontologically and normatively, in a lot of her writings. Her concept of 'individuals-in-relations' has a strong influence on my extension of self-in-relations and I acknowledge this debt.

15   This does not discredit the possibility of self-illusion, or that perceiving a discrepancy between our sense of self and others' ideas of ourselves, may prompt a change in our self-identity. (see Martin ed., 1985).

2 Moral dualism

The chapters following my introductory chapter examine how moral dualism, nature, reason, individualism and moral development have influenced views on gender-related moral differences. As we shall see, a variety of dualisms, dichotomies, polarities, tensions, contrary ideas and contrasts recur with the concepts I deal with. I adopt a literal definition of these terms. By dualism, I mean two independent principles. A dichotomy is a division into two, a binary classification involving pairs. Polarities have contrary qualities. Tensions involve strained relations, where there is an inability to achieve equilibrium. Something that is contrary, is opposed in nature, or tendency. A contrast can have two meanings. It can refer to things set in opposition to show differences of comparison, or it can involve a juxtaposition, in order to show striking differences. All these distinctions are extremely important in this chapter.

This chapter covers an extensive range of historical ideas, hence I have limited my discussion to five points. First, I argue that there is a *gender basis* to moral dualism. This basis permeates ideals of personhood and influences people's practices. Second, I demonstrate the tendency in philosophy to *evaluate* the dualistic principles *hierarchically*. I argue that this evaluation has provided philosophical justification for claims of women's inferiority and failure to qualify as full moral identities. I demonstrate how attributes deemed appropriate to women have been constituted through the suppression and exclusion of women from activities that foster the highly valued traits.

The third and fourth points grapple with various responses to the above two. The third point reiterates that sexual identity is an integral component of personhood. This involves questioning how the ideals of maleness and femaleness affect the relationship between gender and moral dualism. This forms the basis for my fourth point which attempts to clarify the limitations of arguments that affirm a distinctive femininity. I argue that this affirmation operates largely within a space already created for the feminine within our intellectual tradition. A re-assessment of the constraints of this space demands radical changes in our understanding of both female and male moral identities.

In the fifth section, I substantiate the claim that each side of the perceived polarities to be outlined is an essential part of moral existence,[1] and that dualism posits false choices. To incorporate one aspect of a moral contrast into one's sense of self, without the balancing effect of the other, is, I contend, to accept being less than a full moral subject. Rather, I view the pairs as part of the multi-faceted complexity of being human. My refutation of the argument that asserts the antagonistic nature of opposites concedes some continuing tension between the pairs of these dichotomies, but not the impossibility of equilibrium. In extending arguments developed in Chapter One, I suggest means of moving towards a philosophy of *synthesis*. I argue that the ideal of synthesis is related to the ideal of balance in an integrated notion of the self. The actual constitution of this in terms of equality and difference is contentious, and difficult, but its disentangling is a major goal of this study.

THE GENDER BASIS OF MORAL DUALISM

The pervasiveness of dualistic approaches to everyday activities is a constant reminder of the heritage of moral polarities in our consciousness, institutions and practices. They are numerous.[2] We are familiar with the beliefs and practices that business and pleasure do not mix, home and work should be unrelated, that a professional does not accept personal friends or relatives as clients, that clear thought requires an emotional distancing from the object of analysis, and so forth. I seek now to establish the relation between the construction of such divisions and gender.

The sociology of knowledge highlights ways in which we collectively construct social reality (Berger and Luckmann, 1976). If we are led to believe that certain character traits are antithetical, and this belief is internalised early, we tend to act on the basis of the belief and establish our lives in such a way as to confirm the belief patterns. This generates experiences that reinforce the belief and hence one perceives it as 'natural'. As I shall explain, the association of one side of a polarity with maleness ensures that the other side is associated with femaleness. Such an association invites a gender dualism and contributes significantly to perceived and actual divisions between the sexes.

My claim that there is a gender basis to moral dualism is not merely a sociological observation, but a philosophical one. Sociologically, gender constructs make it difficult for people to endure the label of 'deviant' for acting in ways that are reserved for the 'opposite sex' (Glennon, 1979: 26). My task in this chapter is to examine 'femininity' and 'masculinity' as the social construction of gender, and to question the traditional philosophical ideals behind 'femaleness' and 'maleness'.

In order to structure my questioning I make use of Jay's (1981) outline of the association between logical dichotomy and extreme gender distinction. Jay uses basic laws of formal logic classically delineated by Aristotle in his principles of order. There are three such laws pertinent to this discussion. The Principle of Identity states that if something is A, it is A. The Principle of Contradiction insists nothing can be both A and Not-A. The Principle of the Excluded Middle allows no intermediate position: everything must be either A or Not-A.

As Jay points out, the distinction between contradictions defined above, and contraries which are opposed in nature or tendency but not in total opposition', is clear. If for example we hypothesise A to be normative humanity, yet represented by ideals of maleness, and B to represent what is excluded from definitions of normative humanity and represented by ideals of femaleness, several possible scenarios follow. If A and B are perceived to be opposed in nature, or tendency, but not necessarily in contradiction 'continuity between them may be recognised without shattering the distinction' (1981: 44). This resembles a world-view of 'complementarity' that views men and women as two different forms of humans who share important common features. While both forms possess positive value, this view frequently incorporates a corresponding 'equal but different' theme. This unavoidably attributes a hierarchical evaluation to the notion of difference.

Where ideals of femaleness are perceived as Not-A, and ideals of maleness as A, there can be no continuity between A and Not-A, for this embodies the principle of contradiction.[3] To understand the extent of the contradiction, Dewey's elaboration is apt. He writes, 'if, say, "virtue" be assigned to A as its meaning, then Not-A includes not only vice, but triangles, horse races, symphonies, and the procession of the equinoxes' (1938: 192). This means that only A has positive reality. Not-A is Aristotle's privation, or absence of A. I agree with Jay that within this construct 'concepts of femaleness and maleness come into being that have nothing whatever to do with human sexual differences, but follow from the nature of contradictory dichotomy itself' (1981: 4). This is also the logic behind the 'contagion' of pollution. For example, in the Jewish Levitical Law, a man who has any contact with a menstruating woman becomes unclean himself (see Ezekiel 22: 26, 44: 23). Either such rules are arbitrary and meaningless or they are allegories of virtues and vices (Douglas, 1978: 43).

My point in drawing on formal logic is to clarify my argument that this A and Not-A dichotomy can be seen to have a direct connection with gender distinctions. That is, there is a common interpretation by men and experience by women, of femaleness as Not-A, in direct contradiction with ideal notions of the subject as represented by A, or maleness. Anthropologists make it clear that a major function of male initiation rites is to separate male youths from women and children, symbolically affirming not only their maleness, but that they are 'not women' (Warner, 1937; Kaberry, 1939; Ardener ed., 1975; Friedl, 1975). I document in detail in later chapters the western tendency for mothers to push sons toward extreme individuation by stressing their identity as non-female.

Where there is disparity between self-identity and prevalent ideals, internal tensions often prevail. In the case of women, the practical clash between certain polarities places them in a position of 'social marginality', where a person has been socialised into one side of the dichotomy, and then attempts to participate in the other side or to oscillate but never quite 'fits in'. A stark example is women in the workforce, struggling with double or triple work-loads of paid labour, housework and child-care with their seemingly contradictory demands and priorities. Assuming women's early and continuous socialisation into relational roles, and believing they are best suited to the private sphere, women are often at odds with the public world where public morés and ideals of maleness generally correlate. For many women, crises of selfhood are due to their unique location between the public and the private spheres—a major division in modern society.[4]

It is, thus, 'from the vantage point of "caught-betweenness", [that] feminists have begun to question the need for the wide gulf' (Glennon, 1979: 18) between, for example, public and private lives, where the public sphere is believed suited to men, and the private sphere to women. This 'caught-betweenness' involves more than the sense of trying to cross to both sides of the polarity. It involves maximising the advantages of social marginality. By participating in some capacity in both orientations (by inclination or necessity), an individual has an opportunity to engage in comparison of values, structures, identities and life-styles. This leads to an awareness of the precariousness of life, scepticism at popular notions of dualism, and critical insight as to possible changes. Women, living within the constraints of marginality, are in a position to recognise the importance of social change, and the need to explore the nature of dichotomy. A peculiar marginality also affects men who take a significant role in child-care and housework, and who may be caught between, or are sensitive to, the possible contradictions of public demands and private desires.

DUALISM, HIERARCHY AND INCOMPLETENESS

I have established some background to the logic behind gender-dualism, and its association with principles of identity and contradiction. I now look further at the difficulty of conceiving and living with an acceptable middle position. Earlier, I explained the polarity between A and Not-A. Attention must now be given to why women represent Not-A, and men, A. To do this, I examine why there is a philosophical evaluation of certain characteristics normally attributed to maleness and how this results in a philosophical justification of the inferiority and normative incompleteness of a femaleness constituted through the exclusion and suppression of valued moral traits.

I look then at the effect of the evaluations of 'superiority' and 'inferiority'. These two characteristics can be seen as contrary, opposed in nature and contradictory. I am arguing that the evaluation of ideals into these classifications has served two purposes within philosophy. First, it has supported the identification of normative humanity with maleness, and second, it has justified the servility of women. The impact of Judaeo-Christian theology is particularly relevant to this stage of the discussion.

With the patriarchal law of the Old Testament, a symbolic hierarchy of God-male-female prevails (Ruether, 1983: 165). Although the New Testament emphasis is on an affirmation of equality before God, there remains in the theological tradition a distinct ambiguity in the way the *imago dei*–sin relationship is understood in relation to maleness and femaleness. That is, the possibility of equality, posited in the new order, is often obscured by the persistence of a hierarchical scheme of mind over body and reason over passions. Men, as rational beings, are seen in Judaism to be essentially in the image of God. This contrasts with the association of women with the material nature, and the presumption that women are lacking in spirituality. Thus the Judaeo-Christian tradition provides an apt illustration of both a dichotomy (associated with the resistance to change) (Ezekiel 22: 26, 44: 23) and the abandonment of the dichotomy (associated with the vision of a new social order), stating that there is neither Jew nor Greek, slave nor free, male nor female (Galations 3: 28).

What I suggest is at stake, here, is a distinction between essential and accidental properties. Essential properties are those deemed necessary for fulfilling a particular purpose, such as being a moral subject. Being fundamental, these cannot be acquired. Within traditional philosophy, they are perceived as 'natural', containing an implicit value. Attempts to modify essential properties are thus contrary to nature.[5] Accidental properties are seen as neither sufficient nor necessary to selfhood. This is not just a contrast, but necessarily contains an explicit evaluative dichotomy (Tuana, 1983). Within this framework, the 'accidental' property of 'being a woman' means that a woman is perceived as lacking important 'essential' ingredients. As 'incomplete man', she is necessarily inferior.

Lloyd, in unravelling the development of ideals of maleness and femaleness, explains the subsequent evaluative connotations as having been 'formed within structures of dominance—of superiority and inferiority, "norms" and "difference", "positive and negative", the "essential" and the "complementary"' (1984a: 103). If what is valued is identified with maleness, then it is not incidental that most traits identified with femaleness are construed as inferior, or complementary to male norms. In this regard, there are three operative factors that, according to Lloyd, have contributed to the construction of female identity: opposition, exclusion and suppression.

Opposition is defined here as a fundamental tool of moral discourse which presupposes contrasts between various polarities (Unger, 1976: 44). From the time of the Pythagoreans, the perceptual world was accounted for in terms of ten oppositions.[6] These were cited with approval by Aristotle who classifies all dichotomous terms as positive or negative (Lloyd, 1966: 65). By this logic, if the sexes are so distinguished, then there can be only one perfect form. The logic of contradictory opposites decrees that if the 'perfect form' is male, anything not-male is necessarily opposed or negative. This is the rationale behind Aristotle's perception of woman as 'misbegotten male' endorsed by patristic and scholastic theologians. With Plato, again the search for the eternal form is always opposed to its negation. I deal with these specific arguments of Aristotle and Plato in the following chapter on nature.

Oppositional dualism characterises western philosophy. The mind–body split particularly is extremely influential in the objectification of women. With this split, the exaltation of the abstract, or rational, as characteristically human is separated from the physical, which is rejected as less important and projected onto women. Intellectual polarities that evolved from this split have largely maintained themselves with a strong hierarchical dualism.

This dualism relates particularly to ideal character qualities, where feminine virtues are defined in opposition to masculine ones. In addition to the argument about opposition, second and third operative factors are suppression and exclusion. These two factors derive from the oppositional category, and are closely linked. I cite as an example the traditional philosophical view on reason and passion. What I seek to clarify, is that within dualistic models, femininity is often not postulated as complementary, but is defined in opposition to an ideal perfect form which, on close examination, often incorporates the deficiencies in male consciousness. The complication for our purposes lies in the projection onto women of virtues not highly valued in ideals of maleness, and thus not highly valued in ideals of personhood. In practical terms, this involves a rejection by men of their assumed 'lower selves'. The other side to the male claim to rationality would thus be a rejection of the importance of emotional expressivity, and an assumption of the suitability of this for women. This is not just a straightforward equation of women with emotions, or men with reason, but a complex hierarchical evaluation and definition of women through exclusion from valued traits, and a suppression of practices that might encourage such traits.

In extending the example of reason, we note that traditional political theorists accept as a first principle of citizenship the derivation of natural, property and political rights through reason. It was precisely because women were seen to be deficient in the rational capacity that they were historically considered unequal. Wollstonecraft (1972), in defending the rationality and advocating the social equality of women, attacks the view that female virtues were never really comparable with rationally-founded male virtues. With Locke, she maintains that practical virtue is to be attained through reason. She argues that, if virtue for women is different from virtue for men, then morality is relative. Attempts to set up double standards undermine the whole concept of virtue itself (Korsmeyer, 1976: 101). I support Korsmeyer's warning. In claiming the potential of full rationality and complete moral responsibility for women, early feminists were aware not only that centuries of conditioning had denigrated women, but also that, to some extent, women had permitted their accommodation to sensual, dependant and coquettish behaviour. I am not suggesting women voluntarily accommodate themselves to positions of inferiority or subjugation, but that through dependency, or submission to convention and ignorance, women often have not envisaged the possibility of refusal, resistance or opting for change.

Yet, any conclusion that such accommodation is due to female nature misses the complexity of the issue. It is, rather, a further instance of the inhibitory nature of the principle of opposition that is premised on a narrow either–or choice, necessitating the development of chosen traits, the suppression of their perceived opposites, and the exclusion in the case of women, from positions, processes and realms which demand the use of traits considered part of mature moral responsibility. Furthermore, implicit in this instance is an undervaluing of skills developed by women in traditional spheres. This occurs alongside the denial of the practical experience necessary for formulating broad moral judgement.

The content of femininity, with its subordinate status, has developed within an intellectual tradition that involves not just 'a simple exclusion of women, but a constitution of femininity through the exclusion' (Lloyd 1984a: 106). In subsequent chapters I provide many instances of how the affirmation of virtues derived from an exclusion from male thought-styles and practices, ignores the historical development of femininity, which has been defined largely through opposition, exclusion and suppression. Therefore this version of femininity unavoidably assumes the negative or inferior dimensions of moral dualism.

SEXUAL IDENTITY AND PERSONHOOD

Now, the importance of this gender component to dualism should not be underestimated, given that sexual identity is an integral component of personhood. The assertion that sexual identity is an important component of personal identity is not controversial. The translation of this into the context of a philosophical discourse is. Particularities such as the influence of one's sex on identity have not been perceived to be a legitimate focus of philosophical enquiry, and have been ignored or subsumed under the category of 'accidental personal characteristics'. Yet it is important to demonstrate the circumstances in which being a woman or being a man has philosophical significance.

Contemporary philosophical responses to the relationship between sexual identity and personal identity differ. One interpretation is that, because they are both human, there is no significant difference between women and men. Other options are premised on a belief that either men or women are lesser persons, or that women and men are equal but different. I examine these options in more detail in the following chapter. Suffice it to note now that, with the first interpretation, the philosopher, being called to articulate universal qualities of life (Heidegger's search for Being, Husserl's contents of consciousness, Wittgenstein's character of language), assumes that sex-identity is not a primary philosophical concern. It is not valid to conclude from such statements that sexual identity is philosophically irrelevant, but, rather, that most philosophers have not grasped its philosophical importance (Allen, 1976: 107). Allen suggests that it would be illuminating to demonstrate the philosophical significance of sexual identity by considering a Heideggerean analysis of *Dasein* in its sexual dimension, a Wittgensteinian treatment of how questions of sexual self-definition are expressed through linguistics, and a phenomenological critique of the sexual content of consciousness.

In positions that either minimally recognise the importance of sexual identity to personal identity, or ignore its importance, the qualities of reflection, ethical judgement and intellectual discourse are viewed as more crucial to personhood. The association of these qualities with male identity is viewed as incidental. I am arguing that it is not incidental, and that the idea of moral identity within this position masquerades as human, but really only includes men as full persons. De Beauvoir's insight is reinforced by this interpretation, in that 'there is a conflict between being a woman and being a person in the situation where criteria for personal identity are made analytically similar to criteria for male identity' (1975: 110). An assertion by extreme male chauvinists and many radical feminists that sex-identity is always relevant, justifying the separation between men and women, is no better than the assertion of its irrelevance.

I argue that the philosophical significance of gender-based differences should be drawn out. That is, there are some contexts in which one's sex plays an important role. But the point is to discover which contexts are applicable for each individual. This approach explores open-ended possibilities of identity, acknowledging that the developing self is affected by different contexts: historical heritage; culture; socialisation; body awareness; language; personal, psychological and sexual experience; relationships, and so forth. These can be seen as constitutive factors in self-consciousness for a subject for whom sex-identity is an integral dimension.

The question of the extent to which a person can alter or modify contexts is interesting. For some, similar contexts foster similar identities. For others, the awareness of a shared context results in a strong reaction against a similar background, leading to the deliberate attempt to create quite different identities. This suggests a link between self-determination and a conscious choice of alternative contexts that enhance personal growth, although it will not always be clear whether the major instigator for change is the context, the self-determination, or, more likely, a dynamic interaction between the two. Generally, it seems reasonable to assume that different contexts will result in different identities. De Beauvoir's claim that one is not born but 'becomes a woman' need not necessarily be understood negatively as portraying the constraints of socialisation, but can be understood as the need to accept responsibility for becoming an individuated woman who takes seriously the sexual component of her identity.

In summary, mainstream philosophy has not taken seriously the importance of sexual identity to personal identity. While there may be more fundamental dimensions to identity, such as self-respect, integrity and self-determination, I am arguing that sexual identity is a complex phenomenon that contributes to these fundamental dimensions. Other components include body-consciousness, personal experience influenced by one's gender, and individual interpretations of one's body and experiences. Gender and sexuality are often in friction with superimposed cultural stereotypes and individual self-interpretations. Yet, different manifestations of sexual identity cannot be reduced simplistically to 'social conditioning', but should be recognised as part of the enigmatic nature of sexuality. That is, expressions and activities of woman or a man are directly related to different experiences which may arise as a result of having different bodies.

The exploration of difference within this context deepens our consciousness of particular sexual identities. Differences do not negate similarities, but enrich the human arena in which various differences are acted out. The personal affirmation of this has more potential to liberate than denouncing difference in favour of androgens, or the imposition of a dualistic psychology of difference into gendered, polarised beings. Otherwise, we are anaesthetized to the enormous sensuous texture and creative possibilities of being women and men. In assuming personal responsibility for appreciating the sexual dimension to personal identity, we give meaning to the individual manifestation of sexual being.

Gender difference and personhood

How then have other feminists, whose theory and practice have been based on the notion of difference, responded to concepts of sexual identity? A brief summary of trends shows that to feminists like Firestone (1970), Janeway (1971), Millett (1971), Mitchell (1973), Brownmiller (1975), and de Beauvoir (1975) female difference was considered a major source of women's oppression. The rapid growth in consciousness-raising groups focuses on women's experience. Politically, these feminists have a strident belief, articulated by a resurgent women's movement, that 'to refuse to take a stand, individually, or collectively, is tantamount to a "collaboration with oppression"' (Clément, 1984: 130). At a personal level, the reappraisal of differences leads to an increased self-respect among many women. Rather than viewing differences as inadequacies, defects or sources of inferiority, differences can be considered as strengths.

The development of 'Women's Studies' as a discipline in the late 1960s and early 1970s was based on the premise that women's socialisation and oppression results in different types of experiences from men's. Accompanying this, there is an exposure, particularly by scholars in this new discipline, of the partial nature of transmitted knowledge in which the world of women's knowledge and experience is largely omitted. What emerged by the late 1970s, through writers such as Miller (1976), Lerner (1979), Rich (1979) and Griffin (1980), is a concept of a 'woman-centred analysis'.

I am critical of what Eisenstein calls 'the exaggeration of the woman-centred perspective' (1984: 125), particularly for its tendency to lead to a theoretical impasse. By this I mean it fosters a false universalism in gender analysis that over-generalises the commonality of women, disregards specifics like class, culture, or race, and elevates 'women's culture' by invoking a stance where women are considered persons and men less than persons. Just as characteristics associated with women have been undervalued, advocates of this position devalue characteristics associated with men. Any tendencies toward aggression, competition and domination are categorised as animalistic and necessarily male. Compassion and empathy are attributed exclusively to women, and in some cases this specific identity is touted as a means to prevent the destruction of the world. I maintain that an extreme woman-centred analysis has a narrow focus and lacks critical reflection.

GYNOCENTRISM

With this criticism in mind, I probe gynocentrism, a movement which can be viewed as the most extreme version of a woman-centred analysis. I want to demonstrate the inability of a woman-centred analysis to transcend dualism, despite its claims in being sensitive to relationships between objects and people. The fundamental inadequacies of this position are two-fold. First, it unwittingly incorporates entrenched dualism, but with a reversed evaluation from dominant male-centred perspectives. Second, in its most extreme version, it presents an unbalanced perspective, where all masculinity is rejected, and all traditional femininity is celebrated. It is difficult to assess the significance of female experiences as presented by a gynocentric perspective, for the possibility that these experiences may have occurred in a context other than female-defined is rarely acknowledged.

Historically, there are examples of a gynocentric past where social organisation pivoted around women and where femaleness was associated with fertility and primal power (Stone, 1978). Modern attempts to revive this notion of femaleness want female experience to be the major focus of their study and the source of values. As we examine the roots and consequences of this perpective, we note that at the basis of an extreme woman-centred perspective is a rejection of everything associated with masculinity. This is often accompanied by a critique of heterosexuality. There is also an affirmation of female-associated values, particularly as manifest through the relational self and developed through a 'reproductive consciousness'.

It is hard not to conclude that gynocentrism results in subjectivism and separatism. That is, the uncritical embrace of traditional feminine values, simply because they are perceived as feminine, unintentionally reasserts a femininity which I am claiming is defined in opposition to the male ideal. Consequently, ascertaining the actual female contribution to this self-definition is complicated. Furthermore, the implications of this position can only extend to women who support wholeheartedly the rejection of masculinity and the embrace of femininity.

Rejection of masculinity

I examine in turn the ideals of maleness and femaleness within the gynocentric perspective. An important clarification made earlier is important to repeat. I maintain that it is quite inappropriate to characterise the distinguishing features of maleness and femaleness in terms of 'masculinity' or 'femininity'. These categories are social creations, constituted by the social pressures that influence our stereotypical behaviour patterns. I have defined maleness and femaleness in terms of the ideals and character models that influence these patterns. For example, while femininity is defined partly by dress or coquettish behaviour, the constraints of femaleness lie in limiting endeavours and activities to confined ends, thereby creating a situation of contrived inferiority. Richards argues that the complexity of this situation is often obscured because characteristics like 'independence, strength, gentleness, charm, grace, wit, intelligence, success and the like are admired' in both men and women (1982: 193). While sometimes this is so, it does not undermine my contention that more men have had the opportunities (created in significant measure by women) to develop these characteristics that are good in themselves, and gain public recognition. Furthermore, when genuine admiration is merged with socially-constructed ideas of sexuality, nature and domination, such combinations as male success and gentleness or female beauty and strength are rendered unnecessarily problematic.

It is thus helpful to determine what exactly a gynocentric perspective rejects in terms of perceived notions of masculinity. I am concerned to distinguish between a rejection of men *per se* and an opposition to a specific masculine identity which an increasing number of men also oppose. This distinction is not necessarily maintained within a gynocentric perspective. Rather, a common view is that there are no different types of men, as they are all corrupt (Morgan ed., 1970: 514–519). I dismiss this view as counter-productive to the possibility of major changes in relationships between women and men.

Given that much of the rejection of masculinity within a gynocentric perspective is so all-encompassing, it lacks scholarly convincing argumentation. Hence, I can only address the complaints about this type of masculinity in a general way. A typical masculine identity develops when a boy identifies with abstractly defined male standards, while simultaneously separating himself from, and rejecting, emotional characteristics of women. This process lays the basis for an adult autonomy based on emotional distance. As a result, men often differentiate themselves from fellow subjects by exercising power in their relationships.

Dinnerstein (1976), Chodorow (1978; 1980), Benjamin (1980) and Fox Keller (1982) are four important theorists who demonstrate ways in which an extreme sense of autonomy and separateness in typical male psyches are related to the interpretation of woman as 'other', the objectification of knowledge and persons, and links with dominance. While these theorists base their analysis in a woman-centred perspective, they should not be classified as gynocentrists in that they do not advocate the primacy of women nor do they approach the issue of femininity in an uncritical manner. The strengths of their arguments serve as a contrast to the deficiencies of a gynocentric view that simply rejects men for being masculine, and masculinity for characterising the practices of men.

A more substantial critical approach states that the structure of individuality required by the western capitalist market seems to reinforce the type of masculine identity described above (Hartsock, 1983a; Poole, 1985). This has two components. First, the logic underlying the market assumes self-directed, self-interested desires that generally preclude altruism. That is, production exchange and relationships must be conceived instrumentally (Poole, 1985: 18).

When utility maximisation prevails, people also are conceptualised in terms of calculative, competitive modes of behaviour, where optimal market terms are construed as means to ends. Within this situation, it is less possible to conceive of genuinely other-directed activity that considers the well-being of others as a major goal. If the market requires traits criticised as negative attributes of masculinity, it is inevitable that those women who succeed on market terms, do so largely by assimilating these attributes. In defiance of market dictates, other women do cultivate caring work patterns. Second, despite current sociological and economic changes in families, the dominant assumption remains that, within nuclear families, the male should be the main breadwinner, his career being crucial not only to family welfare, but also to masculine identity. The sacrifice made by men is commonly that of forgoing family involvement, whereas women tend to sacrifice careers and a sense of 'public self' in the interests of others, and in congruence with traditional female identity.

What I am trying to convey by this criticism of masculinity is the way in which a calculative disengagement calls into question the development of capacities constitutive of full selfhood. Sexism involves not only a violation of women's integrity, but also represents the distortion of male humanity. Men have not succeeded in actualising a humanity generally worthy of emulation yet a gynocentric perspective does not explain precisely how this has developed and why it should be rejected. Despite such inadequacies, these critiques of male dominance within this perspective, give way to concerted efforts to specify femaleness.

Femaleness

If the gynocentric view does not convince us that the masculine dimension of dualism should be rejected, then we need to explore what it sees as intrinsic to femaleness, and to assess whether such qualities do stand as a better alternative ideal. In a gynocentric perspective, women's construction of the self, primarily in relation to others, is seen to 'provide an ontological base for developing a non-problematic social synthesis', (Hartsock, 1983a: 246) that transcends dualism. This basis is defined by the connectedness and continuity of daily, concrete interactions, in contrast to the divisions intrinsic to dualism. Miller (1976) in reinterpreting women's lives, suggests that emotional traits 'assigned' to women, especially the ability to express and interpret emotions and cultivate co-operative approaches, are developed through interaction with others, but notes that these are human capacities crucial for a flourishing society. The context in which women learn these capacities is often a situation of inequality and powerlessness, which leads to subservience. Yet, in understanding this context, 'the dialogue is always with the future' (Miller, 1976: 27) in order to re-direct experiences advantageously.

That is, Miller proposes using the traditional strengths of women as the 'psychic starting point' (1976: 83) for new concepts of autonomy, unhooked from aggression or violence. This idea of autonomy does not imply the need to give up affiliations in order to become self-directed. On the contrary, it is a sense of self-determination that assumes an interdependence with others, an embeddedness in context, and a concern with the maximisation of well-being, as distinct from market utility maximisation or a preoccupation with individual rights.

According to this notion of femaleness, an affirmation of equality and women's specificity is not contradictory, but seeks to incorporate the context in which femaleness is constructed. This contrasts with the views of some liberal feminists whose sense of equality implies a sameness with men, where the occasional exceptionally successful woman is viewed as having 'passed the test as a good bloke'. Much of this type of equality has been challenged by women who have succeeded in combining public success with conventional feminine characteristics. They have shown that characteristics of team management, and co-operative organisation, though often interpreted as feminine, are not submissive.

Nevertheless, the gynocentric perspective repudiates the liberal feminist concept of equality, and claims to challenge male-defined discourse and practices, rather than merely find women's place within it. Feminists operating in this perspective place the basis for redefining equality in terms of women's specificity within the reproductive network, with an emphasis on nurture, not child-bearing. This emphasis contrasts with other conceptions of reproduction, as a non-feminist example and a feminist one illustrate. Engels gave as the first instance of class oppression men's domination of women for reproductive purposes (1940: 47). In Engels' theory, the production and maintenance of children, rather than women's sexuality, mind or moral characteristics, define women (Foreman, 1977).

Yet some feminists also have negative attitudes to reproduction. De Beauvoir writes of her 'disgust' with the embryo because it initiates 'the cycle that is completed in the putrefaction of death', of the pregnant woman as being 'the prey of overwhelming forces', a creature at 'one with soil and sod, stock and root', with childbirth 'painful and dangerous' (1975: 178, 63, 512, 519, 62). Also, sexually liberated women frequently equate maternal consciousness with false consciousness, viewing it as a 'passive submission to a massive male-chauvinist conspiracy to enslave them' (O'Brien, 1983: 192). With the increasing incidence of feminists in academia, management, bureaucracy, professions and politics choosing not to have children, it becomes difficult for them to comment in an engaged sense on the limitations of a patriarchal motherhood. Any tendency to abstraction is not unlike a man's similar pronouncement. (See Dowrick and Grundberg eds, 1980.)

In defiance of any dismissive line of reasoning, gynocentrists articulate one of the principal differences between the sexes in terms of 'women's possessing an ability which men have not' (Richards, 1982: 162). They argue that social isolation and a pathological loss of self in the service to others has in the past prevented women from grasping this common potential as a basis of strength. As Rich writes, 'I know no woman...for whom her body is not a fundamental problem...There is for the first time today a possibility of converting our physicality into both knowledge and power' (1979: 166). Indeed, she states further that despite a destructiveness of motherhood under patriarchy, the experiential dimensions, the courage, passion, tenderness, the detailed apprehension of human vulnerability can not only be salvaged, but treasured. Equality within this perspective is defined precisely in terms of the opportunity to express female specificity.

This position does not alienate infertile or childless women. It is not just maternity or reproductive potential that is emphasised, but the qualities invoked through nurture that are viewed as the source of the female essence. What is being articulated as a gynocentric stance is what O'Brien (1983: 188) terms 'reproductive consciousness', an aspect of human understanding which is differentiated by gender and culturally transmitted emerging, in O'Brien's case, from her experiences as a midwife. This is therefore not just a common biological factor. Clearly a woman who has borne a child may find it difficult to distinguish the child carried in pregnancy either as 'me' or 'not-me', thus rendering it impossible to extract this 'reproductive consciousness' in abstraction from the woman's sense of self.

This idea of femaleness, as intrinsically associated with connectedness also affects most women with no children, simply because they have learnt what 'being a woman' means. Yet, I disagree that features like intuition, protection, nurture, love, compassion, tenderness, pacifism, fairness and species integration, which are seen to be the products of 'reproductive consciousness', are female qualities, rather than human ones. There is nothing intrinsically feminine to these qualities, but they are exhibited by both women and men, albeit in different degrees, depending on life experiences and different personalities.

Female experience

I have given some indication of gynocentric ideas on femaleness. They are more convincing than the ideas advanced in support of the rejection of masculinity. The typical gynocentrist conclusion on maleness and femaleness differs from my conclusion that qualities appropriate for nurturing emerge with both men and women who are engaged in active care of others. Contrary to my argument, it is frequently claimed that this emphasis on nurture can only be derived from an exploration of female personal experience, and by women's refusal to accept limiting self-definitions. We have seen that the advantage of such a feminist theory grounded in woman's specificity is that it can be critically self-generating, in exposing codified traditions and androcentric models. It is my concern to assess whether a gynocentric exploration of personal experience does free women from the chains of definition by others, and transcends dualism. My discussion also goes beyond the boundaries of gynocentrism.

Historically, personal validity was, for women, derivative from attachment to men (which is why, in popular culture, pity is poured on the spinster or widow). In all feminist perspectives, self-definition is paramount. This is no straightforward task. Take Julia Kristeva's contrary claim that 'woman can never be defined'. She writes 'a woman cannot "be"'...It follows that a feminist practice can only be negative, at odds with what already exists so that we may say "that's not it" and "that's still not it". In "woman" I see something that cannot be represented' (1984: 137). This avoidance of definition seems inconsistent, given the ease with which men are branded by many feminists as phallocentric or exploitative oppressors. Furthermore, Kristeva's notion of 'negative practice' is difficult to envisage. Positiveness seems a more decisive tactic. Nevertheless, one of the most appropriate ways to view Kristeva's statement is to see it as an apprehension of possibility. Yet the uncertainty this response induces in women seeking to understand themselves, their situation, and their relations with others, may result in a 'double ontological shock' (Bartky, 1981: 25). This implies an inability to discern clearly or articulate what is happening precisely, or there is the realisation that one's actual position differs drastically from how others perceive it or how one desires it. In my view, it seems reasonable to conclude that the 'feminist tension is dual vision, that is living in the world as men have fabricated it while creating the world as women imagine it could be' (Raymond, 1985: 85).

Within this 'dual vision', not only are women's imaginations diverse, but the practical struggle of understanding what precisely is a female experience, or what is merely a personal experience, is difficult, something not commonly grasped by the gynocentric insistence on self-definition. I agree with Code that 'there is an entire range of affective experience bound up specifically with being male or being female: experiences of sexuality and of parenthood, of general self-awareness as a physical and emotional being, and some aspects of interpersonal relations, which must of necessity be different for men and for women' (1981: 275). While Code acknowledges that experiences bound up with being male or female suggest there are areas where one cannot easily know what the other does, this does not discredit the possibility and usefulness of dialogue or attempts to communicate these differences. I make a contrast between those who view the exploration of the woman-identified woman as one way to an articulation of historical rootedness, and those who see it as a statement of the primacy of women.

I support the first category, in which women's culture is seen to be crucial in its transmission of an awakened sense of womanhood. Bonds of sisterhood cement a common life and encourage self-empowerment through friendship. This is a valid attempt to reunite the personal and political dimensions of friendship important in the classical Greek philosophical tradition. For Aristotle, friendship has a public nature. Strong ties with others are seen to intertwine the moral and political fibre of the *polis*, constituting more than mere sentiment. Yet grounding a 'Gyn-affection', or emotional, private friendship among women in a mystical 'ontological capability of women to bond with each other is a false optimism that will betray itself' (Raymond, 1985: 89).

Let me explain this. I maintain that the potential betrayal lies in the involuntary maintenance of dualism in supporting conventional principles of femininity, albeit in revamped versions. This retreats into a false universalism, where what is convention is taken as essence. It bypasses crucial differences between women, such as class, race, sexual preference, age, children, and material well-being. As a consequence, the significance of a gender analysis loses its political impact by failing to challenge the social construction of gender dualism.

The second category outlined above supports the primacy of women, and feminism's connection to other struggles for social justice is considered minimal. Female experience is treated as a new definition of 'the ontological good' (Hughes, 1982: 288) from which to derive an all-encompassing woman-centred epistemology. Supposedly liberated from patriarchal thought categories, and freed into new modes of being, this more extreme gynocentric version has a strong influence on feminist theory.

In this second category, two major positions are 'expressivism' and 'polarism' (Glennon, 1979: chapters 3, 5). 'Expressivism', in this sense, involves extreme emotionalism and subjectivism, which is quite different from the philosophical expressivism I support as vital to being a rational, passionate subject. In many ways, the emotional feminist, in her embrace of traditional emotional categorisations, embodies the archetypical woman, or 'female principle'. This is part of the unwitting betrayal discussed above. This can be instructively contrasted with the case of modern power-seeking assimilationist women who adopt a ruthless, calculated individualism, based primarily on utilitarian and pragmatic principles.[7] Apart from physical features, they are probably little different from most of their male colleagues. These women are commonly characterised as using femininity as a tactical approach to manipulate men. On the other hand, the expressivist feminist derives pride and strength from traditional definitions of womanhood. Yet these definitions are little different from many of the traditional variants they attempt to escape from. Such feminists emphasise emotional, experiential components of life, including intuition, which is seen to be not only distinct from logic but impervious to any logical or rational influence. With a stress on engagement and direct expression, they tend to see intellectual discourse as dispassionate and unavoidably abstract. Their alternative articulation of thoughts involves linguistic experiments, often in the stream-of-consciousness mode, based on shared personal, often intimate details. Many feminist expressivists who emphasise emotions, engagement and experience concede that men also develop similar expressive capacities. While some feminists suggest men need encouragement, particularly from other men, in developing these capacities, other feminists suggest that the contrary nature of men's typical experiences inevitably bars the chances of a similar expressivity developing.

'Polarism' also stresses the primacy of women. There is a moderate and an extreme polarism. Both positions take their bearings from a criticism of phallocentrism where male imagery dominates. As Cixous explains, the purpose of phallocentrism is 'to insure for masculine order a rationale equal to history itself' (1984: 93). She explains further that 'phallocentrism is the enemy of everyone. Men stand to lose by it, differently but as seriously as women', thus it is time to transform history (1984: 96). The moderate version is sensitive in its criticism of values and structures defined by men, realising that anger at values represented by many men might be interpreted as a personal attack by those men for whom we have affection.

The more vocal extreme polarists proceed with two premises. First, if phallocentrism rules, then there are no different kinds of men, they are all corrupt (Morgan ed., 1970). Second, because of this first premise, 'the female must be acknowledged as primary, as the source of all life' (Gearhart, 1982: 272), thus 'we take the woman's side in everything' (Morgan ed., 1970: 520). For these extreme polarists, it is not an abstraction called sexism that is responsible for women's oppression, but men themselves, precisely the assertion Cixous carefully avoids. Polarists argue that men's status as oppressors ensures that they are incapable of empathy with women's condition. That is, despite admirable intentions, men engage in discourse from their perspective 'as members of the dominant group. They remain men...in this case they are the "others"' (Klein, 1983: 414). Polarists assert that all contributions made by men reflect the male-centred approach to knowledge, particularly in wanting to define themselves not only in distinction from others, but, by excluding others. Such an approach permits a continuation of an assumed patriarchal right to speculate about the other. While polarists concede that women cannot adequately understand men's experiences, they claim that they make a deliberate conscious effort to subvert rigid distinctions between the subjects, objects and conveyance of knowledge, in a way men usually do not.

The vision of the polarists is of a spiritual rebirth, through the activity of women. Daly, a strong advocate of this position, reinterprets God as a Be-ing (verb) rather than a Being (noun). She correlates this with women's 'becoming' which is seen to usher in the new creation. Daly writes, 'we can do this by be-ing' (1973: 184). Within this position, men are considered the problem, women the solution, hence political significance is given to lesbianism (Morgan ed., 1970). The alternatives for women in this position are to renounce genital sexuality and practice celibacy as a political statement or to choose lesbianism as an alternative model for female identity. As Eisenstein (1984) points out, the explicitly radical lesbian defies stereotypic definitions in renouncing the secondary status of women, and in according primacy to women. Rich writes of a 'lesbian continuum', that includes not just the sexual aspects of a relationship, but 'a range of woman-identified experience' (1980b: 348).

Polarism in this extreme form, represents a pure form of female collective self-sufficiency, as distinct from male individual self-sufficiency and, in terms of my stated objectives, makes no meaningful contribution to changing relations between women and men. Furthermore, the difficulties of defining the uniqueness of female experience remain.

In concluding this section on sexual identity, personhood and the seeming pervasiveness of dualistic tendencies, I make three final points regarding the inability of a gynocentric perspective to counter dualism. My points refer to the related issues of interpersonal interaction, personal experience and human diversity.

First, as we have seen, a relational orientation lies at the basis of a woman-centred and gynocentrist view of moral development. Yet the basis incorporates, in differing degrees, views drawn from a male-dominant, capitalist society with many women involved in prime parenting. For women to equate a relational orientation exclusively with femaleness means they are prepared to accept a definition externally imposed. This type of definition stands polarised to individual self-sufficiency, exemplified in typical male being.

I argue that the construction of the self in relation to others and the type of knowing that affects this being is altered when women adopt prominent public positions and when men assume a significant place in parenting. It is historically premature to specify the precise nature of this revised self-identity. It is possible to conclude that not only is a greater capacity for self-in-relationship fostered through the process of parenting, but the affect on the children's identity is also important. When children have a qualitatively and quantitatively balanced proportion of time from a significant male and a significant female, both of whom practice autonomy in the private and public spheres, interdependence and loving nurture, then the conventional stereotypes and dualism are being eroded in a more conspicuous manner than a claim to female unique relations can provide.

It seems to me that the insistence on calling the relational perspective woman-centred, precludes admitting the possibility of men also developing these character traits. While it is liberating to celebrate what were traditionally devalued aspects of female experience, this stance necessitates a simultaneous critical perspective, so that questions can be raised as to what precisely is being celebrated. Otherwise, there is a narrowness of horizons that prevents self-reflection. It is necessary to remember that the specificity of women's historical identity is inseparable from women's oppression. It is one thing to include those previously denied or marginalised dimensions of female existence, like caring, sharing and nurturing, into the concept of full moral being, but it is quite another thing to direct political struggle to feminise the world or the concept of humanity.

The second concluding point refers again to the nature of personal experience. It is important to determine whether a woman-centred perspective is incommunicable to men, something men can learn from and appropriate into their own lives, or whether it provides a more complete picture than traditional ideas of 'mankind'. While it is difficult to supply documented empirical evidence, it is clear that certain men are engaged in the process of exploring new types of male individuality that are responsive to others and incorporate the emotions, sensitivity and connection with others. Women do not have exclusive rights to a concept of self divorced from aggression.

I see two significant factors operating here. These refer to overlaps in men's and women's concerns and the influence of dialogue and shared ideas. With the example of language, experiments of 'sex differences' seem to indicate that females generally surpass males in their attentiveness to social stimuli, being better listeners, more responsive to variations in interpersonal contexts and more accurately interpreting emotional messages (Lee and Stewart eds, 1976: Part 4). This is cited by some as proof of women's intuitive emotional basis (Fishman ed., 1972). Others seek to demonstrate how much this contributes to the silencing mechanisms men impose on women (Spender, 1980).

Dialogue is the key to increasing the understanding of people's experiences and peculiar identities. I cannot do Habermas full justice, but I cite his critical theory of communicative action, as a positive guideline. He assumes that 'language is the ground of intersubjectivity' (1971: 57) where the 'I' is constituted through acknowledging the 'discourse of the other'. He posits an 'ideal speech' situation premised on the possibility of full intersubjectivity in unconstrained communication, aiming at mutuality, trust and reciprocal understanding. This situation is a concrete manifestation of subjects' mutual recognition of each other. This approach denies the inevitability of tension implicit in dualism, and thus presents a better alternative than an assertion of the exclusivity of a relational orientation to women, which does little to challenge polarities.

A second positive factor operating in relationships between men and women is the influence of 'personal politics'. It seems reasonable to expect that men who have contact with feminists at a political, intimate or work level, are confronted with feminist praxis. Clearly a 'conversion from sexism' differs for everyone. Frequently the strongest feminist consciousness comes in older women who realise their self-betrayal in losing years of a self-defined life (Markson ed., 1983). Anger, as opposed to traditional virtues of humility and self-abnegation, can be liberating, enabling women to assess past mistakes with honesty. Much of the anger is directed against male-defined existence and yet it is essential to avoid adopting a 'reversed female chauvinism' for this might cause us to lose touch with the human face of males and to begin to imagine that women alone are human and males are evil and defective (Ruether, 1983: 188). This is particularly important for fostering unconstrained communication.

Typical male responses to feminist praxis assume varying stages (Tolson, 1977; Chesler, 1980; Pleck, 1981; Spender, 1981). Initially, many men, being convinced of their personal benevolence toward women, find it impossible to believe in women's oppression. The next stage might be co-option, when, being aware of the polarisation, they personalise their suffering in terms of emotional repression and consider themselves 'male feminists'. Yet even when a man's life-style and identity change as a consequence, the 'supportive male' still often views sexism as primarily 'women's problem'. His 'help' for her often does not interfere with his male status and priorities. Men must be willing to enter into risks themselves even if it jeopardises traditional avenues of status. The struggle against sexism is a struggle to humanise ourselves. In stressing the importance of personal experience, I am suggesting that a viable means to transcend dualism is to cease viewing men's and women's experiences as being directed by two necessarily independent, opposed principles.

My third concluding point addresses the gynocentric aim for a unification of diversity. Griffin, using forest imagery, symbolically depicts this stand. 'And we are various, and amazing in our variety, and our differences multiply, so that edge after edge of the endlessness of possibility is exposed... Yet what you fail to know, we know, and the knowing is in us... why we are shaped the way we are, not all straight to your purpose, but to ours' (1980: 220). This recognises the positive power of difference, that diversity is part of strength and within this there can be unity. It is not clear why this is posited by the gynocentrists as a unification of the diversity among women only.

The nature of my questioning is frequently countered by the recognition that knowledge is influenced by a specific sexual position, and occupies what can be called 'a sexualised discourse' (Gross, 1986a: 135). The sexual nature of this discourse is more significant in certain experiences than others. If any distinctiveness can be argued for, any assertion of the feminine principle should not be claimed to be normative for all women (Whitbeck, 1976: 59). A critique of the social construction of gender cannot be simplistically replaced by a claim that women have intrinsic moral superiority. A new codification of sex differences representing women as pure and men as corrupt reverses the typical order of a dualistic world view, while leaving its dualism intact. Such a new codification fails to clearly incorporate the link between history, one's material situation and individual differences. Yet, I support Gross' view that a 'sexualised discourse' can be a vibrant manner of appreciating 'embodied being'. That is, we cannot separate our experiences as men and women from our realisation of being moral identities. A unification of diversity ought not to exclude any person, although, as mentioned elsewhere, we would not endorse sexist practices. We turn now to explain what possibilities emerge from a view of a non-dualistic diversity among men and women.

PHILOSOPHY OF SYNTHESIS

The attempt to formulate a 'philosophy of synthesis' is complex. Yet it is a crucial task, for it directs my entire argument. I offer some guidelines now, but the full progression of this synthesis develops throughout the book. I have demonstrated how a gynocentric perspective affirms a positive female identity, but fails to challenge entrenched dualisms that inhibit the liberation of this identity. I propose the argument that both sides of the dichotomy outlined in list form in foot-note 2 of this chapter are differing dimensions of a balanced moral life. Balance is important in moral life to ensure some harmony of the particular parts in the overall narrative. The conflicting tendencies of parts may not necessarily be incompatible.

That is, I am arguing that the list is of *pairs*, not dualisms, although they have been conceived as the latter throughout the history of philosophy. The pairs may be conceptualised as being 'complementarily coexistent' (O'Brien, 1983: 80). This conceptualisation permits their apparent opposition to be questioned and their interrelation to be exposed. And because it does, the conceptualisation of 'pairs' has an emphasis that's different in kind from the emphases associated with dualisms, polarities, contradictions, contraries and dichotomies which embody the very notions I am trying to surmount: that is, respectively, independent principles, contrasting qualities, oppositions, incommensurable natures or tendencies, and binary classifications.

My proposition does not remove the idea of difference, distinction, or even of tension, but rather of opposition and antagonism. The notion of pairs as being 'complementarily coexistent' does not imply a complementarity between the sexes. A contrast of expressive and instrumental roles, seen as functional aspects of the social mechanism (Parsons, 1951; 1955), is a prime example of what is *not* being asserted. Parsons' contrasts presuppose polar opposites, with choice limited to either–or categories.[8] Reason and emotion, for example, are assumed to be mutually exclusive qualities. According to this view, an increase in one's rational output must result in a decrease in one's expressivity and vice-versa. The exclusive nature of this choice is the 'logical link to conventional views about male and female roles' (Glennon, 1979: 23).

An 'either–or' mentality lies at the basis of marginality, particularly, as mentioned, in the frustration that comes with juggling the conflicting demands of the public and private spheres. For women, this can result in deferring, submissive, private women feeling compelled to act as independent, quick-witted or skilled public workers. Conversely, their identity may be more consistent with the public image and through coercion, choice or dependence to others, they may adapt to produce the socially appropriate private image. Similarly, instrumental, calculative men may find it difficult to adapt to the emotional intensity of the private sphere, experiencing a conflict of self when attempting to do so. For other men, their expressive self may be stultified by work demands and traditional notions of masculinity.

My point is that the 'either–or' mentality contributes substantially to instances of distorted humanity. This mentality delineates restrictive notions of self and constructs dualistic world-views and practices. Consequently, it obstructs authentic interaction, in that individuals manifest pathological masks. To a large degree, each side of the gender dualism depends on the other for what it perceives is lacking in itself. That is, men often fail to integrate into their sense of self emotional traits they project onto women. Many women have not incorporated strong autonomous capacities traditionally claimed by men. Integrated beings have no need to suppress, repress, deny or project negative aspects of the self onto another. My argument calls into question the notion of a 'higher' and 'lower' self.[9]

Yet in the history of philosophy, the alternatives relating to selfhood are usually restricted to an oppositional dualism, or, where this is rejected, combinations of binary pairs frequently result in monism, where one emphasis is reduced by the other. For example, with the mind–body distinction, the tendency within abstract philosophy is for the mental aspect to outweigh the physical: nature, the body, reproduction and sexuality; or within some extreme feminist accounts of the embrace of nature, there is a tendency to exalt these physical aspects at the expense of the mental.

The motivation behind the search for a *monos* is the attempt to discover an all-embracing explanatory mode. Historically, each renewal of the search summons retrospective reflection on the truth or validity of the monisms of earlier views. Is the one Anaxagoras's Nous (Mind)?, Heraclitus's Logos, Parmenides' Being? Is it Plato's Good? Or Aristotle's telic Unmoved Mover? Is the one God the God of the Jews? Or the Christians? (Young-Bruehl, 1987: 210).

The cosmopolitanism integral to the Enlightenment provided the milieu in which people could question the rationale behind such philosophical and religious searches. A new wave of reflection was ushered in. This coincided with the emergence of notions of cultural diversity and mental relativism, basic ingredients of the intellectualism of the French Revolution. The opportunity to reassess 'difference' was ripe. Largely, this difference was still measured in terms of the 'ideal mind', associated with ideals of maleness, my focus in Chapter Four. Given that contrasts are historically mutually exclusive or contradictory, they cannot simplistically be reversed or combined by assertion.

Furthermore, I maintain that it is an illusion to see one dimension of a dichotomous pair as being able to supply the content required to formulate moral judgement, or to provide, by itself, serious guidance in actual moral dilemmas. The area that dualism and monism fail to address is the excluded middle, the complex tension *between* the perspectives which exposes the real complexity of moral experience in general. We can all recall being torn between extremes, and the uncertainty that moral dilemmas invoke.

Thus, in challenging the inevitability of dualism or monism, I maintain that it is through exploring the relationships between pairs that both the mutual dependencies and the interconnections are unravelled. Only then, is the situation created where much of the antagonism between pairs and between people can dissolve.

One option is to argue that it is precisely from the 'middle ground' that the possibility of a philosophy of synthesis emerges. Within such a view, this middle ground is not considered a 'caught-betweenness', in the sense of hovering in a deliberately chosen position while repudiating the definite positions. For those women tossed between the demands of private and public spheres, ambiguity arises from directly conflicting priorities. Any 'caught-betweenness' arises through striving toward the possibility of reconciliation, without the assurance of a solution.

My emphasis differs from a view that defends a 'middle ground' as an important strategical position which precedes and exceeds oppositional categories. That is, a strategy that pivots around the middle ground, embraces the necessity of contradiction to its view, but refuses to accept the possibility or desirability of the resolution of the contradiction. The issues of 'sameness' and 'difference' provide an interesting example of this strategy. A defence of the middle ground maintains that to take 'both sides' leads to a compromise between antagonistic terms or the reduction or subsuming of one by the other. Within this defence, any conclusion that men and women are the same though different is seen as a compromise position whereby either the 'sameness' obliterates significant differences, or 'differences' override shared capacities.

For example, Derrida (1979) maintains that the value of this 'middle ground' is not ontological, in terms of displacing identity with difference, nor epistemological, as creating new approaches to knowing the self, but is strategic, to emphasise the spillage across binary classifications. Gross writes that Derrida recognises such 'deconstruction as, at best, a provisional or tentative untangling of the oppositional strands in metaphysics' (1986a: 133). This process of untangling is particularly used by French feminists to articulate the politics of sexual difference, as a politics of specificity, which, as Gross puts it, 'involves the recognition of the differences between men and women (Irigaray), or the differences within each man and woman (Kristeva)' (140).

I view the exploration of this 'middle ground' as vital, so long as it questions the presumed inevitability of dualism. Understanding the reality of the strain intrinsic to this middle ground, and being alert to the possible pull toward antagonistic extremes, permits us to address relationships and to engage in a reflective, balanced moral perspective without a restless 'hovering', a naive 'taking both sides', or a limiting 'either–or' mentality.

Any revamped versions of androgyny as 'the best of both worlds', reintroduces confusion by linking gender and dualism. When contrasts are accepted as necessarily dualistic, a simplistic convergence reinforces gender dualism and ignores the 'middle ground'. On the other hand, an elevation of this middle position encourages ambiguity. Acknowledging various strains between the contrasts prevents a simplistic complementarity and recognises the real difficulty of integrating both sides of pairs into one's self. It also permits radical challenges to dualism that result in unique interpretations of personhood and difference.

Glennon's comparison of a 'well-rounded person' and an 'integrated person' is useful. She suggests that a well-rounded person segregates aspects of life, such as rationality or the emotions, performing them in sequence, while playing a variety of life roles. For example, a well-rounded woman may manage to balance four non-neutral expressive roles (wife, mother, mistress and hostess) with four predominantly instrumental ones (lawyer, local-council member, club president and school-council member). As Glennon demonstrates, admirable as this may appear, this represents the sum of compartmentalised activities. Furthermore, it has little comment to make on tensions between the roles, such as between wife and mother, mother and mistress or commitments as lawyer and mother. To advocate a 'well-rounded person' as an ideal notion of the subject would be to merely invite men to add expressive activities to their instrumental ones, or to suggest for example that women be more calculative in their relationships.

A *philosophy of synthesis* challenges the segmentation of disparate practices. It is different from an androgynous convergence. It seeks to transform a dualistic world into a dialectical one, where interrelationships are paramount. This synthesis recognises possible tension within contrasts, but repudiates the necessity of antagonism or contradiction. This synthesis permits a radical challenge to dualistic restraints on self-identity. In continuing the instrumental–expressive example cited above, how does an 'integrated person' differ from a 'well-rounded person'? The integrated woman recognises the inevitable tensions between her roles and her self-expression, feeling the pull of one factor against the other, yet never entirely yielding to one at the expense of the other. Each dimension informs and transforms 'in a continual process of dialectical becomingness' (Glennon, 1978: 100). Thus her experiences in each different role inform and are informed by her other experiences.

Some further examples explain this synthetic approach. The relationship between some pairs is clearly connected, as with responsibility–rights, mercy–justice, others–self and theory–practice. With other pairs, like intuition–logic, opinion–knowledge, and sexuality–spirituality, each aspect informs the other. In sexual love, where there is unity of spirit, the self and the other may be virtually indistinguishable. Collective work, whether political, religious, teaching or community also sees the collective–self-interest distinction minimised. With other pairs it is not possible to know one dimension without the other, as with dark–light.[10]

The relationship between some other pairs requires further explanation. Knowledge of the abstract is informed by the knowledge of the concrete and vice-versa. Yet it might be argued that one can know the interior of something without knowing the exterior. While it is strictly true that one might know the inside of a house without ever seeing the outside, or that one can recognise the physical appearance of a person without knowing the personality, it would not be true to say that in those cases one knew the house or person thoroughly. The passivity and activity pair seem superficially to be opposed, but it is possible to be actively passive in the case of rape or uninterested sex, where one is deliberately inactive for the sake of one's safety, sanity or to speed the act. It is also possible to be passively active such as in acts of civil disobedience, where citizens make a political statement by non-violent means.

Possibilities for the immanence–trancendence pair are interesting. Through the emphasis in progressive theology on praxis, a transcendent God is always knowable in concrete terms. Natural beauty is another example. The beauty of a waterfall, cliffs or the ocean have been an inspiration and solace for poets, artists, mourners and lovers, precisely for its ability to transport one beyond the confines of self. With the public–private contrast, difficulty is both conceptual and practical. There is an increasing infringement of private spheres through bureaucracy and rationalisation, coinciding with an increased stress on 'personalising' the public sphere. The relationship between universality and particularity is central to feminist philosophy. Traditionally, philosophers argue that it is only from an 'objective stance' that individual particularity can make sense. This slides into a formalism that ignores content and context. In addition, once the universal is seen to take priority over the particular, or essence over the accidental, then, as we have seen, an inescapable hierarchy emerges, that undervalues the daily, concrete particularities of existence.

I have provided examples of some of the complexities associated with a reconceptualisation of contrasts as pairs rather than as dualistic polarities. I maintain that a philosophy of synthesis has the advantage of understanding its intellectual heritage with all its highlights as well as its shortcomings. A philosophy of synthesis provides a basis for an approach that integrates the full range of human activities. In understanding the contribution of past intellectual thought to female and male consciousness, we can appreciate how both women's and men's lives are often impoverished by stereotypical restraints. Once it is recognised that the full range of human activities is available to all, then an understanding of sexual differences ceases to be threatening. A philosophy of synthesis creates the possibilities from which access to the full gamut of human experiences can emerge.

NOTES

1   The one exception I make here from the list in the following footnote is that of Good–Evil.
2   The following list suggests the major tensions to which I refer. Some clearly overlap. The list has no particular order, except that the first aspect of these tends to be associated with maleness, the second with femaleness. Male–female opposition is at the heart of these contrasts.

Public–Private	Freedom–Necessity
Rights–Responsibilities	Knowledge–Opinion
Culture–Nature	Essence–Accident
Mind/Spirit–Body	External–Internal
Political–Personal	Rationality–Sensuality
Self-Realisation–Nurture	Objectivity–Subjectivity
Fact–Supposition	Self–Others
Light–Dark	Dominance–Submission
Abstract–Concrete	Specificity–Diffuseness
Reason–Passion	Production–Reproduction
Good–Evil	Logic–Intuition

Universality–Particularity	Intellect–Emotion
Justice–Love	Activity–Passivity
Transcendence–Immanence	Instrumentality–Expressivity
Spirituality–Sexuality	Knower–Known

3   A consequence of this principle is the acceptance of infinite variations of the negative, a concept used by theologians to define God in terms of what God is not. This helps to maintain a notion of the infinite.

4   It is possible to see the causes of rationalisation and fragmentation to be a result of numerous factors such as the growth of capitalism, the Protestant Calvinistic ethic, bureaucracy, technology, specialisation, urbanisation, alienation, social isolation, social stratification and class struggle. For one feasible interpretation of changes in attitude that accompanied ethical, economic and social changes in modern culture, see Weber (1958).

5   This general statement on essential and accidental properties merely reiterates the traditional philosophical position. I do not deny that one cannot acquire properties essential to transform one into something else. Furthermore, a severely intellectually handicapped person may be seen to have an 'accidental property', and lacks something essential to selfhood, understood in a maximal sense, but a sensitivity to this person may require a reassessment of essential properties.

6   See Whitbeck, (1976: 57–60). She explains how the Monad was the Principle of Oneness, and the Dyad was the principle of Twoness, derived from the Monad and Space (or the Unlimited). The first aspect is called Monad, the second Dyad. Within this construct, the feminine is seen as the Second of Two Opposing Principles.

Male–Female	Rest–Motion
Limit–Unlimited	Straight–Curved
Odd–Even	Light–Darkness
One–Many	Good–Bad
Right–Left	Square–Oblong

This is also similar to the Chinese construction of Yang–Yin

Male–Female	Constructive–Destructive
Positive–Negative	Heaven–Earth
Active–Passive	Beginning–Completion
Strong–Weak	

7   Moss Kanter (1977) offers a useful analysis of this issue. She argues against the 'women are different' view which maintains that women should strive for political leadership in order to 'humanise' society. She argues that opportunity within corporate management acts as a self-fulfilling prophecy. Those who are given responsibility tend to achieve, but bureaucracies handicap the careers of talented women, in not providing the above opportunities. She stresses the need for structures to change, as well as personnel. Within an Australian context, feminists have made concerted demands on the welfare state to extend women's rights and opportunities. These women working at policy-making level are termed 'femocrats'. (see Franzway, 1986). Opinion varies as to whether femocrats have been co-opted by high salaries and status, or whether they have contributed substantially to social change.

8   Glennon (1979) and Eichler (1980) outline a typical Parsonian 5 fold schema. It includes

Affectivity	Versus	Affective Neutrality
Collective Interest	Versus	Self-Interest
Particularism	Versus	Universalism
Ascription	Versus	Achievement
Diffuseness	Versus	Specificity

9   Berlin (1969: 132) argues of the 'conflict of self', where rational, realistic, idealistic, autonomous self rages battle with irrational impulses, uncontrolled desires and the pursuit of immediate pleasures and passions. After reflection, Berlin suggests the 'lower self' can conclude I was 'not myself', meaning not in control of myself. I argue in Chapter Four that such an emphasis understates the significance the emotions assume in our concept of the self. I also question the tendency to call passions, 'irrational'.

10 A blind person does not see dark as a contrast to light (unless blinded after some sight) but as a nothingness.

3 Nature, women and morality

In the previous chapter, I argued that a dualistic world-view suppressed the development of liberated subjects. The criticism of dualism establishes the framework for the next four chapters. In these chapters, I argue that in addition to moral dualism, views on nature, reason, individualism and moral development significantly influence ideals of moral difference. In this chapter, my analysis of 'difference' focuses on varying interpretations of nature, and how these affect definitions of personhood. These definitions identify some people as naturally primary agents and others as naturally secondary—as little more than instruments, property, defective beings, or non-persons. In repudiating these latter definitions and in attempting to outline a philosophy of the subject that highlights *similarities* between persons, it is valuable to begin with a survey of some influential theories that highlight differences.

In examining human nature, personhood and difference, the conceptual problem of what exactly constitutes a *significant* difference, in anything other than a biological sense, is, as we shall see, enormous. Furthermore, the claim that women and men are significantly different is usually assumed to be a simple statement about women. This utilisation of the concept 'difference', slides readily into notions of 'deviance' or 'inferiority'.

Difference is a relative concept. Just as women may be different from men, men may be different from women, and differences occur among women and among men. A review of gender-specific differences can be viewed on a continuum, between 'maximisers' or 'minimisers' (McFadden, 1984). Such analyses pronounce or minimise differences. While it is not self-evident that difference must be hierarchically scaled, it is difficult to maintain a 'different but equal' concept. Tensions arise in new debates with the feminist demand for *equality* coexisting with the recent celebration of *difference*. A good example of this is provided by Pierson and Prentice, who 'argue that women can be both different and equal, separatist and assimilationist...If this is seen as a demand to have our cake and eat it too, we agree that it is' (1982: 108). Reconciling such tensions is crucial to my philosophy of synthesis.

In this chapter, I analyse the effects of difference and nature on the theme of women and morality. The chapter is divided into four sections. Each section combines both traditional philosophical and particular feminist debates. To initiate the discussion, I outline different perceptions of nature and personhood. In the second section, I examine conflicting views on the conceptualisation of nature and biology. The third section explores the relation between nature, culture and reproduction. My conclusion draws together the implications of the above three issues as they bear on the topic of 'human nature.'

Two major philosophical themes purport to explain natural differences between women and men, and yet hinder woman's development as a moral subject. These themes perceive women relative to men, as helpers and partial beings and as equal but different. Ironically, certain feminist themes of difference reveal three different views of women's moral status, as androgynous, as distinct, or as superior, but remain, in my understanding, an inadequate assessment of moral identity.

Philosophical definitions of women's nature

Two traditional philosophical definitions of women's nature influence ideals of personhood. These definitions present women as partial helpmates and as equal but different. They both have their roots in Judaeo-Christian theology.

Women as partial helpmates

The first definition has two components. It defines women in terms of men's needs, or desires for pleasure, utility or offspring, and also as partial beings. The historical roots of this concept can be traced to the second account of creation presented in the Judaeo-Christian Bible. The first account states that male and female were created together in the image of God. The second narrative states that after having created a man, God declares, 'It is not good that man should be alone; I will make a helper fit for him' (Genesis 2: 18). The distinction between essential and accidental capacities is crucial in traditional philosophy. Some writers suggest that 'helper' carries no status connotations and that the story represents women as derivative in emphasising essential capacities. I contend that within my cultural background the historical association of 'helper' with 'a tool for man's desires' has contributed significantly to women's servility and dependency.

St Augustine attempts to reconcile the apparent inconsistency between the above two narratives. His development of the 'help-mate' idea links the 'tool' notion with that of 'partial being'. Reflecting on women's nature, Augustine concludes that a married woman is in the image of God, being viewed in the light of her husband, but not when she is considered separately, where she is seen as a help-mate, but 'the man alone, he is the image of God...fully and completely' (St Augustine, 1887: 159). The basis of this difference lies in a specific concept of reason. In his *Confessions*, Augustine concedes that women do have rational understanding, but maintains the necessity of female bodily subjection to men. This subjection associates women primarily with sensuality and subordination, and men with both reason and authority (see Augustine, 1887: ch. 32). This assimilation of male–female polarity into soul (reason)–body dualism reinforces powerful gender symbolism, not only affecting marriage, but many other social relations.

Proponents of the view that women are 'partial men' and less capable of moral action derive the principal difference from the claim that women either lack, or are deficient in, some vital ingredient in men's make-up. This is almost always connected with rationality. Aristotle's writings clearly exemplify this view. 'Male and female differ in essence, ability, function, and anatomically...clearly then, the distinction of sex is a first principle' (1979: 35–36). From this premise, other principles are derived. According to Aristotle, the male principle in human conception contributes form, activity and movement, the female principle, matter. He draws a direct analogy between the biological and ethical relations of men and women. The most important difference, he asserts, is in the rational soul. 'The deliberative faculty in the soul is not present at all in a slave; in a female it is inoperative, in a child undeveloped. We must therefore take it that the same conditions prevail also in regard to the ethical virtues' (1972: Book 1, ch. 13: 52). It is not that women's deliberative and moral powers are derived from their biology, it is that he describes women's nature as being defined by the ability to provide matter, or by the inability to provide form, potency or capability. Thus, in natural terms, women are inevitably morally deficient.

Aristotle's 'metaphysical biology' underlies his entire view on human nature which is connected to his notion of a virtuous person. Virtue, being tied to the rational faculty used to intuit true premises of knowledge, is demonstrable in deliberative action, affirming a life in accordance with one's nature. If virtue is dependent on this interpretation of reason, the consequences for women, whose rational faculties are said by some philosophers to be deficient in comparison with men's, is inevitably disastrous. Difference lies in the nature of the soul's capacity and the authority accompanying it, the 'authority' Augustine drew on. An inoperative deliberative faculty presumes a lack of self-control. In these terms (as being by nature equipped to obey men), women can only participate minimally in the ethical virtues. Accordingly, to be a woman is to suffer from 'privation', a term Aristotle uses of something that lacks attributes which, while normally naturally possessed, would not be possessed by the object or person in question. Woman, as 'partial man' thus lacks potency. The influence of this view is enormous.

Aquinas restates many arguments used by Aristotle to substantiate his claim that 'woman is defective and misbegotten' (1979: 69). To Aquinas, a girl child represents a defective human, resulting from an accident to the sperm, imagined to contain the complete male *in potentia*. He defines women's sole purpose as an instrument of reproduction. For all other purposes, man is best served by other men. Aquinas, following Aristotle, again announces that 'man is yet further ordered to a still nobler vital action, and that is intellectual operation' (1979: 69). It is not that women do not possess rational faculties, but that these faculties appear more strongly in the male, reflecting the differences by which the sexes were supposed to reflect the *imago dei* (see Commo McLaughlin, 1979).

Women as different but complementary
A second major philosophical theme stresses complementary differences. 'Complementarity' appears value-neutral in that it attributes to both sexes positive features. Logically, complementarity need not be construed hierarchically—yet, it usually is. However, qualities imputed to 'femininity' do not simply emerge as 'different' from masculinity, but are defined as the male's opposite, negative or repressed elements. Woman, as de Beauvoir expresses it, 'is defined and differentiated with reference to man...she is the incidental, the inessential as opposed to the essential. He is the subject, he is the Absolute—she is the Other' (1975: 16).

Themes of complementarity identify two principles in human nature. The first principle embodies the characteristics seen to accrue to the conscious, active self, where the hallmark invariably is that of rationality, autonomous selfhood and critical judgement. This is usually taken to be the male principle. The second principle is defined in contrast and the feminine is connected with either the non-rational or the irrational, depending on which view of the conscious self is concerned. 'Complementarity' in a context of moral dualism is almost always illusory.

'Complementarity' disintegrates when one dimension of human capacity assumes primacy, and all else is either defined in opposition, or relegated to secondary status. Most of the typically acclaimed differences that supposedly complement the sexes relate to rationality. Traditional philosophers adopt several different approaches to this issue. Some draw a firm demarcation between the whole faculty of thought as male, and the faculty of feeling as female. Others delineate specialisations within thought, so that men are seen to reason logically and articulately, and women are seen to use intuition to reach similar cognitive goals. In this context, sexual specialisation 'can look more or less alarming according to how you treat it' (Midgley and Hughes, 1983: 192).

Yet neither of these approaches satisfies a claim to complementarity, without some hierarchical evaluation. Furthermore, within these approaches, an overlapping of the rational and emotional spheres is logically precluded or actively discouraged. Therefore, the possibility of exploring the 'middle ground', discussed in the previous chapter, is eliminated. The extension of complementarity into a 'different but equal' theme is not the same as a 'different and equal' theme. To generalise, advocates of the 'different' side stress examples of colour, sex, race and religion and advocates of the 'equal' dimension stress moral worth, rights to citizenship and religious status.

Two very different examples of complementary differences are espoused by the Judaeo-Christian view and Rousseau although neither view fits exclusively into this theme. Although Christian symbolism has diminished in Western, secularised cultures, its influence persists. Complementarity is stressed in Biblical passages that provide instruction on interdependent roles (1 Corinthians 11: 11–12). The New Testament attempt to transcend sexual distinctions emphasises the acceptance and equality of all persons in the Kingdom of God (Galations 3: 28). Yet, in terms of interpersonal relations, this is frequently interpreted as 'soul equality, sexual inequality'. To sustain this interpretation, the allegorical relationship between God and the people, addressed in marriage terms (Song of Solomon; Feuerbach, 1957: chs 6, 26), is often cited. The Christ–Church relationship is paradigmatic, not a justification for female subordination and male lordship, unless men want to be elevated to 'gods'.

Rousseau (1977) opposes exponents who regard women as imperfect men. Insisting that men and women are alike in their commonalities, and simply incomparable in all other ways, he criticises those who imply that female traits are defects, and then audaciously suggests that such would be considered defects in men. For Rousseau the 'defects' emanate from major polarities of activity and passivity, strength and weakness, charmed timidity and bold desire. Having supposedly demonstrated that women and men are not constituted similarly in terms of temperament and character, Rousseau's goal is to seek complementarity, and to educate women carefully so they might delight and complement men.

For Rousseau also, reason decides women's nature. Responding to the question of women's rational capability, Rousseau diverts his answer by outlining why the cultivation of reason is not conducive to functions imposed on women like sexual fidelity, obedience, titilation and care for their husband and children. By fulfilling their familial duties, they obtain the respect of their husband on whom they are dependent. Philosophy, abstract and speculative truths are not the proper province of women who are to apply those principles which men have discovered. For Rousseau, sexual complementarity is ideal. He desires women who skillfully incline men to do what women are incapable of doing, and to intuit men's ideas, but men should formulate, appropriate and make use of the ideas. The application of this to women not directly dependent on a man is considered a non-issue, the emphasis being on the combination of men and women. This amounts to a reiteration of the emphases of Augustine and Aquinas.

Where complementarity is within the context of an 'equal *but* different' principle, hierarchy and subordination are inevitable. This idea of complementarity is no more satisfactory than a concept of women's partiality, or helper status, and these concepts prevent the possibility of mutually reciprocated relationships. The resulting duality between men and women, self and other, manifests itself in undue superiority in men or a deep complicity by women exacerbated by their feelings of natural inferiority. The complicity involved is often induced in a woman by the alliance she is obligated to form with those who 'compel her to assume the status of the Other' (de Beauvoir, 1975: 29), due to an emotional, fearful or financial dependence. Androcentric ideals of women's moral nature present a masculine version of moral identity and exclude a feminine input.

Feminism and difference

Many of the recent feminist challenges to restrictive notions of women's nature date from de Beauvoir's *The Second Sex* (1949, translated into English in 1953) and are attempts to provide more adequate explanations of the hypothesis that men and women are 'similar and equal though possibly different'. Despite variances in feminist views, three common explanations recur: the persistence of patriarchy, the social conditioning of women, and power inequalities that emerge as a result of sex-role differentiation. The three views I examine now assume these common explanations and maintain that women and men are essentially the same, that women have distinctive, positive differences from men, or that women are morally superior. My outline is selective. My aim is to clarify whether these definitions of women are more satisfactory than those of traditional philosophical positions. I assess now three particular feminist ideas on nature, personhood and difference—androgyny, distinctiveness and superiority.

Androgyny

The term 'androgyny' has Greek roots, andros being man, and gyne being woman. An androgynous person is characterised as neither masculine nor feminine, but human. Feminist advocates of androgyny do not envisage a sameness between women and men, or an enjoinder to combine feminine and masculine ways of being while still retaining the essential distinctions. Rather, they attempt to transcend stereotypical categories. In repudiating gender polarisation, traits characterised as 'masculine' or 'feminine' are exposed as learned social rules, not the inevitable result of biology. If we pick any trait supposed to be primarily masculine, like competitiveness, aggressiveness or egoism, we will find whole societies of both men and women who seem to lack these traits, and also whole societies that exhibit them (Ferguson, 1981: 49).

Yet, what an androgynous self actually looks like, or acts like, remains vague. It is naive to imagine that the only differences between men and women involve a mere physical awareness of the consciousness of having a sex-specific body, but nothing more. Different experiences and opportunities occur as responses to different bodies. Certainly, 'androgynous people are and will continue to be androgynous men and androgynous women, biologically' (Code, 1986: 51). If the body and sexuality are crucial to our identity, then it seems to me that the nature of being sexual men and sexual women will differ from an idea of being androgynous people. This means that being a sexual, possibly fecund female, will generally result in a range of different experiences and perceptions than those arising from being a sexual male. All attempts to eliminate pernicious normative connotations that descriptive categorisations such as 'femininity' and 'masculinity' normally carry, should be supported. But I withhold wholehearted acceptance of the androgyny ideal because it fails to incorporate the sexual dimension of personhood.

Any value of androgyny seems to be a heuristic one, presenting an ideal encouraging the development of aspects of nature repressed by stereotypical expectations. Within public policy, for example, a formal recognition of the value of traditional female and traditional male skills is important, as manifest through recent equal opportunity policies vying for equal pay (O'Donnell and Golder, 1986). Yet there are problems in proposing androgyny as a political ideal. Popularised versions masquerade as radical concepts, yet at their core is a reactionary enshrinement of stereotypical traits. It is difficult for androgyny to escape being viewed as an 'idealised reunification' (Eisenstein, 1984: 62) of a concept of human identity that should never have been so polarised (Eichler, 1980: 69–71). As a static ideal, it fails to challenge traditional notions of femininity and masculinity. For these reasons, I prefer to advocate, with Jaggar, that 'for me, to be a woman is no more and no less than to be a female human being' (1973–74: 282). The articulation of the 'no more and no less' is an important task. This definition is a more satisfactory combination of shared nature and distinct sexual difference.

Women as distinctive

A second feminist theme defines women's personhood in terms of a distinctive female nature, but gives minimal attention to shared human nature. Three aspects are stressed: androgyny is rejected; a fervent woman-centred perspective is adopted; attempts are made to define female experience in terms of strengths. A useful example of the emergence of this theme comes from an object-relation psychoanalytic framework that aims to understand human nature as a product of social relations in interaction with nature and human capacity.

Within this framework, a central place is given to 'reproduction', defined broadly, as O'Brien (1983) uses it, to include the whole span from conception through to nurturing. Object-relation theorists propose that the acquisition of gendered character-types develops largely as the result of particular reproductive practices which are not determined solely by biology, and hence in principle are alterable. If their psychoanalytic interpretive account is correct, then there is a close 'fit' between infant and adult experience. Only a focus on relations can explain how different psychic experiences structure and are reinforced by women's and men's activities as influenced by the sexual division of labour (Glass, 1978: 66).

For example, Miller (1976), in repudiating the idea that women need to be 'cured' of disabilities developed in male-dominated culture, argues that society needs the qualities it undervalues and relegates to women. She refers particularly to capacities to express and interpret emotions, to cultivate co-operativeness and to encourage co-ordination with others. This emphasis on women's positive qualities also demands a re-evaluation of values traditionally prized in male-dominated cultures. Miller's ideal incorporates a renewed sense of self-determination that rejects aggression or a selfish assertion of individual rights, but advocates a strong self-identity, based on a sense of affiliation and connection with others. She stresses the traditional distinctiveness of women as a moral strength.

Coinciding with this analysis, is a concerted re-examination of the cultural meaning of motherhood. Rich (1979) draws a clear distinction between experiential aspects of mothering—like tenderness, passion and courage combined with frustration, anxiety and pain—and patriarchal structures that restrict the valuing of nurture. Moreover, Dinnerstein (1976), in querying why women almost universally undertake early child-care, probes the implications of this for the development of human character and culture in general. She argues that consequences flow from the fundamental fact that both positive and negative intense early experiences for children occur through being exclusively nurtured by women. These consequences include the association of women with nature, as something to be controlled and manipulated.

Chodorow (1978) likewise, in exploring the fundamental question of why women mother, approaches this as a phenomenon in need of explanation, not a mere natural occurrence. She rejects role theories. Chodorow argues that a scrutiny of intense interpersonal relations reveals how qualities for successful nurturing become embedded in personality. She maintains that anyone who has participated in a 'good-enough mothering' relationship can 'do mothering'. The fact that women do most of the 'mothering' is explained by her belief that females develop a greater capacity for a relational-self.[1]

In briefly summarising these theorists, I want to show how claims of female distinctiveness can be seen largely to result from the development of the capacity to care for others, rather than simply from nature. This is not always spelt out by object-relation theorists. The development of this capacity to care is influenced by early experiences. A child's self-identity moves from an initial sense of unity, usually with the mother or a substitute woman, to a process of separation-individuation. In 'separation', the child develops a firm sense of differentiation. In 'individuation', there is the establishment of character traits uniquely one's own which form one's core identity. Whereas girls tend to develop within a continuing relationship with women, boys in traditional families tend to develop an identity based on an opposition, a notion of 'not-female', and thus develop an exaggerated sense of autonomy that often accompanies the curtailment of expressive capacities. A transformation of this early development through shared parenting may break much of this rigidity. Opinions on this vary from seeing it as 'the key to the liberation of relations' (Balbus, 1982: 312) to suggestions that 'there is something very incoherent in the claim that men must do their "fair" share' (McMillan, 1982: 114).

Nevertheless, the stress on the advocacy of distinct female positive differences is to redress past denigrations of women's traditional capacities. This devaluation is not only by men, but by some women who view any affirmation of traditional femininity as a capitulation to male cultural hegemony. The rescue of certain traditional female traits as potential sources of moral strength is important, but there are two significant, interrelated drawbacks with this achievement that relate equally to feminists and to right-wing proponents of 'women who want to be women'. First, there are significant problems with the glorification of supposedly feminine characteristics. Criteria to determine what precisely is a weakness or a strength remain ambiguous. Furthermore, this lack of clarity within positions advocating a distinctive female nature coincides with powerful, yet irrelevant, symbolism associated with gender difference. Thought is again an appropriate example. In contrast to men's assumed clear rationality, women are often credited with strong intuition. When symbolism is attached to this, connotations of mystery and natural insight develop. The 'intuitive mother' who hears a dozen newborn babies cry and 'knows' which one is hers is difficult to explain in terms other than 'mysterious'. Yet, this elevation of natural intuition is a worrying philosophical idea, for it really constitutes little more than a hunch identified as correct only in retrospect. Now, if that mother is correct in identifying her baby, then people smile and confirm the wonder of her intuition. If she is incorrect, then tiredness, post-natal depression, lack of practice or sheer scepticism will be attributed to her. I am not denying the validity of intuition. Indeed, ample anecdotal evidence could be cited to 'prove' instances of spontaneous compulsion to act in particular ways, where mere coincidence is an inadequate explanation. What I oppose is the symbolic force that can transform a notion like intuition into a natural phenomenon, and in so doing regard it as necessarily 'feminine'. For it has the unfortunate consequence that men regard intuition as mostly alien to their experience, and that women with no particular wish to appropriate it have their femininity queried.

My second reservation about the declaration of women's distinctiveness relates back to my argument in Chapter One that an extreme 'woman-centred perspective', in celebrating difference as a source of moral value, presupposes 'the centrality, normality and value of women's experience and women's culture' (Eisenstein, 1984: xviii). This position reverses de Beauvoir's theory on woman as Other by rendering males the object of analysis and their degree of deviancy from the female the issue to be explained (Lerner, 1979: xxxi). This, I aver, is an important strategy in feminist analysis, which I adopt to some degree in the following chapters. But I try to avoid the slide from distinctiveness to superiority, for this disallows any mutuality in the subject-object relation.

Any tendency toward an unbalanced essentialism should be avoided. At a practical, experiential level, it is consistent to assert that virtues such as nurturing, relational interests, and warm emotional dispositions are predominantly 'women's virtues', in the sense that, currently, more women practice such virtues. Yet, while some women lack these virtues and some men practise them, the notion of how *natural* they are must be questioned. In trying to determine what women's nature is, I have argued that these virtues are not natural traits of femaleness, but ones that have emerged through the practices intrinsic to the social construction of femininity. They can be construed as important dimensions of human nature. This has political ramifications, for when articulated in this manner, the suggestion that what is missing in the public domain is the contribution of women and their specific virtues becomes contentious (Elshtain, 1981; Gould, 1984). What is clearly missing are the virtues. In terms of this issue, the fact that the women are also missing is coincidental.

Women as morally superior

A third feminist notion of natural difference extends the previous position to the point of emphasising the moral superiority of women. This position has two main tenets. First, it asserts that there are innately female modes of knowing. Rationality is denounced as fundamentally male and, thus, flawed. Second, there is an implicit attribution of female superiority to biology, or at least to an assumed female nature. The groundwork for these tenets is based largely on research on sexuality and embryology, including criticising the ideology surrounding men's control over sexual intercourse, positive attitudes to multiple orgasm (Koedt, 1973; Morgan, 1970) and the claim that embryos are anatomically female-like until foetal androgen causes male differentiation. This position views femaleness as normative and maleness as the deviation.

The concept of 'woman-identified woman' initiated revolutionary changes among activists in the women's liberation movement. Many activists view lesbianism not simply as sexual preference, but as an avowed political decision that rejects men. This invokes a modified version of the 'eternal feminine' (see de Lubac, 1971). Just as the Greek goddess, Hera, as 'woman deified', presided over all phases of feminine existence, so too the 'Virgin Mary' is seen to combine virginity, sexuality and maternalism. A prominent supporter of these emphases, Daly, proposes inner journeys for women from a 'male maze' to the 'other world' into an 'Ecstasy of Female Creation' (1978). I maintain these ideas endorse female essentialism, encapsulated in a 'metaphysical feminism', which vocates a 'universal woman', and ignores specificities that define particular women.

In rejecting male definitions of female nature, advocates of this position postulate traditionally unacknowledged modes of knowing, emphasising feelings, emotions, the body and intuition. It is plausible to argue that the relational contexts many women find themselves in encourage responses to emotive cues. Plausibility diminishes when the emotions are posited as an exclusive mode of interpreting the world. The extreme form of a woman-centred perspective paradoxically has an inherent contradiction. It sets out to prove the moral superiority of women, by setting women apart as possessing a different nature. But an acceptance of all women as emotionally intense, reinforces traditional views on which the moral inferiority of women has been based. Furthermore, it assumes superiority simply by rejecting traditional masculinity and asserting traditional femininity, as intrinsic to female nature. Neither traditional philosophical nor feminist definitions of natural differences in personhood mentioned above have provided satisfactory insight into the complexity surrounding the nature of being.

NATURE AND BIOLOGY

In the views outlined above, biological factors are intertwined with ideas of moral capacity. Many debates are misguided in their use of biological data, in their initial premises and in reaching conclusions that tend toward reductionism. In my view, complex historical, socio-political and philosophical phenomena cannot simply be subsumed or 'wiped away' under an all-inclusive category named 'biological difference'. The scientific model of nature is no longer causal and continuous. Yet, much of the literature that aligns nature with biology is accompanied by a concomitant empiricist assumption that differences in social psychology and moral behaviour are necessarily caused by the observed biological differences with which they appear to correlate. There are serious problems with this. When gender differences are seen principally in biological terms, they are viewed as natural, rooted in an unchanging biological basis determining human nature.

We proceed with three ways of conceptualising the relation between biology and women's nature. The first position denies that biology has any real relevance to women's status as moral beings. It asserts the primacy of culture. The second position claims that biology constructs a differential psychology. The third position revels in difference. It attempts to appropriate biological considerations as a solution to articulating women's nature.

Denial of biology's relevance to moral status

A denial that biology is significant to women's status as a moral being can indirectly ignore biological considerations, deliberately reject its relevance or subordinate its relevance to other considerations. There is a fine line between these three responses, and some overlaps do occur. Moral philosophy does at times tend to ignore biology, to reject biological considerations, or to make biology a subordinate concern.

In the western philosophical tradition, the mind represents certainty and the means toward freedom. The body, in contrast, is seen as a source of uncertainty and constraint. Women, in being consistently connected with the body in a more intimate way than men, through menstruation, pregnancy, childbirth, lactation and an association with sensuality, are, in the above terms, in a constant situation of ambiguity and limitation. Given traditional philosophy's devaluation of the body in contrast to the mind, philosophy tends to sublimate, repress or deny the importance of physical passion and body-consciousness. This tendency is not always explicit. Thus, in order to work through the hidden systems of meaning and logic which appear in opaque forms, it is necessary to expose the 'unconscious reverberations in philosophy' (Flax, 1983: 255).

At the root of the unconsciousness in question is the traditional philosophal 'rejection of the process of reproduction as a meaningful principle of social organisation' (Clark, 1976: 52). There is the perception that intrafamilial relations are 'natural', and hence outside the sphere of relevant philosophical discourse. Family relationships are qualitatively different from relationships between actors in the political realm, but this is because the basic unit in political philosophy is not the family, or the person, but the male rational subject within the family. Another root of the rejection of corporeality is the equation of the free political sphere with productive labour and public recognition, and the private sphere with the realm of reproductive labour and natural relations which are perceived as prepolitical. This Greek equation sees public activities attaining an excellence far exceeding that attending activities undertaken in private. That is, value and status granted to public participation is derived largely from recognition by others, particularly those of equal standing to oneself. In contrast, the private stands as a state of deprivation. In these terms, the condition of being cut off from the public realisation of one's highest capacities eliminates the possibility of achieving socially acclaimed value and significance as a moral subject.

Although in western contemporary culture the private realm is valued more highly than it was by the Greeks, so that motherhood is valued for what it offers society, mothers and the tasks of mothering continue to be undervalued. It is not women's reproductive agency that causes oppression, but that this agency has occurred 'within a patriarchal power structure, has been considered a private rather than a social concern, and has been perceived as...defining their very nature' (Okin, 1979: 296).

Where there is a more explicit view that biology is insignificant to women's status as a moral being, moral capacity is characterised in terms of social expectations, roles and functions (Parsons, 1951). Nature is seen to prescribe in terms of optimum characteristics for performing functions. As Okin puts it, to ask 'What are women like?', is like asking 'What are women for?' (1979: 257). This notion of 'functional difference' is, I contend, centred spuriously on nature and convention. If women have pan-culturally been the prime nurturers they 'naturally' seem eminently suited to the task in terms of potentiality, even without reference to biological capacities. A perception of 'naturalness' bolsters existing sexual role-differentiation (Trebilcot, 1977).

It is virtually impossible to separate social expectations from convention. If women are expected to be weak, emotionally unstable, nurturant, reliant on intuition and logically inconsistent, they are perceived in this way, and frequently act accordingly. But to accept as natural the whole gamut of social and conventional expectations and roles is to fail to question their validity. Indeed, it is to foreclose the question and so remain blind to the possibility that the perceptions and practices entailed in the differentiated roles ascribed to men and women may reflect nothing more than prejudice—the sort of prejudice that easily serves the cause of regarding men and women as unequal.

66

Another quite different example of a position that rejects the relevance of biology to identity lies in orthodox Marxism. A Marxist epistemology does not accept social relations as functional givens, but emphasises their role in creating discriminatory beliefs. Yet, despite recognising that biological and social organisation partly constitute each other, the assumption that the domestic sphere falls outside the scope of modern political economics disallows a challenge to the sexual division of labour. Orthodox Marxism relegates women's oppression to an epiphenomenon of class division, thus discrediting attempts to explain the significant commonalities shared across all classes. The socialist-feminist rejection of political economy as a total explanation has had considerable impact on Marxist analysis of women. Socialist feminists accommodate the situation of women in terms of both significant commonalities and class differences so that the 'woman problem' ceases to be relegated to the periphery. Commonalities refer to housework, reproduction and a preoccupation with needs of others. Differences include employment, access to good child-care and house-help, leisure and disposable income. A significant proportion of women remain in low-paid, part-time, repetitive service labour. The careerist bourgeois woman may or may not share common features with her working-class sisters. Useful socialist work deals with the ideological construction of gendered subjects that no longer denies the relevance of biological factors (Scott, 1974; Flax, 1976; Hartmann, 1979; Barrett, 1980; Sargent ed., 1981).

Biology as destiny

Clearly, any view that denies the relevance of biology to female nature has not grappled with the specifically female dimension of this nature. With views that do take account of the relation between nature and biology, there are two major variants. The first states that biology constructs differential psyches. The second variant views biology as deterministic and necessarily limiting one's nature. These variants tend to lead into each other.

The clearest examples of 'biology as destiny' operate within the framework of empiricism. I refer particularly to approaches resembling a Humean conception of the mind (Hume, 1888). These view the mind as formless, passive and receptive to any impressions and sense perceptions of empirical reality.[2] These approaches assume that cognitive development and changes of beliefs are impressed on a supposedly docile, malleable being, through contact with external reality. The distinctive conception of 'objectivity' intrinsic to such an approach, requires methodological controls to eliminate the influence of values, social interests and emotions.[3] It is not merely the empiricist methodology to which I am objecting, but the model of human nature that emerges as a manipulated object of observation with capacities that may not be fixed, but are certainly limited by conditions emanating from experimental scientific constructs. There is minimal reference to an identifiable 'self' as an active, deliberative agent.

There are similarities between typical empiricist conceptions of nature and stereotypical accounts of women's minds and moral status. Both the empiricists' conception of the cognitive subject and women *per se* are commonly purported to be passively receptive to external stimulus. Within this framework, it is assumed that the researcher is actively objective (the stereotypical man engaged in reasoned argument), and the object of enquiry is passive and manipulable (the stereotypical woman—mentally passive and emotionally receptive). When this contrast is presented in a scientific guise it implicitly sanctions the association of political control with a masculine mentality and validates an underclass mentality in women.

Harding (1979) profers three instances to explain this sanction. First, the empiricist inquirer (who may be a woman), like the male stereotype, brings to the enquiry self-direction, firm purpose, determination, clarity, and rational argument. These are all admirable, necessary tactics for any research process. The problem arises when these are posited in contrast to and in abstraction from the object of inquiry. Persons as conceived by empiricists, and women generally, are viewed as passive and reliant on sense perception, rather than as active subjects. While women researchers continue to fall into the traps of the empiricist mentality I am arguing against, those aware of the dangers operate from a different framework. Where men are the object of inquiry, they are assumed to be victims while under investigation. The stereotypical view of women is that she is almost always like this (see Hubbard and Lowe eds, 1979). Second, this imputation of passivity and receptivity to others' directives resembles the situation of the powerless. Their condition is readily manipulated, and their possibility of autonomous activity is frustrated. The third instance of political control concerns manipulation of the object of scientific inquiry as a means of controlling nature. Given the close link frequently assumed between women and nature, the conceptualisation of women as natural 'others', or objects of analysis, takes for granted the social control of women whereby 'others' are kept out of public life (Harding, 1979: 45). This is in contrast to my concept of moral subjects as historical agents, self-conscious, critical, reflective and intentionally acting to change.

Sociobiology is a stark example of the type of empiricism that I am criticising. It obscures the role of conscious human agency. Starting from the premise of genetic selection biological factors are seen to cause social factors in accordance with the dictates of evolutionary adaptation. Sociobiologists draw analogies between genitals and gender. They conclude that differences in sex hormones entering the brain must result in innate differences in nature. Yet differences in physiological states are not necessarily relevant to differences in behaviour, capacity or motivation. For while most women are bio-logically female, and most men biologically male, femininity and masculinity do not correlate neatly with biological sex, nor are all our actions always related to our sex.

The methodology sociobiologists employ to arrive at such conclu-sions as those mentioned above aggregates diverse social behaviour under the label 'traits'. Crucial cultural responses are seen to be the result of biological stimuli. The specific forms in which biological traits are encased are disregarded (Smith, 1983: 92). Aggression as a key trait is seen to include anything from athletic competition, domestic violence, tight Stock Exchange trading to male domination. Yet, brute aggressiveness is quite different from socially acceptable assertiveness in sport, management or personal relations. Within the empiricist framework, the mere fact of aggression is extracted, while complex factors that not only influence behaviour, but define social meaning, are ignored. For example, to characterise football hooli-ganism as mere working-class aggression, without reference to unemployment, economic recession, youth identification and aliena-tion is to make no attempt to understand the phenomenon in its widest sense. By not attending to the contexts within which be-haviour patterns such as aggression occur, sociobiological explana-tions are little more than glib.

When sociobiological arguments are translated into the realm of sexual relations, the familiar conclusion is that relations of domi-nance and subordination between the sexes make sense both biolo-gically and socially (Green, 1982: 124). Goldberg's (1974) position is explicit. Goldberg elaborates propositions about aggression and dominance initiated by Tiger (1969), Wilson (1975) and Fox (in Caplan, 1978). Goldberg advances three tenets of the sociobiology of sex which constitute its methodological programme. First, he draws conclusions about human differences on the basis of animal studies. (see Maccoby and Jacklin, 1974; Haraway, 1978). Second, he pur-ports to find observable psychological differences between men and women that can be attributed to physiological processes (see Lambert, 1978). His third deduction concerns a physiological root of discri-mination. Goldberg concludes that genes and hormones do not just have a differential impact on certain types of behaviour, but, more strongly, determine gender differentiation.

An empiricist and sociobiological epistemology relies on so-called 'natural tendencies'. In doing so, it exaggerates the extent to which our actions are determined by biology, sex or sense perception and ignores social and cultural factors which contribute substantially to our ideals of knowing and being. For example, Wilson (1975) con-cludes that the tendency for men to hunt or go to work and women to stay at home has genetic origins. To make sense of his claim, he must argue that complex relationships that distinguish one society from another are not intrinsic to either hunting, going out to work, or being at home. Furthermore, these accounts of biology as destiny cannot provide criteria for assessing the adequacy of rival accounts of behaviour. In support of the need for adequate explanations of nature and of behaviour, I maintain that it is our reflective, interpretative and evaluative capacities that are vital in grasping the 'meanings and purposes an intentional act has for the actor' (Harding, 1986: 46). These skills have no analogue in empiricist scientific accounts of nature as destiny.

I have suggested that experimenters unavoidably begin with assumptions on the nature of men and women. There is substantial evidence that whatever views the researchers held about the psychology or potential of women were generally confirmed in their research (Weisstein, 1977). Any reduction into rigid categories reinforces prejudgements, so that if our definitions of gender and sex are seen to have biological roots, then they are likely to be seen as natural (Birke, 1986: 73), and thus unchangeable. Contemporary research in anthropology, biology, history, psychology and philosophy has converged to render implausible the assumption that identities, behaviours, desires, roles, or concepts of the self are necessarily determined by sex or reproductive differences.

Nature as solution

A third position views nature as a positive solution to understanding women. This has two different emphases. The first appropriates certain powers inherent in being biologically female. Despite the long tradition of subversive female symbols such as seducers, witches, polluters, and castrating mothers, this position relates female powers to an essential moral goodness. The second view embraces a romanticisation of 'women as nature.'

Women as innately good

The first view invokes the dictum of Demosthenes in the fourth century B.C.: 'We have mistresses for our enjoyment, concubines to serve our person, and wives for the bearing of legitimate offspring' (in Pomeroy, 1976: 8). This dictum remains indicative of much of the popularly assumed relationships between women and morality. There are historical continuities in these segmented archetypes of female existence. For many modern women, choices remain similar to these categorisations of classical antiquity; choices between becoming an intellectual, asexual career-oriented Athena, a frivolous sex-object like Aphrodite, or a respectable wife and mother like Hera. These images of nature reduce women to a corrupt body, are contradictory and impossible to achieve, or are empty chimera, without substance.

These images have theological associations which have survived in secularised forms. Two features of the Hebrew account of 'The Fall' (or humans' choice of evil rather than good) are common to Greek mythology, namely woman's supposed agency in causing evil and the acquisition of knowledge as the temptation. Extreme accounts say that sex is evil, women are temptresses—therefore, women are fundamentally evil. This results in an assimilation of male–female dualism and soul–body dualism, and conditions woman's status as a moral subject, in terms of both her 'natural subordination' to all men and her 'carnality' in the disorder of sin, evil, or unbridled passion. Paradoxically, the imputation of Eve's primeval duping of Adam ensures male hegemony. Her supposed role in causing Adam's downfall became a tool for her intimidation. Symbolically, 'every woman becomes an Eve, indicated as the cause of evil and the corrupter of man' (Prusak, 1974: 97). The other side of this generalisation is that every man assumes an embodiment of spirit to which woman as flesh remains subject. Despite the restoration of women to possible salvation and the impact of the rather different images of the 'Virgin Mother', the ignominy and the need for expiation by women is not erased. Mary did not 'rescue' women, but represents an impossible, contradictory ideal (Warner, 1978). A historical digression explains some of the effects of this ideal, in restoring the idea of women as naturally good, rather than evil.

In medieval thought, natural existence was delineated in a Chain of Being, from God down to angels, men, women, children, animals and plants. Difference meant rationalised subordination. The challenge to this resulted in, among other things, a curious interpretation of women and nature, coinciding in the mid-seventeenth century with the removal of the economic function from the home. Within this historical epoch, a new family type emerged in the new bourgeois classes (Shorter, 1975; Stone, 1977; Banks, 1982; Okin, 1982), where the necessity of women's economic contribution lessened. This family was founded on love, affection and consideration of the individual within a sphere of privacy. It reinforced patriarchal relations based on the premise that women are creatures of sentiment, dependency and domesticity. Religious and political movements contributed to 'a cult of domesticity' (Cott, 1977: 2).

While the Protestant emphasis on domestic virtues was an essential ingredient in the Victorian suppression of women, the later evangelical movements in the UK and the USA played a significant role in changing women's consciousness of their nature in two ways. First, motivated by religious involvement, women extended their activities beyond the family 'in the attempt to "feminise" the public sphere by bringing to it the values associated with the home' (Banks, 1982: 26–27). These values translate into a pursuit of moral reform regarding sexual chastity and a new concern for welfare. Women who appropriate such values reinforce the view that women have different needs arising from their actual or potential role as mothers. Second, education was stressed. Motivation varied according to conflicting views of female nature, and whether education furthered the pursuit of a claim for equal opportunities, or whether it should prepare women for their moral duties as wives and mothers.

The domestic family is thus endowed with sentimental qualities which are considered women's sacred mission to preserve. Integral to such a 'cult of domesticity' is a 'cult of true womanhood'. It is assumed that women's maternal nature ensures a diminished sexual ardour, acting as a moral inspiration to men and as a guardian of children. Through her purity, it is thought she can redeem humanity. The need to protect her from evil to retain such purity presumably justifies her segregation in the home.

These views gained a boost from political theorists like Rousseau and Hegel (see Clark and Lange ed., 1979; Okin, 1979; Lange, 1981; Elshtain, 1981; 1982b; Lloyd, 1984a). Women are then adjudged to lack the need and capacity for participation in public life, other than where it relates directly to family concerns or where supposedly feminine values can positively influence a masculine world. Anyone wishing to register an objection to women's subordination could potentially be accused of being an enemy of a sacred institution—the sentimental family (Okin, 1979). This results in an idealisation of privatised female moral goodness. Women's nature is assumed to be inseparable from nurturing. The 'all-powerful-mother' image is strengthened. She is pictured as either all-powerful and thus responsible for domestic traumas, or powerless and denied the complexity of a life that is the fulfilment of self-agency. Either way, this split self is a myth, perpetuated often unintentionally by compliant women, in the interest of children, men, invalids and the aged (Chodorow and Contratto, 1982).

In these terms, natural goodness becomes defined as unobtrusive selflessness. This tends to render women 'spiritual cripples' (Greer, 1970: 115), in the sense that they are advised to remain within a defined sphere, without looking for varied scope or alternative means to develop self-agency. In the same vein, the pressures on men to be the prime breadwinner have had debilitating effects on some men. While it is morally good to create a healthy family situation, goodness does not consist in the limitation of activity, whereby men are defined as chief earners, disciplinarians or family heads, and women are defined as inspirers, nurturers or sexual playmates. Women who sustain this notion of goodness view these definitions as the natural solution to their moral existence. It is perceived as one way of accommodating seemingly contradictory images of women's nature.

Woman as nature
A different variant of nature as the solution to determining women's moral being is evidenced in a feminist embrace of nature. This may seem strange given previous explanations of feminist attempts to

diminish links between the conceptualisation of nature as female and the oppression of women, particularly where nature is construed as disorderly, chaotic, untamed, or as that which is to be controlled. Two of the clearest examples of this equation of women with nature are supplied by Griffin, who adopts a poetic, allusive style of writing, and McMillan, who writes in a more traditional, philosophical style.

Griffin writes of women, 'We know ourselves to be made from this earth. We know this earth is made from our bodies. For we see ourselves. And we are nature. We are nature seeing nature. We are nature with a concept of nature. Nature weeping. Nature speaking of nature to nature' (1980: 226). I will interpret this by explaining the substance of Griffin's position and the wider implications of her argument. Stylistically, her book incorporates an angry critique and describes an unconventional emotional association of women with nature. The book is a semi-structured collage of apparently disparate materials collected from a wide variety of sources. In order to expose underlying premises, she relies on intuition or what she calls her 'civilised self'. She revels in this as an antidote to thought of the 'civilised man' whose claim to objectivity typically requires a separation from emotion. The book is written as a dialogue between a paternal, detached, bodiless voice that speaks in the form of recognised opinion and absolute truth and accuses Griffin of hysteria and female bias, and an impassioned, embodied voice of other women and natural sources. Griffin's language is vivid, blatant, and intensely physical.

Her content is based on her belief that men see themselves as superior to matter, and thus divorce themselves from nature. Women are viewed as closer to nature which, being devalued, renders them naturally inferior. Griffin deals with the issue of matter by drawing on themes like the land, timber, wind and animals to trace out 'the effect of patriarchal logic on material beings' (1980: xvi). Her 'Separation' is a protest against divisions which are constitutive of civilised men's thought and life processes. Griffin outlines key separations starting from a physical separation from the womb, and including the separation of mind from emotion, and body from soul, which she maintains ultimately represents a self-alienation. Griffin suggests that such separations occur typically through man's separation of himself from nature, his objectification of women and nature, his reduction of women to nature, his power, vigilance, determination of knowledge, control, certainty and terror. The 'Passage' serves as a prelude to the 'Vision' where 'she sees through her own eyes where the world is no longer his' (1980: ix). 'The Separate Rejoined' is an emotionally intense affirmation of woman as nature. Her emphasis here is on mystery, space, time, dreams, rituals, intuitive listening, bodily functions and identification with nature.

While one applauds the forcefulness of Griffin's style, there are problems with both what is being discarded and what is affirmed in its place. Undoubtedly, Griffin's attack is rightly scathing on many aspects of Western civilisation that require criticism and with which I too am engaged. These include the notions 'that woman is what she is in character, charm, body, mind and soul because of her womb alone' (1980: 24), and thus clings to tradition in order to play out her natural roles as good wife and mother. Yet Griffin's symbolism appears to place her in a contradictory position. On the one hand she criticises the association of women with 'natural mothering'. On the other hand, she seems to embrace it: 'We are mothers. (She is a great cow)' (1980: 73). Griffin is also right to attack the notion that matter is passive, inert and imperfect, for this notion assumes that the rational soul is immaterial, 'more noble and more valuable of being than the whole corporeal world' (1980: 17). According to Griffin, this notion implies further that 'nature should be approached only through reason' (1980: 14), which is considered the only way that one can 'refuse to be a slave to nature' (1980: 24), and thus 'nature can be understood only by reduction' (1980: 11), that is, via abstract knowledge and a separation of feelings from thought. But it is in refuting these claims that her approach becomes too extreme.

Let me illustrate. To the extent that she infers all men contribute to the mutilation, anger and exploitation of women, and suggests all women have suffered similarly as a consequence, she over-generalises the position of women—not all of whom have suffered similarly— and does grave injustice to the admirable intentions and practices of some men. Such over-generalised accusations imbue 'feminism with a problematic anthropology about women as well as men...women, like nature become the unfallen innocents of history, victimized but naturally good. One has only to withdraw from the evil world and 'get in tune' with one's bodily and cosmic 'lunar' rhythms to recapture paradise' (Ruether, 1984: 121). This embrace of nature, which is encouraged by Griffin, reinvokes a form of goddess worship. Particularly in agricultural societies, a parallel is drawn between the fecundity of women and of physical nature in general, especially when nature is productive. As nature, women are revered in religious ceremony as the incarnation of natural rhythms. Contemporary proponents of the view stress traditional feminine symbols of women's closeness to nature, nurturing, sensuality, receptiveness, immanence, interdependence and continuity (Grigson, 1976; Starhawk, 1979; Berger, 1985). The goddess and, by extension, women in general are seen to animate nature's creative powers. While this reverses the patriarchal estimation of women's value, its ultimate effect is theoretically regressive in that it reaffirms existing prejudices, and restates a view of women as solely natural beings.

Furthermore, although a poetic mode is valid, the assumption that rational discourse in a more traditional form must necessarily be masculine in character is questionable, as will be argued at length in the next chapter. If one accepts Griffin's premise, it suggests the 'female world' may be unintelligible and incommunicable to men. And, of course, some women too may find difficulty in identifying with many of her images. When an embrace of nature results in women being merged or submerged with nature itself, an unbalanced view of nature results. That is, it leaves women in the physical world of desire and instinct, subject to uncontrollable forces. This unbalanced view diminishes characteristics of nature men and women do share. It renders the task of understanding 'human nature' impossible.

A contrast is offered in McMillan's account of woman and nature which makes use of a traditional mode of rational discourse. McMillan states that feminists correctly perceive that being a woman is a social construction not just a biological one. McMillan suggests that 'the fact that our notion of femininity is a culturally biased one does not, by itself, destroy the legitimacy of the notion' (1982: 59). She asserts that bewilderment over the nature of femininity can be resolved by elucidating the internal relations that exist among the variegated conglomeration of characteristics called 'feminine'. While I also emphasise internal relations, I maintain her understanding of this is often limiting. To understand these internal relations she appeals to a 'way of life' bound to an educative system like Rousseau's that assumes the acceptance of tradition and rules.

McMillan perceptively poses the question of 'how far a woman or a man can be treated both as a member of a particular sex and as a person in his or her own right' (1982: 72). Yet, she intimates that the realisation of a balance between sexual specificity and individuality requires an unlicensed notion of freedom. She counters this by suggesting that even notions like freedom and individuality presuppose a degree of social consensus in being part of our liberal democratic heritage. Her assertion that 'the existence of role typing is an integral feature of any society' (1982: 72) seems, however, to undervalue the controversial formation of our heritage. Just as we do not simplistically accept any idea of freedom, we should not uncritically accept any idea of roles. While McMillan admits that an increased awareness of fluid, flexible roles is good, she opposes role-redundancy, or 'degendering'.

McMillan criticises feminist claims that sex roles based on convention are necessarily inappropriate. She maintains, rather, that traditional roles tend to be correctly based on nature, given the pivotal role nature plays in structuring ethical institutions. Hence, 'it is eminently natural that where we should look...to understand sexual conventions is the inescapable human realities of which they aim to make sense' (1982: 81), especially the issues of birth and sexual relations. Convention is not necessarily arbitrary. McMillan suggests we look at the relations between nature and convention, particularly the fact that 'for women, sex is inextricably bound up with procreation' (1982: 84). She argues that the obvious undisputed difference 'that men beget and women give birth' (1982: 85) is the basis for differential behaviour.

Reinforcing Rousseau, McMillan agrees that women's procreative potential places them in a relation to nature different from men. Indeed, in her view, it positively situates them in a privileged position of being better equipped to tend to infants' needs. She admits that women's reproductive role does restrict them given the specific demands babies make, but asserts that if this is natural then it is a contradiction to suggest that domesticity or reproduction impair women's moral agency. Rather the mother-baby tie is a *moral* relation.

The precise nature of this moral relation is unclear. Do women who choose not to bear children reject their moral potential? Under McMillan's scheme, one presumes they do, for she writes, 'to treat a woman as a person need not exclude, when relevant, an emphasis on her role as mother and wife' (1982: 100). To be fair, she may just mean that when a woman is a wife and/or a mother, these roles influence her personhood, but it seems to imply that without the emphasis on her role as mother and wife she is less than a person. I agree that there are many instances when these qualifications of personhood are extremely important. There are also instances when they are not. This clarification is important. McMillan suggests further that any restrictions that may accompany these roles are based not on mere convention but on nature, and therefore must be accepted, particularly given her claim that there is 'something special about the mother–infant relationship' (1982: 108). That women necessarily have prime responsibility for child-care is, she argues, an inevitability, but one demanding re-evaluation. Whether men actively engaged in child-care are similarly expressing moral relations is, in McMillan's terms, a non-issue. Besides breast-feeding and the more ambiguous concept of bonding, I see no exclusive tasks associated with infant-care that only women can respond to.

McMillan qualifies her position and attacks the notion that being biologically female is oppressive by suggesting 'the tyrant is not man at all but nature' (1982: 116). Conditions of oppression require an enslaving and enslaved force where agency is applicable to both parties. Just as it is nonsensical to prosecute a natural object, like a tree, for falling and killing a child, it is nonsensical to accuse nature of oppressing women. Important distinctions must be made between conditions that arise from nature and those arising from agents. This is a valid point but it ignores the relationship between nature and agency and minimises the way in which meanings attached to nature are themselves socially constituted. Furthermore, it does not consider that the pivotal role she has given to agency is often denied to women, who are not considered moral identities in the same sense as men.

McMillan systematically criticises reproductive self-determination, yet she seems to imply that moral agency emanates, at least partially, from productive or manipulative action that represents a transcendence of self over nature. The mode of being McMillan assumes for mothering is 'inactive action' or 'intentional passivity' (1982: 138), an idea gained from Weil. McMillan seeks to show how traditional feminine virtues, like obedience, humility and passivity, presuppose intentional passivity and thus, in her terms, agency. What is at stake here is whether this concept of intentionality is sufficiently incorporated into her notion of agency. Her form of 'inactive action', a part of what she sees as a 'humble acceptance of suffering', implies that, in avoiding traditional feminine virtues, a woman may 'violate her moral sense of the significance of the natural order' (1982: 141). This infers that agency is derivative from nature.

While not explicit, the further inference one can deduce from this is that women not assuming the 'intentional passivity' which McMillan suggests emerges through mothering, deny themselves agency. I find her conclusion that agency is derivative from nature to be implausible, otherwise any understanding of women's nature is dictated by biology, natural law and convention. This fails to explore the internal relations between nature and custom, the task she set herself. Consequently, the contextual basis and historical development of the construct 'femininity' is not explained and the possibility that a change in context may lead to a change in the nature of women is ignored. There is no acknowledgement that, among others, the Frankfurt School's theory of reification may be applicable here in that the historically produced construct 'femininity' is experienced as a 'second nature' which may actually be an inversion of nature. The question is not addressed of when 'second nature' can be interpreted as 'first nature', or 'nature'.

In this second section of the chapter, we have examined biology, nature, and intrinsic moral capacity. Views which see biology's relation to nature as irrelevant, or as one of destiny or determining nature, have contributed significantly to the idea that women are 'naturally' inferior moral subjects. Clearly, these relations between biology and nature should be rejected. Feminists' views that embrace the biological dimensions of nature as being a positive means to the reconceptualisation of women's moral agency make important attempts to re-evaluate the biological impact on women's lives, but fail to assess adequately the relation between biology and nature. In failing to question the limitations of women's association with matter or the physical world, there is no radical reinterpretation of the relationship. In the following two sections, I attempt to redress this inadequacy, work through the relation, and tie the links together.

NATURE, CULTURE AND REPRODUCTION

In my view, the link between conceptualisations of nature, women and morality lies in a proper understanding of women's relation to their bodies and to reproduction. At first glance, this way of putting it may appear as little more than a reiteration of McMillan's view. However, first glances can be misleading, especially since I am critical of traditional notions of convention, nature and reproduction in a way that McMillan is not.

The examples of Plato and Aristotle remain paradigmatic when considering philosophical moves to associate the mind with everything noble and the body with everything base. For Plato, the body anchors one in a material world and so makes one susceptible to temptations that lead away from the life of virtue and knowledge. It is only the non-material part of a person, namely the soul, that facilitates such a life. In Plato's categories, it is through the powers of the soul that humans are enabled to escape material limitations and ascend to the 'real' world of Ideas, the form of Goodness and true knowledge. Not surprisingly, Plato considers physical love vulgar and vastly inferior to the true love that manifests itself in the soul-attraction that occurs between men. And, of course, on his terms, the internal struggles a person might undergo in trying to decide between the respective pulls of body and soul are to be interpreted as struggles between the lower (irrational) and higher (rational) dimensions of the self. These distinctions intimate 'no mild metaphysical musing' (Spelman, 1982: 113). On the contrary, to be concerned with one's body, rather than one's soul, is to act 'like a mere woman', a creature of nature, and not as a knowing, virtuous spirit.

Aristotle continues these ideas by asserting that woman's basic materiality renders her morally deficient. Virtue, he claims, follows from an intellectual capacity manifest in a character acquired by good judgement and habitual practice. The recognition of appropriate action for a virtuous person comes through the cognitive act of syllogistic reasoning. In Aristotle's view, given woman's assumed pre-eminent materiality, she is seen to be metaphysically deficient with her moral and social aspirations fixed at the low level of matter: thus, the only virtue seen to be appropriate to women is obedience. This not only rationalises moral inferiority—it justifies social subordination. This association of women with matter has had lasting effects on the philosophical and social expectations of women.

Domination of nature

This association is usefully highlighted through the nature–culture opposition which can be understood at a sociological and philosophical level. At the first level, male activities, values and authority are recognised cross-culturally as the locus of cultural value

(Rosaldo, 1979: 22). While 'becoming a man' is typically an ascribed status, distinguished by work and power differentials, 'becoming a woman' is typically a natural process, defined by reproductive capacities. Rosaldo, following Durkheim, presupposes not just that a cultural interpretation of relations is valid, but that social relationships themselves affect cultural modes. This is part of the internal relation McMillan refers to, but which she takes to emerge from nature, thus missing much of its dynamics. Not only does woman's association with nature minimise her association with culture, but it reinforces the way in which she is subsumed in the broader domination of nature.

From a philosophical perspective, the nature–culture opposition has historically specific roots. In medieval times, the idea of the Chain of Being coexisted with other ideas. Nature, although perceived as erratic, was symbolised as purposive. One view saw the origin of creation as hermaphrodite, embracing male and female principles in the universe. Another idea saw the cosmos as an organic unity imbued with a feminine spirit. The earth was viewed as a nurturing mother, sensitive and fecund. An earth-centred universe replaced with a sun-centred one transferred a women-centred focus to a man-centred one.

In later traditional philosophical thought, gender symbolism conceptualises these images of nature. Extreme images of rape and torture are used by Bacon and Machiavelli. It is difficult to accept that such connotations are irrelevant to the intended meanings. A Machiavellian, late-sixteenth-century quote is a good example: 'Fortune is a woman and it is necessary if you wish to master her to conquer her by force; and it can be seen that she lets herself be overcome by the bold' (in Merchant, 1980: 130). As mining and technological interventions increased, a more mechanistic conception of the cosmos developed, so that the idea of nature and manipulable machines meshed (Harding, 1986: 116). Where culture is defined as the systematic transcendence of the givens of natural existence by means of thought or technology, nature is bent to human purpose and controlled in the presumed interests of humanity. Nature becomes culturalised. While women are seen to be closer to nature, the control and devaluation of nature includes the devaluation and control of women (Mills, 1983).

The subjection of women as nature is thus a crucial part of the more general domination of nature. With the advent of modern science, the conquest and control of disenchanted nature became conspicuous—in place of the Enlightenment vision of human emancipation through the mastery of nature. The domination of nature prevailed with women symbolised as nature, and nature as a woman. A suggested reason why this domination and symbolism have been maintained is that early tendencies toward domination start in childhood, particularly in 'mother-monopolised' child-rearing (Balbus,

1982). To test reality as a separate being, a child must court some conflict with the prime caretaker, usually a mother. (The father often enters the child's world at a time when a more definite sense of self is beginning to be established.) One consequence of this is that 'the mother may never come to seem so completely an 'I' as the father, who was an 'I' when first encountered' (Dinnerstein, 1976: 107). Respect for the father often outweighs that for the mother.[4] These early images often extend themselves into an antagonism towards women, based partly on the initial need to submit to women as caretakers, and partly on the separation that must follow if individuation is to occur. There is a tendency, then, for mothers (and by extension, all women) to be 'see as a quasi-sentient being, an undifferentiated part of nature' (Dinnerstein, 1976: 31).

The Frankfurt School offers insight into the untrammelled pursuit of power over nature which leads to an overriding domination in the economic, political, cultural, intellectual, environmental and sexual realms. Horkheimer (1947), Marcuse (1972) and Adorno (1979) agree with Weber (1958) that the extension of a calculating rationality to the 'conduct of life' creates a material culture of domination. Within this 'rationality', nature has meaning insofar as it is instrumental to human purposes: to the extent that people embody the natural (whether women, children or slaves), they are also controllable, and reason becomes synonymous with the process of coordinating means to given ends and takes the form of accommodation rather than insight. Reason, thus, ceases to determine intentions or authorise evaluative actions, and this undermines its status as a critical, substantive standard of values and goals. Domination then operates through the direct manipulation of subjects whose agency is no longer required (Benjamin, 1981: 99). The transformative dimension of history diminishes. Agency is restricted to subduing nature.

The domination of nature ensures a cleavage between the spontaneous, sensuous aspect of self and the reflectively controlled self. Nature is reduced to quantified objects of manipulation and the subject is dominated by a 'second nature'. Socially created roles, conventions, institutions and social processes are comprehended as 'natural'. This results in what Marcuse calls a 'one-dimensionality', where the repressiveness of technocratic rationality posits itself as culturally and normatively neutral, resulting in an inability to comprehend the reality of domination. Instrumental rationality is intrinsically part of the denial, repression or domination of human connectedness with nature. The objectification and domination of women, perceived as nature, thus appears 'natural', and the force of this domination often goes unacknowledged, concealing the true dynamics of many relationships between people. The conviction that nature—and therefore women—exists to be dominated, has a negative influence on both ecological considerations and on perceptions of women's moral character and grossly limits ecological harmony and the scope of moral practices women are thought capable of performing.

Eco-feminism and reproduction re-evaluated

There is a scientific, a general ecological, and an eco-feminist response to the domination of nature. It is beyond the scope of this book to deal with the first two responses in detail. There is now a school of scientific thought that is critical of the stress patriarchal sciences place on understanding nature through domination. This school sees such domination as the consequence of dualism, citing evidence of co-operation among the species, rather than the old paradigm of ruthless, aggressive competition (Augros and Stanciu, 1987). Proponents of this view on co-operation also are critical of reductionism—seeing links between values and knowledge as an integral part of doing science (Rose et al., 1987)—and describe the understanding between science and the social as dialectical. This acknowledges that human consciousness interprets and changes the world and that to understand an integrated relationship, it is necessary to appreciate not only that wholes are more than their sum parts, but that parts qualitatively change through being part of the whole (Rose et al., 1987: 287).

With the eco-feminist response, there are three major ideas. First, there is an explicit connection made between the exploitation of nature and the degradation of women, who are deemed to be 'her' representative. The 'rape' of nature is seen as an apt metaphor. Eco-feminism challenges the exploitative instrumentality, quantification, and will to power which has escalated, with destructive results, in this century. This challenge entails a critique of the objectification of nature and of the male objectification of women.

Second, as a response to the emotional detachment that is part of the objectification of nature, eco-feminism takes seriously an emphasis on the interconnection of phenomena as a viable alternative to reductionism. The model for eco-feminism 'is one of mutually interpenetrating and mutually reinforcing tendencies' (Salleh, 1985: 8). For example, McClintock, while not an eco-feminist, had a strong 'intuitive' belief in the interrelation of physiological cellular events which led her to expound delicate interactions with no master control of cells but a complex interaction (see Keller, 1983). This holistic approach to nature attempts to understand the complexity and unity of nature, not as a conglomeration of parts or a series of discrete objects or persons, but as a *series of relations* between integrated elements.

Thirdly, giving centrality to relations allows us to envisage the possibility of reciprocal, non-exploitative human relationships, predicated on the participation of individuals who are prepared to bypass manipulative, instrumental forms of behaviour in the attempt to

81

formulate more authentic forms of human recognition. This establishes the groundwork for a 'post-instrumental paradigm within which self and other are symbolised as complementary elements of a common whole' (Balbus, 1982: 362). Fostering the development of others is understood as a vital part of self-development.

It is not suprising, then, that the life-affirming sense of being that comes from the act of giving birth is pivotal in eco-feminism, and is a concern common to those who do not have children and those who have. The wider implications of the re-evaluation of reproduction are enormous. 'To reinvigorate the reasons of the body does not mean to reify the body or the understanding of it' (Salleh, 1981: 11). Rather, it invokes an embodied praxis.

I argue that the practical implications of a redefinition of reproduction in terms of shared nurture affect both women's notion of care as a self-chosen moral responsibility, and men's reluctance to participate in care other than in a marginal capacity. This has particular implications for three categories of work: those of labour, product and value. Labour, in transforming nature, is a creative, self-transforming activity often restricted to productive labour. The historical denial of access of women to much of the public productive labour market, means that women and their labour is rendered invisible in terms of public or social recognition. The question of exploited reproductive labour has rarely been couched in terms similar to exploited productive labour. Lange (1976) argues that there has not been an equal recognition of the necessity of democratising the mode of reproduction as well as the mode of production. The process of democratising tasks of reproduction is more likely to occur in households where both partners are involved in 'paid labour' and where there is a commitment to mutual nurture. The re-evaluation of reproduction requires it be viewed as a primary activity of human society not merely a natural pre-political process. Indeed, intention, conscious, direct motivation, and deliberate action are crucial to the reproductive process, although reproductive conventions may more typically be rooted in nature, prejudice or arbitrary views. Nevertheless, reproductive labour is labour, cross-culturally and across class boundaries.

While men are seen as producers of objects, the product of reproductive labour focuses on the continual growth of a new moral subject, not an 'end product', or a well socialised child. This form of 'productive labour' requires a continuity of thought and action that cannot easily be left behind once the labourer is in the paid workforce. This emphasis repudiates a purely economic definition of value or transference of value into social utility. Reproductive workers are often excluded from recognised, publicly acknowledged value. Reproduction is still often perceived as pre-rational, irrational, inseparable from contingent nature—evidence of our animality, not our humanity. To insist, thus, on the participation of fecund women in all aspects of community reinstates the processes of reproduction as a humanly valuable activity. It also attempts to recover the celebratory and social aspects of childbirth and nurturing, more visible in some European and Third World cultures.

Feminists cannot on the one hand demand men's involvement in reproductive processes and on the other claim an exclusive, unique consciousness, implying differential forms of expression and requiring differential modes of analysis. If nurture of others is primarily an ethical concern, then it is an affirmation of human moral agency, appropriate to both women and men. Within this context, value should be accorded to ethical and affective primary bonds like love, trust, friendship and commitment to others. This dimension of nature is a human concern.

WOMEN, MEN AND NATURE

In concluding this chapter, I return to the enigmatic concept, 'human nature'. My argument is that it is possible to defy past static notions and instill the concept with meaning and content. Earlier I indicated ways that women have been seen to lack natural traits designated as 'human'. Phrases like, 'by nature', 'against nature', 'women's nature', 'natural for', 'according to the nature of', have negative connotations for many women. The conspicuous physical differences between women and men render it tautological to argue for sex-differentiated natures based solely on these differences.

Birke (1986) suggests four different interpretations of 'naturalness'. First, 'the naturalness of gender' usually refers to traits dictated by nature. For example, the idea that women naturally want to be mothers assumes an inherent maternal instinct. In a second interpretation, 'natural' can mean close to nature. If women are considered closer to nature than men, the assumption is that they are more likely to be influenced by nature, and are less subject to cultural modification. A third use of 'natural' refers to statistical normality— the idea that something that is commonly done is natural. A statement that it is natural for women to have babies would imply this is in fact what most women do. A fourth distinction combines a statistical meaning with a normative one, for example: most women have babies; therefore, all women ought to have babies. To summarise these four interpretations, 'to say that it is natural for women to want to be mothers may imply biological determinism, closeness to nature, statistical normality, and...what women ought to be' (Birke, 1986: 14). Birke's clarification is indeed useful in understanding traditionally imputed notions of nature, but does not help us to bridge the gap between the imputed, actual and potential aspects of nature.

As for my distinctions, I take the nature of women, *as females*, to be biological, constrained by cultural beliefs about the nature of *femininity*. This is distinct from the nature of women and men, *as human beings*, which defines shared characteristics. Women *as female humans*, specifies sex-specific experiences which reflect social and philosophical ideals of *femaleness*, or more individual interpretations of *being a woman*.

Certainly, once a dialectical relation between biology and human sexual difference is acknowledged, much of the clarity of the distinction between sex and gender is lost (Jaggar, 1984: 39). The example of women's involvement in the care of others highlights these distinctions. If evidence can be produced to indicate sex related differences in behaviour, traceable to a common core of psychological traits, that lead more women than men to involve themselves in the care of others, this can be seen as a historically specific form of nature, influenced by social rather than biological determinants. Yet this feature of 'woman's nature' is only one aspect of her individual human nature and is not necessarily more determinant than all the other factors' (Holmstrom, 1982: 37). Furthermore, this feature allows for variation among women of different cultures and subcultures and the degree to which women do or do not display these features. It acknowledges also that different contexts and socialisation may lead to different experiences and definitions of the self. In this sense, the affirmation of a distinct nature has no evaluative implications, so that if women change, there is no accusation that they have violated nature. Nature itself has changed. If we acknowledge care as an aspect of human nature, then men, in failing to engage in such practices, fall short of their natural capacities.

There is an inseparable interplay between sex and gender. By this, I do not mean that one cannot distinguish between the two, but that generally it does not make sense to discuss one without reference to the other. There are complex relations between our physical constitution, the environment and social organisation. It is not that biological categories cannot be isolated, but rather that even biological propensities interact with culture-specific expectations and symbols. I am suggesting that stereotypical imputations of nature are socially precarious and are predicated on other distinctions, particularly the body–mind, reproduction–production and private–public dichotomies.

Human nature

A dynamic concept of human nature fruitfully accommodates the relations between nature and culture, sex and gender, and the imputation of natural differences, with the potential of nature to change. To clarify, I am not advocating that human nature be understood as the straightforward sum of these combinations. Clearly, an interactive model of differing factors is preferable to a static one. Yet, 'this form of interactionism still has built into it potentially separable components of nature and of environment...even if they affect each other reciprocally' (Birke, 1986: 88, 91).

My emphasis is on the dialectical processes intrinsic to interactive models. I stress the multicausality and reciprocity of factors affecting human nature. Furthermore, I am suggesting that the constituents perceived as natural are not fixed properties of individuals, but involve change and transformation. Gender, for example, extends itself at the individual, structural and symbolic levels, that is, there is a complex relationship between individual concepts of gendered selves, the division of labour and the symbolic association of ideals with gender.

The above processes reach beyond feminist confines. A significant 'paradigm shift', in the Kuhnian sense used to describe major revolutions, is occuring in science (Capra, 1982; Caldecott and Leland eds, 1983). There is an increasing tendency to view nature in terms of transformability and interconnection, where humanity is seen as embedded in nature rather than as standing over it in a dominating posture. With global 'green politics' escalating, we see evidence of a general broader sensitivity to the issue of nature. Developing a 'holistic' framework is not exclusively a feminist concern. Other changes incorporate ecological movements, peace movements and theological holism.

The feminist contribution has been most significant in articulating a 'philosophy of the body', premised on the possibility of developing a non-dualistic theory of the body.[5] Where the division between body and consciousness is broken down one can envisage the mind and body relation as the power of the active body, as distinct from the mind's putative power over the passive body. When philosophy is defined as the struggle to find conditions conducive to a wise, virtuous life, virtue can incorporate various forms of activity, including bodily pleasures. It is as nonsensical to state that one can act only rationally as a disembodied being, as it is to state one can act merely physically, without the influence of the mind. With the removal of traditional philosophy's negative attitudes to the body as mere transcient matter, a concept of the moral subject is freed from a static natural essence.

The Greeks talked of nature in terms of essence and a teleological search for human purpose. Yet, too often purpose entails restrictive notions of function. For example, if a function of women is to reproduce, then a 'good woman' is one who bears children. If this proposition is altered slightly to state that a woman is good to the extent that she fulfills this purpose, it is obvious that no real moral standard is being upheld, only a standard of role efficiency. While it may have been acceptable for Plato to conclude that a good man has an ordered, rationally controlled soul, it can not be assumed that fulfilling a role is necessarily good in a moral sense. Given the evaluative component of our moral capacity, each context must be examined to assess whether what is being portrayed as natural, or purposive, is naturally good. 'A good bomb is one that goes off, but is a good bomb good?' (Pierce, 1971: 171). As Pierce argues further, our pragmatism ensures that 'we often buy without question the latter half of the teleological framework: that good things are those that function well; we fail to scrutinize what we mean by "good"' (1971: 166). Efficiency arguments alone are morally inadequate. It may be inefficient for two partners to share equally in career participation, housework, and child-care without the specialisation of the breadwinner–domestic roles, but to prize efficiency would override freedom of choice, flexibility, equality of opportunity and self-development which are 'higher moral goods'.

To conclude, it may be conceptually useful to relate nature to human purpose if we can also offer a sufficiently open evaluative component of what, in a specific context, culture and milieu, might be a *good human purpose*. I have offered criticism of imputed and actual interpretations of nature. I have concluded that any differences between women and men do not constitute substantially different natures, but that similarities in capacity and motivation suggest a common nature, appreciated best by viewing human nature as human potential, an affirmation of commonality and diversity. Any current evidence that women do not reveal human moral traits of rationality, articulation, deliberation, intention, agency, reflection and evaluation can simply be countered by arguing that 'it is in her becoming that she should be compared...her possibilities should be defined' (de Beauvoir, 1975: 66). To know the nature of something, then, is to have some intimation of potential, and thus to ascertain what might encourage it to flourish. In doing so, we move closer to realising *good human purpose*. This concept of human potential broadens the possibilities of human nature. Politically, this allows men and women to explore and to reinterpret on both an individual and a common level what is meaningful purpose, potential and nature.

NOTES

1　I argue that Chodorow tends to conflate mothering with nurturing. This fails to consider in depth the real possibilities of men being the predominant parent or the increasing attempts to develop equal shared parenting. Furthermore, the viability of a 'relational self' to sustain moral strength will be exposed to a stringent critique in chapter six.

2　Parts of my forthcoming argument have been influenced by Harding (1979). She questions convincingly the adequacy of a restrictive meta-theoretical empiricist programme to explain social and moral life. She refers particularly to theories which restrict explanation to the physical, observable environment, relegating human action to scientifically-explainable phenomena, which can be statistically codified.

3 The translation of empiricist assumptions on objectivity into liberal thought sees the introduction of devices such as 'veils of ignorance', 'rational spectators' and 'neutral discourse'. The myth of scientific neutrality is perpetuated, and the mystification of knowledge misleads the oppressed into believing that knowledge is an inevitable aspect of the status quo, not shaped by active, social agents.

4 Benjamin (1981), argues that the deterioration of a parental authority might be viewed with greater optimism, if the absence of coercion and authority, especially through an identification with a powerful father, was seen to form the basis for autonomous ego development.

The argument of Adorno et al. (1950) that only hard judging fathers can adequately socialise children, seems contrary to his research that harsh fathers do not produce children with critical capacities, but ones who have internalised authority.

Inherent to Horkheimer's (1959) insistence on the link between identification with the father, as a means to individuation, is the denial of women's self-will, and the possibility of a maternal nurturance that fosters autonomy, rather than authority.

5 I am indebted to Gatens (1985), for the thrust of this paragraph. She urges us to 'flesh out' fashionable cliches like 'sex-subjectivity', and 'rendering the body meaningful by discursive practices', rather than tossing them around like fads. Also, in being concerned with human differences, clear attention must be made to biological constraints in nations afflicted with famine, disease, poverty, illiteracy, inadequate contraception and health care, compared to the privileges of the affluent west.

4 Reason, passion and objectivity

The previous chapter demonstrated the historical association of women with nature and the body in contrast to the association of men with culture and the mind. Of great importance is the fact that women's alleged preoccupation with the 'non-rational' is often used to justify their inequality with men, especially since the criterion of rationality is the one most commonly employed to assess human value. In this chapter, I undertake a critical examination of what male-oriented philosophy understands reason to be, and suggest how our understanding of reason can be greatly improved by going beyond the confines of such philosophy.

I develop my argument in five major sections. In the first, I draw out implications of the arguments of previous chapters which reinforce my contention that reason is commonly understood in masculine terms. Secondly, I document some of the important historical changes in philosophy's conceptualisation of reason, which have contributed to reason's construal in predominantly male categories— categories which are reinforced through their correlation with the abstract methodology of modern science. In the third section, I offer some critical reflections on why 'feminine' ideals have been dissociated from reason. I look in particular at the customary philosophical move of associating women with passion and moral disorder, and also comment on definitions of rationality, irrationality and non-rationality. Fourthly, I demonstrate the influence of gendered selfhood on the association of rational objectivity with autonomous masculinity. This amounts to a serious critique of the pretensions of rational objectivity in its typical guise. In the fifth section, I intimate some ways in which the dilemmas presented in the above four sections can be overcome through a concept of the rational, passionate self.

GENDER, PHILOSOPHY AND THE MASCULINIST PERSPECTIVE

The critique of reason directed particularly to ideals of the rational subject, is crucial to my entire critical emphasis, since without it, the alternatives I propose seem unnecessary, or of minor relevance. One of the principal arguments of this chapter is that reason is not as universal as is claimed, since it is typically associated with masculine ideals and defined in a manner that excludes ideals of femininity. Such a charge of exclusion is necessarily political, yet trying to convince sceptics of this masculinist basis in customary philosophical conceptions of reason is a daunting task. The belief that philosophy's concern is with human nature rather than with 'particular' and 'applied' social questions (Gould, 1976: 5) remains strong. Not only do most philosophers consider that appropriate philosophical subject matter is universal and abstracted from particular differences, but, reason is also often considered to be the epitome of a universal concern.

There is a dispute between philosophy's claim to universality and the contrary claim that talk of universality is hollow if it occurs at the expense of philosophical indifference to differences. Gould (1976) notes three possible responses to this dispute. One reiterates the claim to universality by regarding differences between women and men as matters of social, cultural or historical interest but not of philosophical interest. This is because being a woman or a man is considered an accidental occurrence, not an essential one, and therefore sex or gender cannot in themselves qualify as philosophical categories. Another response denies the basis of such an affirmation of universality by depicting sex differences as essential and not accidental to human nature. In this view, then, sexual polarity provides the fundamental categories of human nature and 'woman' thereby becomes a rudimentary philosophical concept. I have been critical of these two responses in earlier chapters for either failing to incorporate particularity into personhood, as in the case of the first, or imbibing an implausible version of essentialism, as in the case of the second. This leaves a third response for which I have already indicated support. In its terms, a shared universality is admitted and consideration is also given to the particularities of human nature as manifest through expressions of potential influenced by social and historical circumstances. In effect, this third response advocates a type of universalism that endeavours to accommodate differences, not ignore them; and it recognises differences as philosophically relevant not because they imply some sort of feminist essentialism, but because they significantly affect notions of personhood.

Now, if it is valid to accept a 'concrete universalism' (Gould, 1976) which does not entail consigning particularities to philosophical limbo, then there are important connections between women's concern with oppression and liberation and traditional political philosophical ideals associated with reason, such as consent, emancipation, equality, freedom, justice, solidarity and personhood. And, if this is so, the failure to recognise such a connection implies a misconstrual of reason in masculinist terms. It is a misconstrual of this sort that helps to explain why women are excluded from the full range of possibilities and responsibilities that derive from the categories 'subject', 'person', 'moral identity' and 'citizen' which are so central to the western intellectual tradition; indeed, the category 'woman' has alone been sufficient to differentiate from the category 'man' which has been synonymous with 'person' or 'human being' (Elshtain, 1975: 459). Furthermore, a misconstrual of reason treats the natural propensities (or, pejoratively, disabilities) which putatively characterise women as women as sufficient to deny women full personhood.

A masculinist misconstrual of reason underlies cases of women's explicit exclusion from domains to which men are given free access. But there are more subtle ways, too, in which this misconception of reason can contribute to women's marginalisation and trivialisation. For example, within moral and political philosophy, what is not said, or what is avoided, is often as significant as the explicit context (Flax, 1983: 249). The official language of male-oriented philosophy frequently hides a bias against women that effectively deprives them of their legitimate entitlements as human beings, even when it does not seem expressly intent on doing so.

In order to clarify the different ways in which a masculinist misconstrual of reason can negatively affect women, it is helpful to distinguish between sexism and genderism (Keat, 1983). Both are certainly pejorative terms. However, whereas sexism refers to acts of discrimination against women or unwarranted differential treatment of them, as in cases of their explicit exclusion from certain realms, genderism does not necessarily connote such overt anti-women sentiments. Instead, genderism assumes a privileged status for gender-specific characteristics—perhaps even unwittingly—without being justified in doing so.

Let us take the familiar claim that rationality is the basis of intrinsic human worth and respect. A sexist instance of the masculinist interpretation of reason occurs when it is maintained that only men are fully capable of reason, since the rational inferiority of women is thereby inferred and unequal treatment of them condoned. While a straightforward response to such sexist misconstrual may involve showing how the initial claims about women's lack of reason are mistaken, as Mary Wollstonecraft, Harriet Taylor, John Stuart Mill and others do, the overall theory informing the claims remains unchallenged. To mount a thorough challenge here requires recognising that a genderist misconstrual of reason may also be at work, that is, where the prized characteristics of rationality expressly form part of the ideal of maleness, but not of femaleness. In such a situation, the supposedly valuable human capacity of rationality is defined in gender terms. And if this is what is happening then a good deal of critical analysis needs to be developed at the genderist level.

So a critique of sexism often needs to extend into a critique of genderism. A failure to make this extension leaves too much unsettled, or, at least, encourages a lapse into an unquestioning acceptance of received canons of rationality. Consider, for example, Aristotle's conflation of the categories, 'male' and 'human' and his definition of them in terms of reason. Aristotle's articulation of what constitutes the highest good for a human being (*anthropos*) entails excluding women from its achievement. Women are, in his view, constitutionally incapable of attaining such excellence: sexual difference is a first principle relating to a qualitative difference in human faculties since men alone, in virtue of their full possession of reason, are equipped to attain the highest human good. Now, evidently, Aristotle's opinions here are open to the criticism that he is guilty of a sexist misconstrual of reason. But is such criticism sufficient? Let us see.

It might be said, for instance, that the obnoxiousness of Aristotle's position is overcome, that his overt sexism is corrected, by retranslating his celebrated definition, 'man is a rational animal', into nonsexist terms that apply equally to women. Thus we could envisage the following syllogism:

Humans are rational animals.
Xanthipe is a human.
Xanthipe is a rational animal.

Given this retranslation, Xanthipe's rationality can be deduced syllogistically just as easily as Socrates'. This is a considerable advance on Aristotle's sexist conflation of the categories, 'man' and 'human'. To concede this, however, is not to suppose that a critique of sexism itself is adequate. What is left unexplored is the (almost overwhelming) tendency in universal models, which purportedly represent both sexes, for the specificity of the feminine to be subsumed under masculine terms. But it is precisely this tendency to which we need to be alert when considering the concept of rationality. It is not just women's arbitrary exclusion from the domain of rationality that needs opposing, but also the way this domain is constructed. That is why a critique of sexism frequently needs to extend to a critique of genderism.

A critique of the genderist misconstrual of reason is, not surprisingly, much more difficult to effect. It sets its sights on a 'theoretical misogyny' which is hard to locate because it requires being able to render visible the invisible. Theoretical misogyny is so deeply ingrained in the thought-patterns of western philosophy that it is not easily made conspicuous. Despite such difficulty, I aim to expose theoretical misogyny by clarifying the extent to which certain received epistemological and moral theories are not gender-neutral, even if their advocates suppose otherwise. I can then legitimately criticise the conception of rationality dominant in western philosophy as genderist, 'precisely because it has assumed a privileged status for those gender-specific characteristics (Keat, 1983: 20) associated with masculinity. I will endeavour to expose both sexism and genderism.

REASON AND CHANGE

In order to explain how reason has been construed in predominantly male categories, I wish to clarify significant historical changes in the understanding of reason, from a substantive Greek concept first, through Cartesian changes second, and third, to reason's association with scientific, abstract forms of knowledge. I explain how the aspiration to a concept of reason common to all has led to an abstract rationality that cannot incorporate concrete, contextual contingencies of daily experience, which are important to moral existence. Furthermore, success in the modern world is defined commonly in terms of the rational, public citizen who bears traits typically classified as masculine.

Reason has an important influence on ideals of moral identity. As indicated, definitions of a good person have been fraught with naturalistic fallacies. Claims about how women ought to be and to behave are based typically on assertions of how women appear to be and to behave. This purportedly neutral description of women mistakenly identifies the 'good' woman (and thus, concomitantly, the 'fallen' woman) with natural propensities (Midgley, 1981). This diminishes the distinctly evaluative feature of 'goodness'. The recognition that such assumptions are not neutral provides a useful basis from which critically to assess ideals of 'good moral identity'.

There is little dispute within traditional philosophy that the most significant requirements of being a good person hinge upon reason. Reason is understood here not only as a criterion of truth and a means to assess beliefs, but as a prime character ideal. It may seem contentious to claim that what is true or reasonable or ideal frequently varies according to our sex. Reason purports to relate to the 'real nature of the mind' in which, as Augustine expresses it, 'there is no sex.' Yet to ignore the gender input into reason, is to refuse to unmask the essential maleness behind what Lloyd aptly calls, 'The Man of Reason' (1984a).[1]

Highlighting this maleness is not prompted by 'reverse chauvinism'. That is, I do not imply conversely any distinctively female criteria for reasonable belief, although I examine, in the following section, certain feminist claims to women's intuitive truth. Rather, at stake is the 'wider context of ideas and ideals of reason which frame epistemological questions' (Lloyd, 1984b: 20) and significantly affect ontological dilemmas. Tracing this historical development does not require the discarding of either reason or theory, but makes use of the resources of both for critical reflection. A specific motivation for this task concerns the genuine practical and conceptual conflicts women experience between femininity and ideals of reason. 'Rational women' often feel ambiguity and conflict between the importance of theoretical abstract thought to ideals of rationality, and accepted ideals of femaleness including an emotional orientation. Once women refuse to accept one at the expense of the other, the urgency for clarification grows.

Reason and the Greeks

There have been substantial changes in the philosophical understanding of theory, knowledge and rationality. The Greek term *theoria* refers to a form of contemplation aimed at truth. Consistent with all forms of contemplation, this necessarily entails a disengaged perspective, in that it does not try to understand things as they impinge on us, as with 'our ordinary stances of engagement', but claims to offer a higher view of reality (Taylor, 1985b: 136).

Within an intellectual culture, theoretical understanding is related to rationality. The translation typically used for the Greek word *logos* is reason. For both Plato and Aristotle, reason is taken to be the condition of really knowing something, evidenced through its articulation. Plato makes it quite clear in *The Republic* that to have real knowledge of something, *epistéme'*, is to be able to provide a clear account of it, *logon didónai* (1971: 245; 273). That is, the claim to have a rational grasp of something should coincide with the ability to articulate it. For the Greeks, rational articulation encapsulates the links between a view of the universe as meaningful order and that of understanding and attunement, or knowledge and wisdom (Taylor, 1985b: 142). Contentment as a rational being relates to grasping the order intrinsic in human purpose. As Taylor explains, 'to say that man is a rational animal is to say that this is his *telos*, the goal he implicitly is directed toward by nature (1985b: 142). This affirms the link between knowledge, wisdom and rationality.

The Greek theory of knowledge is a reminder of a type of rationality that can be called 'substantive', and is not the focus of my critique, nor the major input into the construct 'The Man of Reason', despite its sexism and genderism. But outlining it shows how deep within our philosophic tradition is women's exclusion from the full status of rational being. We saw in Chapter Two how the primary Pythagorean contrast between form and formlessness aligns maleness with the active, determinate form and femaleness with passive, indeterminate matter. The conceptual and practical ramifications extend far beyond any reproductive analogy, to, for example, a Platonic distinction between mind, as the principle that understands the rational, and matter, which is deemed to play no part in the contribution to knowledge. Indeed, in a stronger sense, matter, having overtones of femaleness, is construed as something to be transcended in the more important search for rational knowledge.

In *Phaedo*, Plato has Socrates describe from prison the intellectual life as one that cultivates the rational soul. The true philosopher

> is entirely concerned with the soul and not with the body...While the soul is infected with the evils of the body, our desire will not be satisfied, and our desire is of the truth. For the body is a source of endless trouble...We make the nearest approach to knowledge when we have the least possible intercourse or communion with the body...And what is purification but the separation of the soul from the body? (1955: 157, 159, 160, 161).

While the cultivation of reason stays central to a Platonic life-style, the later Plato incorporates non-intellectual elements into the life of the soul, so that reason becomes a passionate, creative, productive faculty. The formal arena is judged also by Aristotle as the proper object of knowledge, attained by exercising the intellectual faculty, yet not construed as the soul's escape from the body.

The idea of the divided soul maintains itself historically. In the first century, Philo assesses moral progress in terms of reason's supremacy over the influence of sensual passion. Philo's philosophy involves a synthesis of the Platonic notion of reason's corruption through the senses, with a Judaic account of women as sensual seducers. To assert that women symbolically represent the non-rational aspects of human nature does not necessarily imply that women are irrational, but it is Philo's pejorative attitude to women that enables his allegories to function (Lloyd, 1984a: 25). In these terms, woman's distance from the superior contemplative form of reason qualifies her as feminine (Lloyd, 1984a: 13). To attain moral progress through reason, 'lesser' traits, characterised as 'female', are to be set aside.

Greek concepts of nature and reason tie understanding to an attunement to one's nature as a rational being, in contrast to the modern scientific view, which dissociates them. These views have not only different goals, but incompatible norms, and are, hence, incommensurable in many ways. The scientific study of reality has accompanying technological spin-offs, and claims to achieve greater knowledge of physical nature through its dissociation of understanding and attunement, but actually tends toward domination and a disregard of the personal meaning or symbolic activity such reality might have.

The attempt to identify separate activities highlights differences between modern and Greek approaches. With the latter, understanding and attunement cannot be separated. 'You cannot know the order of things without loving it, nor the other way round' (Taylor, 1985b: 144). That is, if one accepts that there is purpose in the universe, and that one's rationality is the capacity to grasp the order of being, then there is an intrinsic relation between wisdom, understanding and rationality. Rational discourse requires a justification of this understanding and is made meaningful through shared articulation. This idea of meaningful order has been corroded and is seen largely as illusory in the light of 'real' scientific knowledge.

Cartesian foundations

A historical jump from the Greeks to Descartes reveals stark contrasts and factors central to modern philosophy. Descartes' *Meditations* (1980) is seen as the *locus classicus* of the conviction that philosophy's quest is to search for an Archimedean point upon which knowledge can be grounded. This quest is more than a device to solve metaphysical and epistemological problems, for underlying the 'Cartesian anxiety' is the haunting fear of intellectual and moral chaos. Therefore, while an Archimedean point may have appeal as the quintessence of scientific method and as a metaframework for evaluating and justifying all theories, it represents an impossible dream, that of possessing absolute knowledge and intellectual finality.

For our purposes, it is pertinent to locate two major features of Cartesianism that have entered mainstream philosophy. The first is a rigid separation of the mind from the body, in a way that is different from the Greek notion. Second, there is an altered conceptualisation of reason. The Greeks require the subject to engage in intellectual self-purification, an internal dialogue where previous unproven judgements are suspended. In Cartesianism, once the Archimedean point is supposedly discovered, this serves as a foundation to build a solid edifice of knowledge, justified only by an appeal to reason—but reason is now divorced from the concept of meaningful order, intrinsic to Greek notions of rationality.

First, consider the changes in the mind–body split. Seventeenth-century rationalist philosophers sharpen the mental division of labour between the sexes in strengthening the antithesis between mind and matter, and in demanding the shedding of the sensuous from thought. Lloyd suggests that the Cartesian search for the clear, distinct and rational, quite separate from the emotional, sensuous and imaginative, invokes dichotomies of what were previously 'contrasts within the rational' (1979: 24). Aristotle, like many theologians, concedes the possibility of a 'rational desire'. There are many instances of feminist attempts to demonstrate that non-rational characteristics are certainly not irrational. Rather, they can be seen as contrasts *within* the rational sphere.

We need to look further at what changes this contrast into a dichotomy, for the conjunction of the Cartesian downgrading of the sensuous with the mind–matter distinction introduces new possibilities of polarisation (Lloyd, 1979: 24). This separation of the mind and the body which is associated with the separation of men and women and is used to justify separate functions is powerfully reinforced when such a separation is justified by a theory of the mind. We have noted the tendency for reason to be assigned to men, and the emotions, sensuality, intuition and the imagination to be considered appropriate for women. 'Within a context of sexual inequality, the division between reason and the non-rational is confirmed at both philosophical and practical levels. This division reflects and re-enacts the division between the sexes. The stage is now set for the emergence of the Man of Reason as a male character ideal' (Lloyd, 1979: 25).

The offence here lies not just in consolidating a contrast into a hierarchical polarisation, but in the exclusivity of the valued position, that is, its deliberate exclusion of women. 'It is not because male nature is rational that men become rulers, but it is because men rule that rationality is assigned as a male trait' (Gould, 1976: 22). The other side to this is that 'it is not because women are intuitive and aesthetically sensitive and because these traits are of secondary importance, that women are assigned a subordinate role, but rather because women are subordinate' (Gould, 1976: 22), hence the traits are undervalued. The realm of the sensual to which women are assigned is precisely the space which the Cartesian 'Man of Reason' needs to transcend to ensure 'true knowledge'. This space indicates the appropriateness of a 'different kind of intellectual character, construed as complementary to "male" Reason. This crucial development springs from the accentuation of women's exclusion from Reason, now conceived in its highest form—as an attainment' (Lloyd, 1984a: 50).

The nature of this attainment can be precisely defined. While reason was viewed as a distinctively superior human trait, it could be categorised in terms of a potential that humans could strive to realise. The seventeenth-century changes meant that reason is considered not as a distinguishing human feature, or a fulfilment of nature, but as a skill to be learned as a particular methodical approach to knowledge. For Descartes, method is less a reasoned approach than a precisely ordered abstract mode. In the context of his metaphysics, with the radical separation of mind and body, rational method became divorced from its previous associations with public pedagogy, disputation and public discourse. The emphasis on public debate shifts to private abstract thought, the 'pure thought' that lies at the heart of abstract scientific thought.

This thought concerns itself with the search for certainty and the control of nature (and here this includes its association with women and the body). Devoid of particularity, personal experience or subjective content, nature is known only as the abstract object of an abstract *cogito*, where knowledge is inextricably intermeshed with domination (Flax, 1983: 259, 260). Matter ceases to be perceived as that which has to be dominated so as to attain knowledge, but as the object of knowledge, now construed as the power to manipulate and transform. The symbolic associations of femaleness with matter and nature, where nature is seen as mysterious but controllable, act as more than symbolic metaphors. They affirm the idea that men, who can rationally know nature, have a rightful dominion over women, perceived as nature.

This 'male achievement' involves repudiation of the intuitive thought-styles attributed to women which are assumed to be unsuited to the abstract, systematic rationality defined by the Cartesian paradigm. This repudiation does not necessarily infer that women are incapable of rationality—indeed praise is offered for their understanding of the familial world within their grasp. Yet, because the nature of this intuitive knowledge cannot be rigidly systematised in abstract terms, the ideals of rationality appear further to downgrade women by precluding women's possible attainment of them.

The implications of a theory of rationality such as Descartes', which aims at demonstrating that true objectivity and real knowledge are attainable and that what cannot be distinctly understood does not constitute true knowledge, extend beyond an epistemological debate. If the intellect is seen to be unaffected by background, or personal attributes, sense experience is acknowledged to contribute a possibility of knowing simple or personal natures and is thus kept from being a threat to this impersonal objectivity (Thompson, 1983: 11). As Thompson points out, Descartes' construct attempts to obliterate individual idiosyncracies and overcome the limitations of human, physical beings who actually feel, desire and relate. This demands a detachment from concerns of daily existence, to ensure uniform conclusions are accepted. For those immersed in domestic organisation and nurture, such a detachment is impossible. Princess Elisabeth, a regular correspondent with Descartes, complained that her household and social duties made philosophical reflection difficult. Propriety also prevented her conversing with and visiting intellectual men. The 'Man of Reason' is compelled to detach himself from the mundane and to rise above bodily influences. This is not possible for women for whom the menstrual cycle, pregnancy, breast-feeding and menopause are reminders of bodily influences. Even if it is conceded that women have the same mental capacities as men, this does not mean much if women are constitutionally unable to use them properly (Thompson, 1983: 12). What is crucial here is not just the distinction between intellect and the passions but the distinction between true or real knowledge as opposed to a common-sense knowledge requisite for daily living.

To summarise, for the Greeks, the mind provides access to the true order of things; that is, it enables humans to achieve an attunement with the order that encompasses them. According to this order, desire, matter and the body have a place, albeit a subordinate one. By contrast, Descartes states there is no order 'out there' from which to derive human purpose, but that the mind generates its own order. Accordingly, there is no hierarchical scheme which grants desires or the body a place, even a lowly one. What is introduced then is not so much a mind–body split as such, but a break from a vision of order in which both mind and the body found their respective, but different, places. For our purposes, a major implication of this is that it does not give desire and the body any significant place at all.

Reason and method in the scientific age

I highlight certain shortcomings in past ideals in order to understand the impact of history on current ideals. Hence it is now necessary to explain why many Cartesian assumptions have persisted, and in what way these are contrary to my argument. I want to examine the modern preoccupation with method and scientific rationality, and the development of an instrumental rationality.

As explained, method for the Greeks is a clear path to be followed, a reasoned way of pursuing activities. Philosophy concerns determining the right way to live. Through processes of argumentation and dialogue, rational accounts (*logon didónai*) are given, with the aim to harmonise *logos*, what and how one thinks and speaks, with *ergon*, what one is and how one acts. This is an emphasis on *phronēsis*, practical wisdom which involves the habit of deliberating well. Within philosophy, such questions of being cease to be primary after Bacon, Descartes, Hobbes and Locke. The major questions become epistemological: 'how do we know we know?'; and 'what is the status of our knowledge?'

A preoccupation with the methods of science assumes that what is knowable through rational inquiry is known through the application of scientific, objective methodology (Gadamer, 1981). Furthermore, it is assumed that rational methods require a disengagement from the object of enquiry. This methodology is applied particularly to nature, thought of, by analogy with machines, as manipulable. This is particularly evident where 'the expert' assumes a 'god-like' status. When individuals are faced with a barrage of technical 'experts', they often feel dependent, helpless and confused in establishing their self-identities. This is not surprising. 'Experts' often relegate non-quantifiable, personal or ethical aspects to a secondary status as not merely incompatible with objectivity and rationality, but totally incommensurable with them.

The question of what form reasoning, as a process of making sense of individual and communal life, can possibly take when technical methodology permeates a culture, remains open. Significant responses to this question emerge from other than feminist politics. Wolin (1972) argues that the *vita methodi* has deformed our understanding of political judgement. Feyerabend (1975) is critical of the 'deification' of science in contemporary life. Gadamer (1975; 1981) argues that an obsession with method distorts the ontological character of understanding. His emphasis on the interpretative structure of human life contextualises his hermeneutics, as the art of explication. Bernstein also is critical of the 'intellectually imperialistic claims made in the name of method' (1983: xi). These responses are animated by a practical–moral concern about the potential threat a preoccupation with method may pose to moral judgement. An emphasis on dialogue, debate, conversation and communication both presupposes and fosters a personal and civic solidarity which is absent where culture is defined as a manifestation of instrumental and abstract rationality.

Instrumental rationality
The modern understanding of reason typically views rationality as an instrument for determining efficient or effective means to a determinate end, where acceptable activities include technical application, manipulation, and control (Bernstein, 1983: 46). The 'subjectivist' component of instrumental rationality means that what is 'rational' depends on the effectiveness of the self to pursue ends that prove rewarding, regardless of the integrity of those ends. In this context, being rational means making choices that coincide with self-interest, and someone who acts flagrantly in violation of personal interest can be viewed as irrational in avoiding preference-maximising behaviour.

Weber (1978) draws clear distinctions between the subjective and objective categories of reason. He distinguishes between a 'subjectively rational' transaction, which is purely instrumental, and an 'objectively rational' calculation, which is purely quantitative. Intrinsic to this distinction is the belief that a 'pure' rationality, which is predictable and based on regulated rules, is possible. While the above 'subjective' element is largely synonymous with whatever is classified as private, idiosyncratic and arbitrary, he concedes that if people act subjectively rational, then they can expect subjectively meaningful behaviour from others (Weber, 1978: Vol. 2: 1,376). These expectations exist where there is a mutual agreement in a 'voluntary association', and some accountability, but such 'meaningful behaviour' often represents little more than the acknowledgement of private subjective preferences.

Under such constraints of instrumentality and rational formalism, the emphasis is on observed predictability and goal-directed behaviour. As we have seen, reason in a pre-modern sense is understood in broadly evaluative terms. The type of instrumental rationality under critical review here is incapable of yielding value judgements that defend a substantive rationality or support a conception of the good society. This basic disjunction between formal and substantive rationality, between reason and moral conscience, is unique to modernity. Procedures are divorced from ends, and are regulated by mechanisms that are indifferent to substantive values.

Weber explains the emergence of such mechanisms in terms of

modern capitalism, which is governed by instrumental market exchange—the systematic pursuit of profit through calculation and methodical self-control—and in terms of ascetic Protestantism, which fosters sober, purposeful devotion to the task at hand and a scrupulous work ethic. The work-oriented individual Weber has in mind affirms his or her humanness through efficient, ambitious, productive work. To an instrumentalist, the ideal self is detached, objective, self-assertive, self-oriented, and achieving. This 'instrumental, rational agent' assumes an appropriate impersonality, which is part of the objectification of structures of power. A disjunction may be experienced by this person when activities invite emotional expression. Some women mistakenly assume that access to the business, professional or political worlds is facilitated simply by overcoming the fear of success through adopting instrumental orientations. Consequently, many 'successful women' assume a functional rationality, an emotionally neutral objectivity, and concentrate on task orientations.

There is a very real possibility that the interpersonal relations of such women may become inbued with similar attitudes. Where this occurs, there is a strong tendency for marriage or de facto relationships to be defined and lived out on the basis of contractual terms, and for other social contacts to be 'slotted in' at one's convenience and calculated according to their likely utility. Insofar as this is the case, we have a clear example of life in general being assessed in a calculative, self-interested fashion. One suspects that this cost–benefit approach to life lies behind the choice not to have children that is taken increasingly by some career-oriented women. Possibly, such a choice is not solely a feminist statement on women's right to reproductive choice, but is also an absorption of an instrumental, calculative mentality which insists so stringently on the rationalisation of time and energy that little place can be found for children.

I suggest further, that in the modern view, a logical calculative approach extends beyond instrumental individual relations. It seems feasible to go so far as to talk of an 'internalised social ego' that erodes expressive, communal orientations. Weber's notion of *Zweckrationalität* (instrumental rationality) incorporates the idea that abstract, depersonalised modes of interaction have replaced older communal modes based on common beliefs and values. While the degree of commonality varies in different historical milieus, pervasive disenchantment has become a feature of modernity. Rationalisation becomes part of a generalised social form. This instrumental rationality, unconcerned with its ends, replaces a substantive reason which morally evaluates its goals. Furthermore, an 'instrumental rational orientation has become degendered' (Benjamin, 1978: 54) in that it has been internalised by men and women, although it is more typically associated with masculinity.

We have seen that mainstream philosophy operates with conceptions of reason and objectivity which are considered the opposites of emotion and subjectivity. We turn now to explain why traditional philosophy tends to regard passion, emotion, intuition and desire as not only morally inferior to reason, contemplation, objectivity and abstract knowledge, but as indicative of moral disorder, in distracting from 'higher moral goals'.

I begin with some conceptual distinctions between the contrasts to reason typically thought to inhere in the irrational and the non-rational. When something is described as irrational—let us say a series of propositions—it usually means that it is logically inconsistent, incoherent or ambiguous. Here a contrast to reason exists in the sense that the irrational constitutes a failure to satisfy reason's legitimate requirements. When something is described as non-rational, however, no such failure to comply with canons of rationality is implied. On the contrary, the category of the non-rational, which customarily includes such features of human experience as intuition, emotion and faith, refers to an area over which reason has no rightful claim to sovereignty. Thus, it is not uncommon to be told that intuition, emotion and faith defy strictly rational explanations and are properly understood as extra-rational rather than irrational. Obviously, it is sensible not to conflate the irrational and non-rational and it is important to oppose the customary philosophical elevation of reason at the expense of non-reason. Besides this opposition, I intend vindicating certain 'non-rational' features and calling into question their alleged antagonism to reason.

With this in mind, we explore first why passion has so frequently been associated with moral disorder and seen as a threat to moral stability. Aristotle, Plato and Rousseau provide us with clues, and I avoid repetition of their ideas dealt with elsewhere. To Aristotle, nature does nothing in vain. It is nature's intention that the rational should always control the irrational. This may appear unproblematic, yet, placed within a context of contrasts, differentially valued, not only do rational and irrational stand in opposition, but so also do spirit and matter, men and women.

The implications of these contrasts impute women as passionate, unstable beings. In Aristotle's view of reproduction, form, which is necessary for agency, is provided by the male principle to the receptive females who merely provide raw matter. The importance of the spirit–matter dichotomy can be related to his political ideal of organic unity, where 'the whole must be prior to the parts' (1972: 29). To Aristotle, this means that, within the unified soul, the rational should be in control of the irrational. He specifies the parts of the soul by analogy to particular relationships, such as child–tutor, master–

servant and husband–wife. The relationships obtain between rulers and subjects. In systematically emphasising women's materiality, as opposed to spirituality, Aristotle does not necessarily imply any irrationality of women, but rather that the deliberative capacity of their rational element lacks authority and therefore is easily overruled by irrational tendencies. In Aristotle's terms, women, in lacking full rational deliberation (assumed to be 'natural' to men), are incapable of full moral goodness and thus should be socially subordinate.

It is not outrageous to suggest that reason should have some influence, if not authority, over the physical or passionate dimensions of one's self. But in order to conclude that nature intends men to rule over women, Aristotle 'has also to say that nature intends the rational part of the soul not to have authority over the irrational part in the case of women' (Spelman, 1983: 23). Such an assertion is not at all conclusive, unless Aristotle knows how nature intends this. The suggestion that rationality prevails in men, whereas in women it is deficient, finds no justification in nature. The sexist proposition is not the assertion of the authority of the rational part over the irrational, but exemplifies Aristotle's association of rationality with men and non-rationality with women.

Reason is philosophy's prime tool in the search for wisdom and moral progress. Passion, in contrast, is identified with disorder and moral instability. For Plato, an understanding of Forms establishes what is abstract, eternal, universal and worthwhile. The Ultimate Form for Plato is to know the Ultimate Good, the light by which all else is intelligible. To apprehend the light requires being in control of the body, for material concerns, or passionate entanglements with other persons, jeopardise the acquisition of knowledge. Reason thus should dominate these 'lower' aspects of the self. The social arrangements of *The Republic* reinforce the internal control of the passions, with its communal property, controlled mating, parents not knowing their own children and so forth (1971). Education is to prepare potential philosophers to see the Forms, to foster rational capacities and to ensure the sublimation of passions. This radical disjunction between the mind and body leads to an identification of the body with moral chaos, and the mind with the capacity to dominate the passions. The body thus is placed under the control of a desexualised reason (Flax, 1983: 268).

A historical jump to Rousseau reveals the persistence of these notions of passion as disorder. As with Aristotle, Rousseau connects convention and purpose. He defines women's nature in terms of natural, sexual and procreative functions. These functions are still seen to distinguish women's life and potential in relation to men. Rousseau categorises men in terms of creative rational thought, and categorises women in terms of sensual, sexual or procreative activities. This typical categorisation of women is not without its contradictions, demanding women to be both the inspiration of romantic, sexual love, and the guardian of marital fidelity (Okin, 1979: 126).

In *Émile* (1977), Rousseau states that God endows both sexes with 'unlimited passions', but equips men with the capacity of reason to ensure control of passions, and women with modesty as a restraint. Reason, Rousseau acknowledges, is a delicate potential, requiring nurture. Sophie's education thus is directed toward 'what nature intended', that is, that she should be someone who pleases and is subject to men. Women's rational capability is to help men perform their functions more appropriately so long as it ensures no distraction from women's appeal to men. Pleasant conversation with Émile will not pose a threat to his ego. Nonetheless, gaps in Sophie's knowledge are desirable, since they ensure Émile the pleasure of remedying this.

Passion, disorder and the family

More detail is needed to explain the myths that women, being uncontrollably passionate, are responsible for much social and moral disorder. This requires particular attention given to women's traditional position in the 'family' defined loosely as an intimate domestic unit. First, I draw on Pateman's argument that, within civil society, women who are granted citizenship are still considered unsuitable for political life, since is considered dangerous for the state to be in female hands. Pateman traces this conclusion to the early development of liberal individualism where individuals began to be perceived as rational equals. Despite the appearance of equality, questions remain as to who possesses requisite natural capacities for participation in civil life. Those who lack such capacities are commonly assumed to be a threat to the social polity. The intensity of the threat is exacerbated by the real and imputed relationship between women, nature and the family. Given that the family commonly is viewed as a natural entity, it may be comfortable and convenient for some women to conclude they cannot transcend natural inclinations in the manner civil society demands. Such a conclusion should not be ridiculed, for in a real way the family does stand in stark contrast to the demands and conflicts of civil life. The particularistic family 'stands opposed to the impersonal, universal, "conventional" bonds of public life' (Pateman, 1980: 24). This conflict remains unresolved for many people.

The contrast between a Rawlsian sense of justice as the first virtue of social institutions and a Hegelian concept of love as the first virtue of the family highlights the above conflict. Rawls states that individuals who develop a sense of justice and morality of order will more readily maintain rules of civil association. If it is assumed that women are naturally 'incapable of developing a sense of justice, the basis of civil association is threatened; it contains within itself a permanent source of disorder. The threat is all the greater because the natural morality, of deficiency in moral capacity of women fits them only for the "natural society of domestic life"' (Pateman, 1980: 24). The family is simultaneously the foundation of the state in nurturing citizens, yet antagonistic to the state in subordinating public interests to particular concerns. In these terms, women's internalisation of the idea that they have a deficient sense of justice, reaffirms in them an inward sense of disorder which many women may attempt to compensate through activities like fastidious house cleaning. This internalisation may also prevent many women from leaving the domestic sphere. While there may be an imputation that women are a potential source of weakening the growth of justice in male kin, their socialisation of boys is not seen as problematic.

Hegel declares that 'love, the ethical moment in marriage, is by its very nature a feeling' (1973: 122). For Hegel, feeling is not only subjective, but capricious. He emphasises 'spiritual bonds' which rise above the 'contingency of passion'. Family life based on love exists outside the realm of reason. For Hegel, morality is the zenith of reason in which love has minimal place. What is crucial for our purposes is the devaluation of the emotional dimension intrinsic to family life, and the notion that, because feelings and love are not indicative of rational reflection, judgement and knowledge, morality must be independent of affection. A major purpose of the family is to foster human growth. Intrinsic to such growth is the development of emotional stability. Yet, if women are seen to imbue instability, then even their role in this development is jeopardised. We look further at the nature of intuitive knowledge, to show that non-rational characteristics need not be antagonistic to reason.

Intuitive knowledge

Behind the strict contrast between reason and emotion, or rational and intuitive knowledge, is the fallacious notion that intuitive knowledge is actually pre-reason. An intuitive judgement draws on the experiential basis of knowledge, rather than on abstract reason, science or a theory of the mind as the absolute gauge. I argue that any intuitive ability women may have is not an innate faculty, but one that develops through having many life experiences based firmly within a relational nexus, where there is a strong need to draw on factors other than the purely rational. As such, it is a learned faculty and underdeveloped in many men. Art provides an interesting example of this point. Artists, writers and musicians generally accept some artistic conventions, although they rely heavily on intuition for inspiration. The existence of a vital community of acknowledged artists and critics enable us to distinguish 'good' art from 'bad' art. It is possible to make sense of spontaneity and intuitive knowledge, without lapsing into notions of feminine wiles, magical powers, natural rhythms or subjectivism. Emotions and intuition are not merely experiential instincts, but can be subject to critical scrutiny. This critical reflection permits an appreciation that people's perceptions of situations vary, as do cultural norms defining appropriate responses to, for example, anger, grief, joy or public expressions of intimacy.

There are two main approaches in feminist theory to this idea of intuitive knowledge. The first approach is basically 'anti-rational', declaring unashamedly that women are less rational and more dependant on feeling than men, and that no benefit would be gained in being equally rational. The second approach refutes natural female emotionality but rejects traditional accounts of rationality, for being identified with the instrumental, quantitative, technocratic concept of reason that emerged from the seventeenth-century scientific revolution. I provide a detailed account of this type of rationality in the following sections.

As critics of the first position, with its reliance on intuition, de Beauvoir, Greer, Millett and Friedan adamantly declare that domestic activities inhibit women's success, as they require minimal use of the intellect which public activities are based on. Forthright advocates of a revised view deny this notion that domestic activities do not require the use of reason, and include contemporary French feminists Delphy, Irigaray, Clément and Cixous. They admit that traditional perceptions of rationality lend themselves to activities men are currently better at, but maintain that men's grasp of reality is inadequate, hence these perceptions should be rejected. As Irigaray asks, 'Can female sexuality articulate itself even minimally within an Aristotelian type of logic? No...unless precisely as an "undertone", a "lack", in discourse' (1977: 62).

These critiques are very revealing, but it is difficult to argue against traditional philosophical ways while refusing to use familiar logic and rational (albeit modified) discourse. In response to this problem, some challenge the impossibility of articulating female sexuality by pointing to instances of females who *are* successfully articulating it (Pargetter and Prior, 1986: 109). The problem with this response is that it fails to question traditional conceptions of reason, that is, it does not address what is being articulated and how it is being expressed.

McMillan (1982) argues that a traditional 'rationalist sense of reason' is narrowly construed and impotent in solving many of life's crucial problems. Further, she maintains that, where reason is seen to encompass broader categories, it is within these extended areas that women particularly are favourably endowed. Her attempt to oppose the rationalist ethic is focused on Hegel's categorisation of family life which is important, as noted earlier, but is considered inferior to civil life, the one being based on love, the other on reason. In attempting to reveal the inadequacy of rationalism and to avoid a position of ethical relativism, McMillan supports a view which grounds ethical judgements in a high valuation of emotions that is not totally subject to caprice.

She suggests three guidelines to moral conflicts. First, in determining what constitutes a 'good decision', even classical decision-theory concedes that rational action requires a concept of rational belief and a theory of value. Reason, or subjective valuation alone, is insufficient to provide a basis for moral choice. Second, reason can be brought to bear on emotional dilemmas, just as one's emotions influence rational decision-making. Third, while an emotionally-based decision may sometimes be as appropriate as coin tossing, drawing straws, or relying on opinion, when reason and emotion clearly conflict—often a decision based solely on emotions will prove inadequate.

I concur with McMillan's three guidelines, but I hesitate to endorse the conclusions she draws using mothering as an apt example of a reliance on intuitive knowledge. I agree that this form of intuitive knowledge is learnt through an apprenticeship of practice, role-modelling and spontaneity, with some deference to those skilled in the trade. But I consider that confusion is generated when distinctions are not drawn between reason *per se* and narrow conceptions of reason, or between intuition and intuitive knowledge. Drawing such distinctions is difficult. In the instance of parenting, one may not readily be able to articulate why one responded to a child in a particular way, nevertheless, this is not to deny that there are clear grounds for our responses. While it may confirm the reality of intuitive knowledge, any movement 'to the claim that intuition may function as an alternative to reason is just to commit a fallacy of ambiguity' (Pargetter and Prior, 1986: 115).

There seem insufficient grounds to abandon the distinction between intuition and reason, although in some situations the distinction is more conspicuous. The clear differences between rational knowledge and intuitive knowledge do not lie in an inner psychic state, but with the type of justification and mode of articulation offered for the respective judgements. For example, with a public debate, typical instances of a confrontational, aggressive male versus a reconciliatory, co-operative female reveal differences in the mode of reasoning and arguing, not a difference in rationality or natural potential. As such, the aggressor may also be a woman, and the conciliator, a man.

The content of rationality is influenced by the numerous human activities in which it finds its expression, therefore, definitions of rationality must extend beyond the abstract to include the conditions of reason. Scholarly attention to female experiences has revealed cognitive aspects of intuitive and emotional life, as Elshtain, Gilligan, Hartsock and Ruddick testify. Writers like Chodorow, Flax, Jaggar and Okin suggest that an insistence that men's lives are enriched by performing traditional female tasks, revalues the cognitive basis of the emotions. It also permits an exploration into whether certain activities foster particular traits. Once the cognitive basis of emotions is acknowledged, the constituent desires, passions and reasoning processes are open to critical challenge and to change.

This differs from a feminist identification of women solely with emotion and intuitive nature, which is counterproductive. The mistake lies in the assumption that reason must always be patriarchally defined and hence, to avoid being absorbed by a rationalist mentality, one should ignore reason. Anti-intellectualism (or a romantic fusion with nature) mystifies emotions. In doing so, it fails to recognise that anger, awe, disgust, hope, fear, jealously and joy are not 'pure feelings', but are rooted in social contexts, where some rational interpretation can be offered even if the initial expression appears solely emotional. That is, there are reasons why we are angry or joyful. The irony is that, by accepting historically bound definitions of reason and emotion, emotionalist feminists with seemingly radical politics actually adopt a fundamental, patriarchal dualism which their politics claims to reject.

What is required is the active questioning of traditional distinctions, and this includes both reason and emotion. This section has critically reflected on why feminine ideals associated with the emotions have been disassociated from reason. To reveal a genderist perspective on the rational subject, we must identify further how rationality formed part of the specifications of masculinity.

OBJECTIVITY, RATIONALITY AND MALENESS

The association of subjectivity, emotion and the body with femaleness exists alongside the association of objectivity, reason and the mind with maleness. I extend Code's idea that when 'the knower as well as the known, is accorded epistemological significance' (Code, 1984: 29, 30), the active nature of the knower comes into play. When knowledge is seen to have a context, the gender dimensions of knowledge become especially salient, and include the power relations that influence the construction of knowledge. First, I argue that the association of gender with rationality reflects, and is a reflection of, gendered personalities. I then elaborate the nature of objectivity and autonomy which are crucial components of stereotypical masculinity.

Gender and rationality

In our search for a normative practical rationality, we have discovered constraints imposed by gender-differentiated norms, that is, by characteristic modern understandings of what constitute appropriate masculine or feminine belief and action. We have concluded that 'rationality has been conceived as transcendence of the feminine' (Lloyd, 1984a: 104). What needs further questioning is the hypothesis

107

'that the distinctive masculine perspective that has heretofore defined "human rationality" is not only one-sided but also, in some respects, perverse' (Harding, 1984: 44). Also, the claim that feminist moral reasoning may differ from a masculine model in an important *qualitative* sense is crucial.

The danger in asserting a distinctive female intellect or moral character is that the structural features underlying gender will be misunderstood. The affirmation of the value of 'the feminine' occurs, ironically, in a space defined by the intellectual tradition it seeks to reject (Lloyd, 1984a: 105). I do not deny the strengths within femininity—my point is that traits like patience, resolution and negotiation have often developed as reactions to exclusion. Other negative responses include passivity, hysteria, voluntary isolation and uncertainty of self. The positive responses strengthen character. The negative responses contribute to the loss of self-confidence. It is important to question how the model for knowledge-seeking came to be so connected to capacities that have been disproportionately attributed to men, and how this model distorts our understanding of a rational person. Unless this model is understood, any divergence is viewed as a failure of moral growth. In terms of my feminist project, if it can be shown that the accepted notions of freedom, rationality and individuality are male-defined, and that the motivations behind a rational culture are masculine pursuits, then neither women's integration into these pursuits, nor their appropriation by women will lead to women's liberation or human emancipation. Alternatives are essential.

Gendered identities
The rationalist model of knowledge can be explained further in terms of its association with gendered identities and I draw again on object-relation theory which describes how infants 'objectify' or model themselves in order to establish identity and form relationships. From an initial symbiotic unity, the infant begins to discover others, and creates a self-identity and individuation usually as distinct from the 'mother world'.

The typical scenario presented by object-relation theory is that girls are encouraged to develop an identity within an atmosphere of attachment to others and emotional affection. The resultant sense of self is often merged with others' identities, contributing to the formation of a relational self. This encourages a sensitivity to others' needs, an openness to persuasion by others, and a concern to maintain connections. Imputations of fragile ego-boundaries exist, given that relationships are sought at the expense of personal autonomy.

A sharp contrast is evident in the typical socialisation of boys which tends to emphasise their separation from others, independence, autonomy and self-control. This often occurs through an opposition to unity with the mother. That is, with rigid gender distinctions, boys become masculine by ensuring they are non-feminine. This necessitates a repression of emotional affiliations. What emerges is an objectifying sense of self, where other persons are perceived as disconnected from themselves.

These stereotypes of boys and girls occur in 'mother-monopolised child-rearing' with the 'father-breadwinner' disengaged from active participation, except as an authority figure. An increasing number of people view these stereotypes as unnecessarily rigid and limiting to creative potential. Nevertheless, the elaboration of the stereotypes in the works of Chodorow, Dinnerstein, Rich and Balbus, provide useful causal explanations for individual and social tendencies and expectations. Defiance of these extremes in a shared parenting situation reveals the potential contradiction between the unreality behind the extremes and the intransigence of rigid cultural gender constructs. Another shortcoming of this explanatory approach is that it tends to stress a self-other distinction, rather than a self-other relation. In doing so, it postulates an energy output that is either directed toward the self or directed toward another, making it impossible to represent caring about the self-in-relation-to-others (Whitbeck, 1984: 72) which is the emphasis I favour.

Objectivity and autonomous masculinity

The explanatory approach does account for links between the typical early psychosexual development of males and females, and their identity, beliefs, practices and approaches adopted to relate to other people. My discussion is unavoidably limited to my cultural background as a white Westerner. We examine the specific input of objectivity, first, and then autonomy, into stereotypical masculinity, and contrast an objectivist approach to the object of knowledge with a feminist analysis which, although not subjectivist, centres on the subject concerned with procuring knowledge.[2]

The intricate intermeshing of cognitive, emotional and social forces that embrace most human situations supports both the historical conjunction of objectivity and masculinity, and the assumed disjunction between objectivity and femininity. In its extreme forms, objectivity is associated with facts, power and masculinity and is conspicuously removed from subjective feeling and the world of women and love (Fox Keller, 1985: 8). The pattern is often set from early childhood and this has little to do with any intrinsic sex differences: it is the intricate contexts of beliefs and practices that most influence the meaning of maleness or femaleness.

In belief structures and practices that rigidly separate subject and object, it has become virtually canonical to insist that knowledge of objective reality is yielded only to those who display the proper characteristics of anonymity, neutrality and individual separateness. These are characteristics encouraged in common patterns of childhood development for boys: the aspiration to objectivity is bound up with a boy endeavouring to define his own identity by separating himself from the prime parent. The danger is that emotional growth is predicated on the maintenance of separateness and a rigidly defined autonomy.

Alternatively, a feminist perspective, like other holistic perspectives, attempts to integrate subject and object components of life, and bases growth in a knowable reality in which the subject is already involved and intimately connected. For many women, their distinctive experiences occur within the personal-private sphere, 'so that what it is to know the politics of women's situation is to know women's personal lives' (MacKinnon, 1982: 534). To procure knowledge of such lives necessitates approaches to reality that are sensitive to the particular, individuated, intimate dimensions of life. An objectivist approach that is emotionally distanced from the subject of knowledge, is, in this instance, misplaced, and inadequate.

An objectivist mentality emerges from an image of self as autonomous and separate from others. I wish to make explicit this capacity for extreme objectivism which develops alongside a gendered self and hence represents 'the cognitive counterpart of psychological autonomy' (Fox Keller, 1985: 71). The dilemma this parallel of objectivity with autonomy presents is that, within the context of moral dualism, objectivity, a positive human attribute, becomes construed as objectivism, and correlates with masculinity. Subjectivity, another positive human attribute, is construed as subjectivism, and assumed to be a feminine perogative.

What is the nature of the autonomy that correlates with this objectivism? There is a tendency to confuse or even to equate autonomy with a separation based on an independence from others. Object-relation theory admirably stresses the development of self-in-relation-to-others, but its fundamental flaw lies in its preoccupation with autonomy as a developmental goal. There is the tacit implication that it is an 'either–or' situation—autonomy or relatedness. This restricts the notion of a balanced self, a self incorporating variegated parts.

While an understanding of boys' rigid autonomy explains the equation of autonomy with personal distance, it does not explain so clearly why this perspective tends to confuse objectivity with domination. That is, individuals preoccupied with an objectivist autonomy often have access to public power or are likely to seek control over others despite the human costs involved.[3] Why is this so?

In acquiring a sense of autonomy, there is some tension between the development of an *autonomous identity* and the need for *recognition by others*. The tension is, I suggest, dissolved by a balance of these two postures. Nevertheless, as I have shown, the process of differentiation is commonly split into two differing stances, the traditional female stance which overemphasises the relinquishing of self and the traditional male stance which overemphasises self-boundaries. Neither leads to a balanced subject, but to extremes of submission or rational control. Furthermore, when there is an extreme opposition between autonomy and dependency, the gap between men and women tends to be very wide.

Benjamin (1980) explains the emphasis on difference over sameness, on boundaries over fluidity, on separateness of individuals over relations with others, in terms of the psychic tendencies in which the basic elements of modern rationality are situated. This emphasis correlates with a radical dichotomy between subject and object, promoting extreme individuation and contributing to objectivism. As a result, there is a strong assertion of self which readily obliterates the personal reality of others.

Where others are readily considered as objects physical, mental or emotional violence are extreme ways of asserting control, of negating the other, and of establishing firm self-boundaries. While we often deplore instances of this in domestic violence, child pornography, prostitution, racism, imperialism or totalitarianism, that is, where the specific objectification is blatant, it is less readily acknowledged in calculative situations of employment, domestic tension or personal relationships where the objectification may be more subtle. Yet these are all instances of what Benjamin calls 'rational violence', a calculated objectification, where 'the other survives only as an object, not another subject who can recognise' (1980: 166) the other and be acknowledged also.

I endorse Benjamin's explanation that at the root of such domination is the 'splitting of autonomy from recognition, independence from moral dependence' (1980: 167). When the affirmation that 'I am not you but me' takes place within a context of reciprocity and freedom, there is no fear of losing self-boundaries, or any striving for mental omnipotence. Rather there is the discovery that an awareness of self and other develops as an interdependent process. Mutuality and interdependence are vehicles for moral self-growth, and autonomy is 'rescued' from its propensity toward the denial of the recognition of others. Furthermore, it is through the recognition of a subject's actions that meaningful selfhood is communicated. This is a major Hegelian thrust. Hegel writes, 'self-consciousness exists in and for itself when, and by the fact that, it so exists for another; that is, it exists only in being acknowledged' (1979: 111). Confirmation of the self also enables us to develop a sensitive appreciation of others' subjectivity.

Hegel states the possibility of mutual recognition between subjects where both engage in contradictory elements of negation (denial) and recognition (acknowledgement). While it is hoped that the polarisation of these two moments, of negation and recognition, is transitory,

111

Hegel claims they are a necessary part of the dialectic. Some may ask, why is there need for the negation, even if momentary? It makes sense when we recall that contradictory emotions are invoked in intense moments of selfhood, whether birth or death, self-loss or self-awareness, creativity or confusion. Expressing our humanity means we will experience, often simultaneously, fear and excited anticipation, pain and joy, hope and loss, anger and love. 'True differentiation...is a whole, in tension between negation and recognition, affirming singularity and connectedness, continuity and discontinuity at once' (Benjamin, 1980: 161). In the yearning for recognition, to be known and to know others, persons are able to achieve a wholeness, combining the impulses for differentiation and recognition and refusing to accept these as necessarily opposing impulses. This is premised on the compatibility of the desires for intimacy and independence.

RATIONAL, PASSIONATE SELFHOOD

So, is it possible to synthesise reason with passion within a contextualised ethic? I maintain that it is, and have accordingly sought to develop a conception of a rational, passionate selfhood. This development requires a reformulation of moral identity—an enormous task even to begin. From a reconceptualisation of the basis of knowledge, through the objectivist versus subjectivist debate, and a reconceptualisation of the nature of being, through a contrast between an abstract and a concrete universality, emerges a view of moral identity that sees autonomous agency as an empowerment, stresses the context of intimate mutual recognition, and encourages differences in selfhood.

Objectivism and relativism

The debate surrounding objectivism and subjectivism provides an interesting starting point for this discussion. J.S. Mill (1963; 1973) argues that the human sciences can be understood as moral sciences. Dilthey (1976), in meeting this challenge, tries to reveal a distinctive subject matter and method that would achieve 'objective knowledge' and still be appropriate to the *Geisteswissenschaften* which clearly requires explanation and understanding. The human sciences need interpretative devices that can rationally explain human behaviour, yet be flexible enough to allow for individual differences.

Still underlying many contemporary debates is the belief that the only viable choice is between a form of objectivism and a form of relativism. The options are posited as an objectivist, 'permanent, ahistorical matrix or framework to which we can ultimately appeal in determining the nature of rationality, knowledge, truth, reality, goodness or rightness' (Bernstein, 1983: 8), or a relativism, 'understood as relative to a specific conceptual scheme, theoretical framework, paradigm, form of life, society or culture' (1983: 8). Kant's attempt to ground the categorical imperative in a universal, objective, moral law is a prime example of the objectivist option. But it is relativism which presents the major challenge to reasons' claims to universality and truth.

Claims to consistent neutrality or relativism locate the basis for knowledge in self-evident truth, individual feelings, instinct, intuition or communion with nature. What is the problem with such subjectivism? First, modern relativism may deny reason its due, but in fact 'intensifies the function of rationality as self-rationalisation, control over impulses, and the observation and organisation of the self' (Benjamin, 1978: 39). Secondly, the authority of knowledge cannot rest in individual preference or psychological mood. To be answerable only to oneself dissolves socially beneficial distinctions between good and bad, and so collapses ethics as a set of values shared by a community. This extreme relativism results in the inability to make reasoned judgements about values and goals other than based on one's own preferences. What is at stake here is the subjective dimensions of reason and the objective ends to be served. Where there is a separation of 'subjective reason' from 'objective reason' (Benjamin, 1978: 39), the balance between subjectivity and objectivity is disturbed. The scales tip toward subjectivism and it becomes easier to rationalise a calculative objectification. Under the guise of relativism, an abstract rationality prevails.

These issues raise important questions regarding personal values, context and where reason should be most appropriately situated. I have criticised objective, supposedly neutral forms of knowledge based on scientific models—particularly the dichotomy they posit between the object and subject of knowledge. As I have argued, to affirm the importance of feelings does not necessarily entail a denial of objectivity or rationality. Furthermore, objectivity need not be limited to activities perceived as independent of feelings. Emotions have a firm cognitive thus rational basis, influencing value orientations which endow the world with meaning, coherence and moral significance. A clear distinction can be made between what is subjective and what is judgemental. The assertion that 'I like novel X' is subjective, but not contentious, unless it is a lie. The claim that 'I think this novel is entertaining' is judgemental, for it demands I provide reasons to support my assessment. What is important is the relation between this judgement and the reasons given. In all instances, it is a matter of balance between rational objectivity, and passionate subjectivity.

As for ideals of knowledge, I am advocating a shift from rigid models of rationality based on permanent, unambiguous rules, to a *practical rationality* that emphasises character ideals, exemplars and judgemental interpretation. This model accepts engaged, reasoned bases for particular actions. Differing interpretations highlight its flexibility. Indeed, 'there is no ahistorical, asocial, privileged vantage from which to assess either the projects or the construction of reason that arise from them' (Ruddick, 1987: 241). The concept of 'objective rationality' need not be an abstract, intransigent, rule-demanding device, but can act as a guide to practical rationality, or when to apply rules. For example, with surgeons, teachers, judges, and parents, the precepts behind medicine, education, law and parenting are not fully understood until they are applied in a context. Furthermore, each particular context throws up the possibilities of different applications, interpretations and conclusions.

This process enables us to grasp the relevance of a 'historically situated reason' (Gadamer, 1981: 274) as it emerges within a living tradition. In drawing on Aristotle, Gadamer reminds us that moral being is not equated with a type of objective knowledge where the knower stands over a situation, but it involves a deep embeddedness in the situation itself. While knowledge of technical skills for crafts can be learnt and applied, moral knowledge is acquired through situations requiring a right action. Guiding principles cannot be dogmatically taught—they are schemata that must be made concrete in the situation of the person acting. This adaptability is not subjectivist, though it does rely on personal experience and interpretation. Requiring deliberation, moral knowledge is experiential—moral judgements may alter with different individual dilemmas. Gadamer's critical appropriation of Aristotle's insights, posits *phronēsis* as an important challenge to scientific knowledge. Furthermore an emphasis on practical wisdom permits a positive distinction between ethical pluralism and ethical relativism. That is, it contextualises ethics.

Abstract universality

Such a synthesis between rational objectivity, and passionate subjectivity has enormous bearing on the balance between an abstract and a concrete type of universality. The articulation of an abstract universal subject represents a major moral advance, that is, it specifies the criteria of certain rights, claims and obligations possessed in virtue of being human. Since, as Gould points out, this ideal is 'based on the view that what is essentially human determines the equal ontological status of all human beings in all societies,' (1976: 16), it provides a means by which societies can be critically assessed in terms of overcoming inequalities.

Whatever its strengths, an abstract universality falters both in practical contexts and where differences that can be shown to be constitutive of the self are classified as 'accidental'. In terms of this first weakness, a distinction between an abstract concept of equal treatment of all persons and a concrete case of sex discrimination can be shown to be more than just the inadequate application of a universal principle. It lies, rather, in the difficulty of applying the formal principle of universality to every concrete situation. Further-more, the abstract conception presents the individual as consisting of invariant purposes, wants and interests. It cannot take seriously the idea of individuality. When reason is categorised as an 'abstract universal' faculty, it becomes hypostasised as an entity existing inde-pendently of social relations or individual variances—and precisely because it does it proves itself incapable of dealing with important human factors that cannot simply be banished to some nether world ungoverned by rational principles.

The second major weakness of an abstract universality, an exten-sion of the first, is its inability to incorporate differences, perceived in this framework as inessential. As demonstrated, the abstractness of the universal principle provides no certain bridge to the concrete, hence the possibility of there being a concrete component to the principle of universality remains unaddressed. Kant (1964) provides a specific example. To be moral is to be 'purely' rational and entails obedience to a moral law that has been rationally prescribed as universally binding on all rational agents. Pure, practical reason alone is capable of determining the 'categorical imperative' that attends moral law, and the will to act in accordance with it. To be feasible, Kant's position requires an unconditional goal of absolute worth. The foundation of this goal is the idea that rational nature exists as an end in itself. Moral action consists in respecting precisely this. To such an end, there can be no variation.

Concrete universality

Against the deficiencies of an abstract universality I counterpose concrete universality, which concerns itself with the individual and social differences that must be included in a notion of personhood, 'not simply as accidents, but as aspects which constitute the universal or the essence itself' (Gould, 1976: 26). As Gould explains, this universality must be seen to be constituted by both the features humans share and those which are individuating. If we accept a 'unity of differences' or an 'internally differentiated unity', then we also accept a dynamic interplay between the universal principles. Such an emphasis highlights the role of creative agency in history.

The application of this for ethics requires a reformulation of concrete universal norms that takes into account commonality and relevant differences. While the very notion of 'relevant' is controver-sial, its determination is necessary to specify conditions for applying the norms. The philosophical task requires critical reflection on ideas and the social context from which they emerge, and it is from this basis that a critique of rationality makes sense.

Furthermore, it is from this basis that it becomes impossible to accept that the rational subject can be established in abstract. On the contrary, it becomes evident that the rational subject must be able to incorporate particular differences. Being a woman, or being a man is not merely an abstract property, but is dependent on, among other things, a network of relations with others. Indeed, even the properties we have believed to be essential to 'rational males' or 'emotional females', develop through such relations. 'Men become men, and women become women, in the course of these interrelations. In this sense, the relations are "internal", or constitutive of the very properties themselves' (Gould, 1976: 28). A respect for persons requires us to regard individuals in their concrete specificity. Conceiving the individual as a particular person places the emphasis on the 'source of (yet to be discovered) intentions and purposes, decisions and choices, as capable of engaging in and valuing certain (yet to be discovered) activities and involvements, and as capable of (yet to be discovered) forms of self-development' (Lukes, 1984: 146). In doing this, a concrete universality acknowledges the realisation of human properties like rationality and passion within actual situations. Also, it brings together many and varied purposes, possibilities and potentials that make up human nature.

Rational, passionate selves

A synthesis of reason with passion, objectivity with subjectivity, alters our understanding of knowledge and of being. It injects new possibilities into moral identity. Let me summarise three major features of this identity: autonomous agency as empowerment; the mutual recognition of rational, passionate selves; and the encouragement of differences. First, a revised understanding of autonomy leaves behind a 'static autonomy' that pursues knowledge and being by severing subject from object. On the other hand, a 'dynamic autonomy' aims at a mode of being that relies on our connections to the world around us (Fox Keller, 1985: 117), without being threatened by them. Being able to act on one's own volition does not imply one has no need for others or that one is not influenced by them. Instead, dynamic autonomy requires a struggle to establish what are real human needs and how one can avoid harm to persons. The practical concern is with choice, deliberation, a tolerance of conflicting viewpoints, and the judgemental quality of rationality.

I can only briefly allude to the links this reinterpretation posits for reason, autonomy and freedom. The Frankfurt School, for example, in following Hegel, focuses on freedom as reason's intuition of itself. In following Kant and general Enlightenment thought, their emphasis is on release from self-inflicted bondage, where resolution has been frozen. This School and its followers adopt the idea that thought is so liberating that 'the attempt to identify the emancipatory potential in the present is the rational project' (Flax, 1978: 210). This project requires a rational refusal to accept constraints, whether natural or social. Furthermore, it is only in conjunction with other self-actualising selves that freedom can be assumed to be a principle of communal life. As the Frankfurt School's critique of 'pure reason' reveals, if reason is construed simply as the activity of the self-reflective subject, it can be shown to be markedly deficient as a means of bringing about freedom and autonomy. Reason needs to be firmly grounded within an intersubjective context. As is clear, the advocation of a flexible, practical rationality and of a more dynamic idea of autonomy is by no means purely a feminist contribution. Those striving for alternative conceptions of reason aim to pave the way 'to a more historically situated, non algorithmic, flexible understanding of human rationality, one which highlights the tacit dimension of human judgement and imagination and is sensitive to the unsuspected contingencies and genuine novelties encountered in particular situations' (Bernstein, 1983: xi). Such conceptions try to interpret, to understand and to explain the nature of human meaning and action in order to present a fuller, more holistic moral identity.

The ontological basis of this conception is a specific notion of the person, and of agency. We have cited evidence of the standard form of the knowing subject as a disembodied, non-historical, non-sexual, non-social subject. I have argued that to reinstate the concept of a person as a knowing subject implies a principled subject who views personhood as a moral category. Clearly this is not always the case. Putting the knower strongly into the knowing process may lead to a concept of a moral science or to an immoral science. The implications are profound, leading to an active moral critic. My point is that our values, beliefs and ethical orientations are not merely subjective or passive value judgements, but *Weltanschauungen*: they endow life with meaning, and suggest paths of action. In this context, to be devoid of a value-orientation is to be devoid of character. As Weber argued, the dignity of the 'personality' lies in the presence of the values around which life is organised (see Brubaker, 1984: 63, 94). I am arguing that a concept of agency that stresses a life of moral significance embodies a self-empowerment that emerges from understanding and affirming our connection to the world. This positive empowerment incorporates an autonomy that repudiates separateness, control or domination. This has enormous political potential in that empowered persons refuse to be manipulated, coerced or exploited. When this potential is redefined in terms of mutual interests and well-being, it provides scope for radical consequences in relationships in the private and public domains.

Mutual recognition acknowledges give and take between two subjects as the prerequisite for both love and knowledge. Where there is mutual recognition, there is a sense of self as being differentiated from others, despite being intrinsically related to others. Without a firm sense of self, there is a submission to others or an attempt to assert the self through control of others. Rather than a strong personality, this control represents weakness: the need to dominate arises from anxiety about impotence. The alternative—taking pleasure in another's autonomy and inclinations—provides evidence of a sense of self defined simultaneously in relation to and in differentiation from others. The facilitation of this dynamic autonomy through parenting and/or other relationships removes the need for symbiotic fusion, alienation or domination.

What place do reason and passion have in the context of mutual recognition? Clearly, there are different degrees of desire, and different types of intimacy. While *eros* or sexual desire, does not always incorporate *agape*, or a charitable orientation, insofar as *agape* incorporates *eros*, the sexual dimension remains subservient to the prime consideration of the other person. This does not underestimate the strength of erotic urges, but it ensures there is no sexual exploitation of others.

What is the relationship, then, between sensual desire and reason? Within the moral rationalist tradition, the relation between reason and desire is antagonistic, characterised by a Kantian morality of reason, a utilitarian morality of desire, or an emotivism where morality is a matter of taste impervious to criteria of objectivity. Clearly, the desire for love or affection cannot be approached from a universalist view such as a Kantian categorical imperative. The demands and requirements differ. Reason is seen in public thought, form, rules, and ideas, while desire manifests itself in private feeling, content, substance, ends and events, yet reason is informed by desire, as desire is by reason. Intimacy is exclusive, directed to particular lovers, friends and relatives. 'No lover could claim that any rational person in his or her (objective) position should love the person he or she loves' (Weston, 1984: 187).

Moral conflicts are difficult precisely because there is a real tension between what we want and what we perceive we ought to do. The problem moral subjects face is how one can be reassured that what is wanted is what ought to be desired. With Kant, no moral worth can be attributed to action emanating from natural inclination, only from duty. Of course some actions springing from natural passion have no intrinsic moral worth, such as the desire to eat chocolate, but it does not logically follow that all acts of desire are morally inferior. A spontaneous gesture to buy a box of chocolates for someone we love can be seen as a principled, passionate action. Yet, the possibility that passionate acts have moral value is ruled out *a priori* by strict rationalists, because of the assumed opposition between reason and emotion. In these terms, it is deduced that actions stemming from natural or emotional inclinations are not capable of genuine moral goodness.

Schopenhauer points out that a Kantian assertion that only acts based on rational duty are good opposes Christian morality where love is primary: without charity nothing profits. While Schopenhauer assumes egoism as the major motivation, he takes sympathy, as 'identification on our part with others...so their interests become in a sense ours' (1965: 148), as the only genuine moral motivation and means to go beyond egoism. With compassion as a cardinal virtue of morality, a different picture from the rationalist view emerges. Acts springing from love or distress can be viewed as principled acts, not just as acts of duty. That is, the real demands of duty cannot properly be understood if one is incapable of feeling genuine empathy. Schopenhauer exhibits his traditionalist tendencies by admitting that, in this regard, women are weaker in reasoning but superior in sympathetic inclinations (1892: 109). Even if the contention that women are more involved with the emotions and inclined toward compassion is true, it does not prove either than women do not reason, or that reason and desire are antagonistic. Rather, I maintain with Young-Bruehl, that 'reason without desire is empty, as desire without reason is blind. Even when the two are in tension, in conflict, neither wins' (1987: 215).

Finally, rational, passionate personhood is concerned with the facilitation of positive relationships and thus fosters the appreciation of differences disallowed by an abstract universality. This makes political use of the differences claimed. Cultural definitions of maleness and femaleness as polar opposites undervalue differences. When a dynamic notion of autonomy is premised on the continuity between persons, differences between self and others can be viewed as sources of deep enrichment, and appreciation is encouraged of the range and complexity of the human imagination. Where difference constitutes a principle for understanding, multiplicity is acknowledged. This provides a starting point for relatedness and the milieu in which rational, passionate personhood may thrive.

NOTES

1 My indebtedness to the clarity and strength of Lloyd's argument will become evident.
2 Fox Keller (1983; 1985) argues along similar lines. I acknowledge where I am indebted to her. While her venture concentrates on the practices and body of knowledge around science, her application concerns itself with the effects of scientific knowledge on what it means to call one aspect of human experience female, and another male. The alternatives she offers overlap with many I advocate.
3 While undeniably men have dominated in this realm, I contend that some aggressively ambitious women also fit this category. Interestingly, these women rarely have children. First, there is the assumption that children are incompatible with the life-style and demands of 'success', which is a major reason for 'successful' men's minimal participation with children. Second, it is difficult to maintain rigid autonomy, where frequent attention has to be given to daily needs, desires and development of dependant others.

5 Liberal individualism and the individual

I now want to consider in more detail a few of the cardinal themes of liberal individualism which constitute a challenge to my idea of rational, passionate selfhood. I do so for two reasons. The first is that many of the notions upon which liberal individualism rests are deeply embedded in our culture and recognition of their inadequacies is not easily won. The importance of this cannot be overestimated: if the vision of women and moral identity that I am pressing for is to have much credence, then cherished aspects of the liberal individualist tradition that has done so much to shape Anglo-American-Australian thought and practice have to be abandoned. The second reason for concentrating on liberal individualism is that its influence has even permeated the ranks of feminism; indeed, it has shaped the direction taken by a certain sort of feminism which gained prominence in the early 1960s.[1] This indicates the depth of the challenge liberal individualism makes to the position I am advocating. For, to the extent that certain feminists freely appropriate liberal individualist categories, it implies that I have to establish my case not only against those liberals who care little for talk of women as moral subjects, but also against those who care deeply.

Now, it should be noted that liberals emphasise the importance of individuals in different ways, not all of which are targets of criticism in this chapter. Certain of these ways are evident, for example, in three broad schools of liberalism: rights-based, utilitarian, and social or developmental. Rights-based liberals, such as Locke, Dworkin and Rawls, think that individuals are granted the respect they are due when they are recognised as possessors of fundamental rights which society should not violate. Utilitarian liberals, such as Bentham, James Mill and J.S. Mill, reckon that individuals' importance is affirmed when they are permitted to be judges of their own interests. The idea is that individuals are basically self-interested beings who seek to satisfy those desires that maximise pleasure and minimise pain. Social or developmental liberals, such as T.H. Green, Hobhouse and, arguably, C.B. Macpherson and Lukes, maintain that the most significant thing about individuals is their potential to develop as morally self-conscious beings, given the appropriate social and political conditions.

Quite clearly, there are notable differences among these schools of liberalism on the question of what a respect of persons' individuality should amount to. For instance, both rights-based and social liberals typically criticise utilitarianism's stress on self-interest as an insufficient basis for establishing the worth of individuals. Then again, utilitarian and social liberals are both similarly sceptical of the tendency of prominent rights-based liberals to assert that the basic rights to which individuals are entitled are pre-social in origin. Furthermore, rights-based and utilitarian liberals suspect there is something awry with social liberals' insistence that individuals flourish best through their involvement with others in pursuit of a common good for society.

These instances of divergence among liberals could be multiplied, but cannot be pursued here. For my purposes, the noteworthy divergence is that between rights-based and utilitarian liberals on the one hand, and social liberals on the other. That is to say, when I refer to liberal individualism, I have in mind either rights-based or utilitarian liberals, but not social liberals. This is because both rights-based and utilitarian liberals conceive of individuals as independent beings for whom social co-operation and interaction is a convenient means of securing essentially individualistic goals, whereas social liberals do not.

I intend to criticise the extravagant emphasis on individualism found in much liberal theory, and not liberal theory in itself. Throughout the chapter I refer to liberal theorists, of rights-based or utilitarian persuasions, who espouse a specifically individualistic, independent view of the moral subject which contrasts to the communitarian, interdependent view I am advocating. Accordingly, I omit discussion of the perspective of social liberals who, in spite of their liberalism, echo a broadly similar conception of the moral agents' constitution to mine. Thus, I focus on individualistically-oriented liberal treatments of rights, independence and self-interest.

In this chapter, then, I examine liberal individualism in general, then liberal feminism in particular. I argue that dimensions of liberal individualism block out an appreciation of what I take a convincing account of women and moral identity to consist in, and that liberal individualism incorporates ideas that are susceptible to damaging criticism. Consequently, liberal feminism is implicated in the general flaws of the liberal individualist programme, and its prescriptions for women fall short of what is required. This represents the shortcomings of a theory that slides from an admirable support of the individual to individualism itself. The discussion begins now with a treatment of four interrelated themes of liberal individualism, that is, individualism, autonomy, solipsism and rational choice.

121

LIBERAL INDIVIDUALISM

Fundamental to liberalism is the belief in the ultimate worth of the individual as a person possessing intrinsic value who should not be subordinate to the will of another. The protection of individual rights, self-interest and autonomy are important liberal goals, and an appreciation of these goals as valid for all individuals facilitates tolerance. Put broadly, there is much that is intuitively appealing about this statement of the importance and worth of individuals as persons. I do not intend to undermine this statement. What I do want to criticise, however, is the abstract individualism that assumes human characteristics are properties of individuals given independently of particular differences between people and their social contexts. Clearly any conception of individuals requires some conceptual abstraction, but this is different from an abstract conception of individuals.

There are different variants of individualism. With the German variety, respect for individuals is not always thought of as a threat to social solidarity, but to be one of the latter's chief aims. My emphasis is on its Anglicised association with classical liberalism, which directs itself to maximising freedom from interference by others, and to a lesser degree on the Western association of liberal democracy with capitalism, which accepts the inevitability of conflict betwen competing individuals.

In general terms, the idea of individualism within liberal individualism affirms the intrinsic dignity of the human, where every rational being exists as an end. The qualitative uniqueness of individuality is stressed. The individual is accorded autonomy, or the self-direction whereby an individual's thought and action is self-propelled, and not determined by external agencies. Any pressures and conflicts this individual might confront should be subjected to critical evaluation and resolved according to the intentions the individual articulates after independent reflection. Privacy, a clearly defined area in which the individual should be left alone, is valued by this individual. While the above ideas are all basic to the dignity of moral beings, I address my criticism to the *abstract* notion of the individual as bearer of the above features. This abstract notion is seen by liberal individualism to determine behaviour, and specify interests, needs and rights. In addition, my criticisms address the *individualistic* notions of individuality.

Despite variances within theories of individualism, there is a common ontological and ethical commitment to the individual. By this, I mean that moral value is attached to the individual *per se*, rather than to the community or to the self-in-relations. Indeed, the first premise of liberalism is the idea that the individual possesses a subjective existence and will prior to any expression in society.

Individual choice is prized as an indispensable means of respecting the right of individuals to construct personal, rationally based moralities. Often, what reinforces this sort of individuation is the belief that the 'first source of each person's knowledge of the world is his or her own senses' (Arblaster, 1985: 25). Consequently, as much liberal theory presumes that all values are simply private values, it cannot provide the grounding for a life in common (Elshtain, 1978: 36). Part of the 'poverty of liberalism' (Wolff, 1968) lies in its failure to appreciate the intersubjective dimensions of moral subjectivity.

In my view, this poverty relates in particular to the dominant liberal model of an individuated sociality which, in attempting to resolve conflict between individual and social interests, assumes that the individual has priority over the community. This assumption is conspicuous, for example, in the seventeenth-century social contract theories of Hobbes and Locke which have helped to shape the liberal tradition. Hobbes and Locke assume individuals relate to society in external and instrumental fashions. The external relationship implies that social participation does not alter individuals in any essential way: personhood is putatively given to individuals as individuals and is not a socially-derived achievement. Social relations also have an instrumental character, especially for Hobbes, whose influence here can be seen in utilitarianism. As Hobbes put it, individuals are concerned chiefly about their own interest and so are eager to make 'mutually beneficial bargains' in 'reckoning consequences', based on the 'highest value' they can attain as 'esteemed by others' (1974). Accordingly, formal, legal and contractual arrangements among people are encouraged and approached instrumentally, the aim being for each basically atomised individual to clinch deals which are maximally self-benefitting.

Whether such a picture of the individual's relation to society provides an adequate basis of social co-operation is highly questionable. Whether, indeed, it is compatible with democratic ideals is also doubtful. The comparison between an individual 'as a consumer of utilities, an infinite desirer and appropriator', with a developmental concept 'as an enjoyer, exerter, of uniquely human attributes' is indeed stark (Macpherson, 1973: 24). But such difficulties aside for the moment, the immediate point to be stressed is that the various entitlements Hobbes and especially Locke thought belonged to individuals as individuals and which it is society's responsibility to protect, are often in practice not extended to women. One might expect, at the very least, that a translation of such a conception of individuals into the popular language of democratic citizenship would give practical, universal recognition to all members of the polity as social, equal 'individuals', having all the capacities implied by this status (Pateman, 1983: 211). And, yet, as Pateman reminds us, there has been a serious failure of contemporary democratic theory—with its language of freedom, equality and consent of the individual—to acknowledge that women are conspicuously excluded from references to the 'individual'. Furthermore, in the context of liberal civil rights, public success is seen as the actualisation of this individual. Many women, relegated to the 'natural' realm of a domestic household, are effectively excluded from this fulfilment, and fulfilment in any other sense is often not acknowledged within liberal individualism.

With this brief background of liberal individualism, I address three further questions. What is involved in the liberal value placed on individual autonomy and rights? Why does this individual tend to think of himself or herself as a self-sufficient being? How does this autonomous individual make rational choices? We seek to discover why these features run counter to the feminist goals I am proposing.

Autonomy and rights

In Kant's classic formulation, autonomy is the state of being subject only to self-created, self-imposed obligations. The basis of this autonomy resides in the rule-making propensity of the 'rational will' which adopts as its own principles maxims that can be universalised— 'Autonomy of the will is the supreme principle of morality' (Kant, 1964: 108). The contemporary understanding of this emphasises the right not to be the object of another, and to have maximum freedom to determine personally what is true and good, where knowledge is viewed as the product of individual minds. This understanding oscillates between differing views. Take for example Lukes' differentiation between autonomy 'as self-determined deciding and choosing on the basis of consciousness of one's self and one's situation...and the extreme and intransigent moral pluralism implicit in ethical individualism' (1984: 156). Lukes' first idea of autonomy is profoundly influenced by moral guidelines that suggest means toward reflective self-consciousness and a situated individuality. With the second version of autonomy, moral value is placed on the subjective preference of the individual, not on any specific normative ethics. A reciprocal respect for one's own autonomy and the autonomy of others, relies on the integrity of individual judgement and self-consciousness as in Luke's first idea of autonomy. This fosters a respect for individuality that is different from individualism.

This respect is sometimes suppressed, for a liberal goal is to leave as intact as possible the individual's right to self-definition. To cater for a maximum respect of separateness, liberal societies provide mechanisms for adjudicating between the competing or conflicting claims of individuals. For example, an emphasis on non-interference reinforces the conviction that the state ought not discriminate among varying conceptions of the good life. Within this framework, the state claims neutrality on views of human nature, and thus can offer no rationale for moral preference other than fostering self-interest, with a sprinkling of altruism thrown in for good measure. It has little to say on what a good self-definition might resemble. The respect for separateness is essential for understanding a concept of privacy and self-determination, but, as an overriding premise, it ignores the interdependence of people, their historical character and human vulnerability or disability.

This ideal of non-interference can be seen to reflect the type of masculine morality that is premised on an emotionally distanced autonomy, untempered by a positive commitment to the care of, and responsibility for, others. This notion of autonomy 'presupposes and reproduces indifference to inequalities of power and situation' (Bologh, 1984: 381), precisely because it can block out its effects on others. To reiterate, a differentiation must be made between *individuality* which recognises the social factors shaping individual potential, and *individualism* that either ignores these intersubjective factors, or, in placing the autonomous individual at a premium, undervalues them.

Another root of liberal individualism relating to this idea of individualistic autonomy is the importance of the possession of individual rights. Explanations as to how these rights are acquired vary with different theorists. For Locke (1963), a notion of rights is tied to the law of nature, which he ties to God's law, and a law of reason, accessible to every 'man', by virtue of his rational capacity. The purpose of the state is to ensure the protection of God-given natural rights to life, liberty and estate. For Rousseau (1973), political society is manifest through the mutual recognition by individual contractors as equal possessors of rights. Whatever the various explanations as to the legitimacy of rights, dilemmas lie in the potential conflict between the pursuit of equal value of all individual rights, and the freedom to act without being interfered with. Some limitations on individual freedom are necessary to secure basic conditions of freedom premised on an equality of respect, because unlimited freedom represents a license for anarchy. Yet such a respect is appreciated only when the individual can identify a common link in personal interests and others' interests, thereby acknowledging shared interests to which individual ones may, if need be, become subordinate. Rigid individualists, in embracing ethical individualism, have difficulty in accepting the rights of others as a personal restraint and hence may be intolerant and excessively egocentric.

The failure to apply political-legal rights to women and children is due largely to the failure of most liberal theorists to include women in references to the individual. For example, while Locke's 'life' extends clearly to women, 'liberty and estate' are not effectively extended. Also, if political society for Rousseau is in a large measure legitimated by the mutual acknowledgement of separate contractors all equally possessing and claiming rights, then, in these terms, the suppression of women's public activity (or their confinement to the domestic sphere) prevents their making of contracts, affirms their inequality vis-à-vis autonomous rights and inhibits the mutual recognition of equals that might otherwise ensue.

The political challenge to sexist discrimination in the public sphere, and the struggle to procure rights are vital, but, as I have shown, the notion of liberal rights is premised on a concept of citizenship tied to the autonomous individual. While, ostensibly, this individual is not presented in liberal individualism as exclusively male, in reality, it usually is. This concept of the individual, which entails political rights and autonomy, may be thought to give expression to liberty and equality. While that may be so in principle, the reality is that the political rights which the concept celebrates are appropriated by those who already have access to liberty and equality. It is this access that has been blocked for women. Furthermore, because the 'personal' is seen by many conservative liberals to have minimal place in politics, legal reformism, though crucial, has been insufficient to secure actual sexual equality (Mitchell, 1976). Contradictions remain between the daily oppression of many women—in household labour, child-rearing, domestic violence, sexual exploitation—and their theoretical civil equality.

Similarly, a superficial concern with 'equality of opportunity' presupposes straightforward equal rights, but this assumption of equality here obscures the actual constraints which prevent people from grasping the opportunities which are supposedly at their disposal. Policies of equality of opportunity rooted in individual rights *alone* cannot incorporate the complex network of opportunities and constraints that actually exist. In failing to incorporate these factors, the principled concern for abstract rights undermines what I take to be the primacy of equality of respect. This is a contrast of emphases between concern for the individual and concerns for *individuals within communities*. Two contrasting feminist views highlight this dilemma. Elshtain argues that a shift in focus from a consideration of 'rights' or 'opportunities' to a concern with what persons are (or ought to be free to become) facilitates an understanding of the obstacles which militate against the emergence of human potentialities (1975: 472). In other words, the emphasis moves from abstract rights to the concrete situations people find themselves in, where actual rights may be denied, suppressed or granted.

On the other hand, McMillan writes that 'the demand of women, particularly mothers, for the right to pursue their interests without qualification and uncontested ought to be regarded as abstract and groundless... To treat a woman as a person need not exclude, when relevant, an emphasis on her role as mother and wife' (1982: 99, 100). While McMillan's view re-evaluates the maternal role positively, the emphasis on the significance of biological or socially conventional differences has disturbing implications. McMillan suggests that legislation for equal rights culturally compensates for unfair restrictions women might be subjected to by their reproductive role. She disputes the accusation that this role is a source of injustice. Her position retains naturalistic assumptions and does little to stipulate what treating a woman as a person might mean, other than affirming her possible 'roles as mother and wife', roles increasing numbers of women do not slot into, or slot into in modified ways that are incorporated into an all-encompassing sense of self. While categories like 'mother' and 'wife' have meaning in relation to a child or a man, and hence do repudiate the social atomism implicit in an abstract individualistic rights view, the emphasis on such categories yields an indecisive view of persons because they exclude other categories important to being a woman, like 'lover', 'friend', 'colleague', 'neighbour'. Elshtain's attempt to articulate a concern with persons in their own right (in contrast to persons with rights) incorporates both particularity and commonality and is a more realistic idea of dynamic autonomy than an abstract or conventional autonomy.

Self-sufficiency

A concern for persons in their own right is not possible where the primacy of rights relies on an atomist conception of the self-sufficient individual. This notion maintains that human capacities need no particular social context in which to develop, and hence is not attached to other normative principles concerning what is good for humans or conducive to their development. Rather, there is the assumption that each individual is expert in identifying and maximising self-interest. Questions of the good, as such, are not as important as the individual's reliance on personal judgement. In these terms, criticism can only be directed toward its grounds of rational inconsistency. Within such a framework, the moral dilemmas that arise from competing rights are seen to be resolvable only through formal, abstract modes of thought.

Yet, even the possibility of this resolution is complicated, because this mode of thought frequently coincides with the acceptance of solipsism as a plausible ontological viewpoint. Solipsism considers that only the solitary self is knowable as the only existent thing. Other people are isolated from the individual in question, or are assumed to have competing interests. Within this view, the purpose of civil society is to ensure that solitary beings with independent or opposing interests and needs can maintain their self-interest and prevent conflict. This view generally coincides with the belief that innate aggression, conflict and selfishness are endemic to the human condition, rather than co-operation, consensus and consideration of others. 'Value' is defined in terms of individuals' wants or interests leading to power struggles, resulting in domination or submission. The alternatives appear to be total engulfment or isolation.

This is a modern phenomenon. For Aristotle, such a notion of individual self-sufficiency and solipsism is neither desirable, nor possible. To him, it is axiomatic that the community is considered prior to the individual. The opposite axiom is held by modern liberal individualism. This fundamental difference affects its conception of human nature, of the relation of individuals to society, social goals, political values, practical policies and specific choices. The emphasis on rights and formal equality defines personhood in terms of 'being free from all relationships and responsibilities except those ones entered or accepted voluntarily' (Elshtain, 1975: 467). This permits people to give priority to friends over commitments to relatives. In liberal individualism, there is a conspicuous failure to accord value to relationships or to sentiments formulated through interaction with others. Consequently, the possibility of co-operation and community is accepted as, 'puzzling, impossible, problematic' (Jaggar, 1983: 24). When individualistic tendencies are dominated by market relations, with the alienation of capital-based labour, the anti-community bias is exacerbated.

Individualistic rational choice

In the previous chapter, we examined views of modern rationality that consider the mind as a calculating, interest-maximising machine. We saw that these views reduce the subject to a self-interested being, and rationality to methods for discovering what constitutes personal preference. I have argued that the high value liberals place on the free, autonomous individual militates (often by emphasis rather than intention) against the promotion of a communal consensus of well-being, or what might be called 'civic virtue'. I refer particularly to relativist notions which hold that individuals can make rational choices but cannot or, indeed, need not give rational justifications for any particular rank or ordering of ends. This interpretation of rationality permits each individual maximum freedom to ascertain personal needs and desires. Political institutions are considered 'neutral', or independent of any particular conception of the good life, or of what gives value to life (Dworkin, 1978: 127). For the modern rationalist, value is often reducible to price or quantification. Hobbes was explicit—someone's value lies in a price (1974: 150). Power is reflected in this price, the ability to have others succumb. I have demonstrated how an autonomy that readily abstracts from emotional or personal situations lends itself just as readily to a domination and objectification of others. Such an autonomy is more likely to occur where an individual is socialised into accepting a concept of self which is defined in opposition to others, such as the self-sufficient, individualist cited above.

Problems implicit in this modern rationalist view are made explicit in Gibson's (1977) discussion of Rawls. She translates Rawls' hypothetical construct into a voluntary, master–slave and a voluntary sadist–masochist society. She maintains that no matter how inegalitarian or exploitative these may appear, the liberal conception of rationality provides inadequate grounds for *morally* condemning these societies. This may appear extreme. Rawls places a priority on liberty and equality of opportunity, but Gibson's point here is to emphasise where a priority on freedom-of-choice, without a notion of good, may lead. She claims it is impossible to formulate a value-neutral account of rationality, advocating instead references to normative approaches to personhood and human good. I concur with Jaggar's conclusion that, 'if Gibson's argument is correct, then liberal scepticism, the insistence on what Rawls calls the thinnest possible theory of the good, itself begins to seem irrational' (1983: 25). That is, in terms of fundamental ethical questions—such as what constitutes a moral subject, what are real human needs and what objective criteria might fulfil such needs—formal rational choice theory translates human needs into an abstract language that not only eliminates passion from the preference calculus, but provides a minimal ethical framework in which to resolve such moral dilemmas.

Rational economic man

The 'rational economic man' (Hollis and Nell, 1975), an ideal construct within capitalism, provides us with a vivid example of the type of individualist I am criticising. I link this construct to the idea that an abstract masculinist world view has a great deal in common with the ideology imposed by commodity exchange (Hartsock, 1983: 242). 'Abstract masculinity' is defined to include the separation and opposition of culture and nature, abstraction and concreteness, and the hostility evoked when social relations available to the self are maintained by opposition, each struggling for recognition. The major features of the 'rational economic man' are shaped by the dictates of the capitalist market and may affect financially ambitious women as well as men. These features include the maximisation of profit, pleasure and materialism, and may be accompanied by the tendency to be ruthless, calculative or exploitative in the pursuit of the desired objects. Those influenced by these tendencies reduce the variety of human passions, desires and capacities to the urge for economic gain.

The capitalist market provides a space for the congregation of independent, self-sufficient and frequently hostile beings. Paradigmatic connections between people tend to be extrinsic, instrumental or conflictive, played out in competition and domination. Relations are entered into in order to perpetuate self-interest. 'The Other's status as Other is maintained' (Hartsock, 1983a: 39). The framework behind such relations cannot sustain a fruitful sociality. Within such interactions, nothing is actually owed to the community. Any existing concept of community is fragile, a by-product of arbitrary but shared desires and the calculative search for private gain. As Weber suggests, the rationality and impersonality dominant in market relations defies fraternal ethics. He cites the market community as the most impersonal relationship of practical life into which humans can enter given its 'matter-of-factness' or orientation solely to commodities (1978; Vol. 1: 636).

An egotistical conception of rational choice falters in connecting economic and moral terms. Sen (1977), in criticising the foundations of classical economics, suggests that an economic theory based on a universal egoism cannot account adequately for the allocation of 'public goods' such as a park or a library. He advocates replacing the model of the 'economic man' with a notion of human behaviour that acknowledges not only the rationality of self-interest, but the individual's commitment to groups. Wolff (1968) similarly criticises proposals that the criterion of individual want-satisfaction can be used to measure the good society. Communal values are a vital dimension of the public good irreducible to the sum of individuals' private desires.

I argue that the grounding of the 'rational economic man' lies in a moral emotivism that cannot incorporate a meaningful concept of the moral subject within communal life. Yet, to be fair, it does not claim to. Let me explain. There are ample instances of certain types of self-interested activity, where a value, a price or a cost-benefit analysis can legitimately be placed on an object and where the exchange that might occur involves no exploitation, such as a fair price for a hand knitted garment or baby-sitting in exchange for lawns mown. With the 'rational economic man' outlined above, similar considerations of moral justice, equality and mutual satisfaction do not necessarily occur. There is minimal moral basis to his activity, other than subjective preference. This does not mean that there are no reasons underlying these preferences or that they are necessarily immoral. My point is that individual rational choice in this form primarily assumes interest maximisation. In this context, chosen preferences may run counter to 'real' interests, that is, wants may themselves be a product of a system that works against human interests (Lukes, 1974: 34). Undoubtedly, the determination of what really constitutes human interest is enormously difficult.

Habermas (1977b) throws some light on this. For Habermas, the concept interest, as a means toward enlightenment, is meant to mediate reason with the faculty of desire. The basic orientation of such interest is rooted in work and interaction, and Habermas highlights three interests. The first, technical interest, refers to an individual's relation to nature and features rationalisation, strategies and causal explanations brought about by technical, analytic knowledge. The second, practical interest, refers to symbolic interaction within a normative order, of ethics and politics. This interest is linked to the existence of a reliable intersubjectivity of understanding, via linguistic communication and involves the interpretation of intention, goals, values and reasons. Interaction has a cognitive interest in mutual understanding and a practical interest in securing a precarious subjectivity. Habermas suggests that the development of this interest is blocked by, among other things, the belief in instrumental rationality and technological control. Central to Habermas' view of an understanding of reason and knowledge is the primary emancipatory interest, or the interest for self-actualisation through concrete political lives. This involves the critique and the exposure of power structures that constrain communication, and the concomitant pursuit of self-reflection out of an interest in emancipation.

While some may criticise the feasibility of informing subjects about what interests it is rationally desirable to possess, a synthesis of reason and passion, as we concluded in the previous chapter, is more likely to define moral activity as a dynamic communicative relation. Dynamic, first, because it is potentially liberating to synthesise traditionally perceived oppositions, and secondly, because creativity emerges with communicative intersubjectivity where people actively work together. The capitalist market mentality plays a significant role in preventing the realisation of this synthesis.

In summary, I have linked four dimensions of liberal individualism: the priority given to the individual, the importance of autonomy, the solitariness of this autonomous individual, and the parallels that can be drawn between this rational autonomous individual and the rational economic man. The concern expressed about the above four links has its roots not only in a critique of individualism, but in a vision of *individuality through community* (Gould, 1978; 1988), a concept of *self-within-relations*. Liberal individualism works counter to the feminist goals I am advocating.

LIBERAL FEMINISM

Liberal democracy and liberal feminism share a common concern with individuals as by nature free and equal to each other. Indeed, the major goal of liberal feminism is the application of liberal principles to women as equals to men. This has two components, namely, the extension of liberal conceptions of the individual to include women and the attempt to have women accepted into the public realm on equal terms with men. The historical roots of liberal feminism lie with the early suffragists, Wollstonecraft, J.S. Mill, Taylor and Cady Stanton. They argued that women, like men, are rational beings. While we have seen some problems with the liberal model of rational individualism, we have also acknowledged a progressive core relating to the self-determinate individual. It was

131

the hope in the progressive core that spurred early liberal feminists to foster the wide acceptance of the idea of women as rational individuals.

Yet, tension between political and moral theory and feminism is, I maintain, most acute in the liberal tradition. Exposing this tension highlights the contradiction between liberalism as patriarchal and individualist in structure and ideology, and feminism as sexual-egalitarian and collectivist (Eisenstein, 1981: 3). This tension is due largely to the rigid demarcation liberalism makes between the State, civil society, and independent beings on the one hand, and the family, private life and interdependent beings on the other. The liberal individual contracts into society, bears citizenship rights and obligations, consistent 'with the "public" character of mind, as distinct from the "private" character of passions and desires. What is peculiar to particular minds is supposedly left behind when abstract individuals enter the public realm in which they are formally equal' (Lloyd, 1983b: 27). Within liberal individualism, there is a rigid distinction between the socially constructed public rights of individuals as citizens and the putatively natural private demands of the family with rights invested in its male head, or uneasily in women. Furthermore, as demonstrated, while men are defined in liberal theory as persons with individual potentials, women are defined in fixed biological, sexual and familial terms (See, 1982: 185). Much of the viability of the liberal public individual relies on domestic maintenance in the family unit which typically reinforces functionalist conceptions of women.

Our concern is to highlight a major consequence of the institutionalisation of liberal individualism, and the establishment of universal suffrage, namely the practical contradiction between the formal political equality of liberal democracy and the social subordination of women, especially the subjection of wives within patriarchal marriages (Pateman, 1983: 208). The existence of liberal formal equality is belied by the persistence of deeply rooted patriarchal assumptions which militate against substantive structural social change and actual equality. Let us assess liberal individualist feminism, examining equality, marriage and contract relations.

Liberal equality and gender difference

In the latter part of the twentieth century, the liberal feminist emphasis is placed on the principles of individual equality and freedom. Features of these principles include the vote, legal and civil rights, the right to contract, to education, to work, to property, to political participation. A major problem in this contemporary analysis relates to the issue of what is the most useful appropriation of a principle such as equality. This is a crucial issue but I make no attempt at a comprehensive treatment of it. (see Jaggar, 1973–74; Code, 1986; Thornton, 1986). Rather, I examine this principle in relation to the contradiction between the formal recognition of women as free and equal individuals, and the constraints of women defined as wives and mothers within the family or as natural unequal beings. I thus examine the compatibility between equality and difference.

My claim, along with Brennan and Pateman (1979), is that there are problems with feminists appealing to an abstract notion of equality, or to an individualism that ignores the importance of historical realities, particularly when related to 'the married woman question'. The liberal conception of the individual as a separate and autonomous being whose relations are either extrinsic or accidental, and who is only accidentally differentiated by history, race, personality, age, culture, race, class, or sex, supports the theory of abstract individualism which forms the foundation for the liberal principles governing relations within the public sphere. With these principles, a split within the individual between abstract rationality and personal desire is reflected in the split between the public and private spheres. Insofar as women are deemed less capable of rational, abstract thought and more tied to others by sentiment and compassion, they are seen to be 'naturally' located in the private realm of the family.

In order to remedy the limitations of this naturalistic assumption, early liberal feminists show that women are indeed capable of sophisticated reason. As Wollstonecraft states, 'ignorance is a frail base for virtue' (1792: 108). In encouraging women to cultivate their reason, they are encouraged to 'bow to the authority of reason, instead of being the modest slaves of opinion' (1792: 92). Wollstonecraft's argument is that rights accruing to men, by virtue of their status as free, rational individuals, ought also to accrue to women. Part of the struggle to assert this aims to counter the notion that the participants regulating the public sphere as fathers or husbands actually represent women.[2] A simple claim that, in virtue of this rational capacity, equal rights should be extended without discrimination or adaptation assumes an uncomplicated homogeneity. Clearly, rights should be applicable to all, precisely because the possession of these rights affirm human dignity and can be called moral rights since they *are* applicable to all persons. They can be said to affirm one's personhood. There is a fine line between the translation of basic welfare needs into universal rights, and rights into a concept of care that ensures a *moral community of rights-bearing persons*. The limitations of an emphasis on rights-bearing individuals 'seems to require that women and men become more alike...it seems to require that women become more like men...social conservatives are not alone in thinking that such a change would be a real loss' (Thompson, 1986: 100).

The nature of this loss lies precisely in the ignoring of all difference, so that exciting differences go unrecognised and the equal treatment of unequals still results in inequality. The necessity of an unequal treatment, or a positive discrimination in order to strive for equality is a recent awareness. One response to the dilemma of inequality can be found in McMillan's defence of tradition. On the basis of conventions bound up in the development of tradition and an understanding of self and culture, she maintains that the most favourable situation for women in combatting inequality is to accept simply that they bear children and thus should be educated as potential nurturers. Her complaint against the neutralisation of sexual difference is directed against those who ignore the significance of experiential biological dimensions. Now, I agree that 'a woman does not regard herself as an individual who just happens to be a woman' (Thompson, 1986: 102), especially if her life revolves around her growing awareness of what 'being a woman' really means. (This applies similarly to a man's perception of himself). McMillan's response appears merely to sustain the conditions in which sexual inequalities are perpetuated and which prevent rights from being meaningfully appropriated.

To adopt a liberal insistence on equality as an abstract principle, applicable without differentiation, diminishes the real possibility of politics being substantially affected by feminist issues arising from women's lives or by other social groups' demand for a redress of historical inequalities. Yet, it is not entirely clear to me that the assertion 'the personal is political' is an adequate antidote to an abstract application of equality to homogenous beings. It undoubtedly disarms a tradition of knowledge which, through its severance of public reason from private passion, has confined the possibilities of knowledge and experience. Also, in treating the personal as political, esteem is accorded to women's reality and legitimacy sought for appropriate methods to explain this reality (Coltheart, 1986: 112). But for sexual differences to be substantially recognised, prime significance should not always be granted to the private or domestic sphere. To argue for practical equality in the private *and* public spheres, without working through the sexual dichotomies *between* these spheres, serves to relocate women's secondary status from the private sphere into an additional sphere. That is, in a situation of actual inequality, where there is a diminishing but persistent gender division of labour, references to women's equal political status belies the reality of her possible oppression in the private sphere. A close analysis of the relationship between these two spheres is necessary to clarify the concept of equality and difference within a just society. The mere assertion that 'the personal is political' is an inadequate response, meaning different things to different people.

To undermine the rigid distinction between public and private, there needs to be a shift of emphasis from equality and fair treatment of abstract individuals to equal freedom (Tapper, 1986: 42) as particular individuals. This prompts an articulation of the opportunities available to individuals on the basis of unique, often different needs, in a way that is not possible with formal notions of fairness. Arendt reminds us that equality for the Greeks is not concerned with justice as in modern times, but is seen as the essence of freedom to act in a public space, 'to move in a sphere where neither rule nor being ruled existed' (1974: 33). While this type of equality may be ideal in the Greek situation, it necessarily ignores the question of the nature of equality in the non-public spheres, where freedom is as essential to human agency as it is in the public sphere. Presumably, most of us would not want to obliterate entirely the distinction between the public and private. Most of us prize the retreat to a sphere governed by affective ties in an informal, relaxed space after time spent in a formal, rule-regulated environment.

To highlight some of these dilemmas concerning the relationship between equality, justice and the public and private spheres, I contrast a Rawlsian response to 'equal freedom as autonomous individuals' with an alternative feminist one. Rawls refers to individuals in the original position as 'heads of families'. In an early formulation he accepts the inevitability of inequality and adheres to the public-private distinction intrinsic to liberalism. Can liberalism survive the removal of its patriarchal blinkers? (Green, 1986: 29). Take Rawls' principles of justice which state that, first: each person is to have an equal right to the most extensive basic liberty compatible with a similar liberty for others, second: social and economic inequalities are to be arranged so that they are both (a) reasonably expected to be to everyone's advantage, and (b) attached to positions and offices open to all (1971: 60). I assess these principles by exploring further the notion that the inequality of liberal individualism is mainly rooted in the different relationships men and women develop to the nurture of others.

In this vein, Green suggests that an alternative reading of Rawls might involve individuals in the original position who, instead of centering on concepts of justice as public, social principles, would opt for principles of justice most conducive to 'regulating a shared responsibility for and enjoyment of members of the younger generation' (1986: 31). Green is sensitive to woman's role as a child-bearer, and concedes this role may diminish the range of options open. Yet, inequalities with natural origins are not generally deemed unjust by Rawls. In trying to re-evaluate the mothering role, Green attempts to compensate for any diminished freedom women may experience by suggesting the exclusivity of 'mothering' as a primary good not readily available to men. If this 'good' is to be understood broadly as the nurturing of natural relations of affection, the development of cultural and moral values, the sense of identity within community, and the strong identification with significant others, then I am unclear as to whether Green is really suggesting any more than McMillan, that is, a strengthening of convention.

135

On the contrary, Green suggests that her reformulation leads to a radical restructuring of family relations. Part of this reformulation would involve a marriage contract where, with the allotment of rights and duties, the bearing of children would present no more of an impediment to women's freedom than to men's. This assumes a mother's greater ability to satisfy the needs of very young children and thus the 'fair' attempt on the part of fathers to compensate mothers for any loss of freedom they incur (1986: 32). In Green's account, this compensation attempts to defy the tendency for it to be considered a *prima facie* duty for a mother to limit herself because of her children where a father's liberty is generally not curtailed to the same degree. One wonders what, apart from breast-feeding, 'a mother's greater ability' might involve, and precisely what form any 'fathers' compensation' might take.

While Green's motives are admirable, I am sceptical of the suggestion that liberalism can do justice to the equal status of men and women as free rational individuals through the introduction of principles of justice within the family. Justice in the main involves some variant of the Aristotelian notion of 'giving and receiving one's due'. One can be a 'just individual' and live a life according to duty and not love, though this defies personalist notions of compassion. Intimate relations rely on individuals who are prepared to give 'beyond one's due', if one defines 'due' in terms of formal, minimal expectations of justice. One generally does not look after sick children, senile parents or invalid partners, merely out of duty. For Rawls, it is perfectly consistent for the just individual to be basically egotistical, given his emphasis on the social benefits of self-interest. The liberal state's function is to ensure that the competitive means to maximise personal self-interest is just, through legal mechanisms for adjudicating claims. In my view, where prime emphasis is placed on the individual, there is no vision of the political community that permits a substantive sense of civic virtue, for the groundwork of a life in common is dominated by a self-interested predatory individualism (Elshtain, 1982c: 141). For these reasons, I conclude that formal equality and justice are inappropriate principles for family and intimate relations.

Liberalism, marriage and contractual relations

The interpretations of the celebrated liberal tenets like equality and justice are problematic in a feminist context. The difficulty lies in the emphasis in liberalism on the individual, and the translation of this, sometimes unwittingly, into an emphasis on *individualism*. This dilemma is particularly pertinent in what constitutes an embarrassing problem for liberal theory, namely the question of 'married women'. In our contemporary situation this includes de facto relationships.

The embarrassment lies in the contradiction between formal equality and practical oppression, and highlights problems in the relationships between the public and private spheres. The two major issues of contention are authority and contract, and I deal with them simultaneously.

These issues are best focused in the question why a free and equal female should always place herself under the authority of a free and equal male (Brennan and Pateman, 1979: 183). The view that individuals are 'by nature' free and equal contrasts with the traditional seventeenth-century position that people are naturally bound in a hierarchy of subordination and inequality. To be consistent, the advocation of equality means that women should also be considered 'free and equal', but we have seen how other considerations, such as 'nature' and the 'individual' being historically construed as male, work against this. Furthermore, the growth of these ideas arose in the context of a closely defined patriarchal theory. With the emergence of the liberal state, a capitalist market economy and social contract theory came a systematic patriarchal theory that affirms the family as a basic source of authority relations (see Schochet, 1975).

The common denominators between liberal theory and patriarchy involve contract, consent and exchange based on a free, equal individual. On examination, it becomes clear that this individual is almost exclusively male. There is a failure to address how the assumed 'naturalness' of a husband's authority over a wife is to be justified without giving up some basic principles of liberal theory. Liberal individualism assumes that individuals entering, say, Locke's contract are the fathers of families. While it is assumed that men are naturally capable of governing a family and participating rationally in political life, women are seen to be naturally subordinate and lacking in rationality (or at least authoritative rationality), assumptions which preclude the latter's active political participation and limit their activity to domestic maintenance. Once the existence of women as individuals in their own right is recognised, this mythical assumption of the total unity of the family's interests is exposed. A notable exception to these attitudes is provided by J.S. Mill (1869) who argues that the traditional marriage relation is an unjustified aberration from liberal principles of individual rights, freedom, choice, equality of opportunity and the recognition of merit. He and Taylor (1970) advocate a more egalitarian partnership centred around the negotiation of personal terms of association.

Contractual relations

These issues of authority and the 'married women question' should be placed more specifically within the context of the emergence of civil society, with particular emphasis on the contractual relations that are constitutive of it. Within liberal theory, the notion of a social contract plays a vital role not only in securing an individual's rights, but in preventing a war of 'all against all' that might arise when self-assertive individuals assume their own interests have priority over others'. Social contract theory employs a concept of individuals which entails a qualified mutual recognition of others' individuality, although, Rousseau's version of the theory is something of an exception since it exhibits a more communitarian stance.[3] Within the context of civil society, and within most liberal thought in general, the recognition of others implied by contractual relations is a matter of convenience which depends on the agreement of each to serve as a means to others' ends in the hope of advancing their own. But such a pact of convenience gives each individual the licence to withdraw from the situation of mutual dependency, which constitutes merely 'an abstract and generalized fraternity' (Yeatman, 1984: 156). While mutual exchange is seen to serve the specific needs of specific subjects, mutual indifference to the specific expression and particularity of others' individuality abounds.

How does this notion of contract apply to family groupings, typical masculine individuality and women within civil society? The crucial issues concern the abstraction of persons and the persistent distinction and difference of emphasis between the private and public realms. The abstract basis of the individual within liberal individualism ignores specific relational dependancies and does not incorporate a particular content into its notions of individuality. This ensures that the family is bracketed out of the domain of civil society, except when the state chooses to encroach—in education, health, welfare, and law. The public realm generally concerns itself with 'non-specifically disclosive individuality' (Yeatman, 1984: 157). Specific, expressive individuality is consigned to the private sphere, and considered irrelevant to the construction of the abstract individual. There are three typical responses to this construction. Some individuals accommodate themselves readily to this split self and oscillate between a typical public and a typical private mentality, such as the careerist who adopts a rigid work/non-work division. Other persons who spend much of their energy with others in the private sphere affirm through a combination of love, duty or fear the physical and emotional maintenance of children and public individuals, and feel remote from the demands of an abstract fraternity. Housewives come into this category. Their commitments to work outside the home include volunteer activities in kindergartens, school canteens and libraries. A third group of both women and men attempt to resist the 'either–or' mentality, aiming for a balance of commitment to themselves and to others in the private and public spheres. This is evident particularly where partners are engaged in shared parenting and paid work.

The pertinent point here is that a contractual basis for civil society or for relationships is premised on a notion of equality that is unsympathetic toward particular differences. Such a stance cannot appreciate that an enunciation of difference may associate one sex with the freedom of willing, and the other with following the former's willing (Yeatman, 1984: 159). This 'willing individual' has been the independent male, dependent for personal recognition on public activity and private confirmation through female others, whose status as autonomous subjects has been frequently denied, although the *individualistic* careerist woman who tends to avoid long-term intimate relations preferrimg casual, instrumental liaisons also fits this category of the free, calculative individual. Nevertheless, there is a contradiction in the denial of women's autonomous subjectivity, given their special role in confirming the specific individuality of masculine wills, through the socialisation of young boys. A standard reply to this dilemma is that in obeying her 'master's' will, the feminine other adopts his will as a substitute for her personal differentiation.

Given this framework, the formal entry of women into the public domain remains a problem full of inconsistencies. The point of access to the public domain of political life is as a rational individual who can sustain an abstract detachment in public modes. One response to this requirement results in the enforced acquisition of typical masculine standards by some women ambitious to advance their careers in male-dominated professions. Yet, on the other hand, there is the expectation from liberalism that perhaps women may make a distinctively 'feminine' contribution, while simultaneously meeting criteria of 'public' life which have traditionally presumed that containment (Lloyd, 1983b: 27). To what extent an affirmation of distinctiveness in public spheres posits a viable alternative to the contradiction between the ideal liberal individual and the ideal feminine woman is controversial, and not always made clear within liberal feminist thought.

Contract marriage

It is useful to examine whether problems inherent in liberal individualism are resolved by a contractual conception of marriage. While much of this discussion is relevant to de facto relationships or homosexual partnerships, the exception lies in the difference the legal component makes as a public, legally binding relation. Until recently, marriage has been institutionalised through ceremony, speech acts and religious symbolism, with any contractual basis being grounded in conventional role ascription. To contract into marriage was to consent to its status requirements. Yet, as demonstrated, what is contained in the traditional status as wife, namely, her submission to those in authority, exposes her inequality and denies her the possibility of meaningful consent. This status works against her claiming rights she is legitimately entitled to, as a participant individual of liberal theory.

Hegel, in discussing contract, argues against viewing individuals just as contractors in that it abstracts from concrete social relations (1973: 36, 37, 58). A significant defect of the contractual marriage is that it is viewed by many as merely the public recognition and regulation of natural sexual inclination' (Pateman, 1984: 82). In responding to these types of issues, Hegel argues that a specific form of ethical association is created in the family. Whereas the individual appears in abstract form in liberal theory, disguising particular individuality, love aspires to know the self, strengthen individuality and affirm the person's autonomy. Moral recognition is the key here. Yet, for Hegel, the family revolves around the sphere of immediacy, so that women within this sphere cannot develop the consciousness of particularity required to qualify as an individual subject.

Contemporary attempts to organise 'contract marriage' vary, but all imply free, equal, self-determining persons who have developed the consciousness of particularity Hegel refers to, and who negotiate to formulate a mutually advantageous contract. According to divorce lawyers, this notion of contract marriage has taken particular significance in 'reversed-role relations', where the woman as chief earner and property owner seeks to ensure her financial dominance in anticipating the possibility of divorce. Clearly, in an environment of rapidly changing relationships, alternatives are essential. Yet, caution is needed, otherwise contracts may reduce intimate relations to marketable commodities. Nevertheless, within egalitarian, non-instrumental relationships, there is a potential basis for the development of a philosophy and practice of what Pateman prefers to call 'personal association', where bonds of loving mutuality enable a recognition and an enrichment of individuality. Then, she suggests, the marriage contract can represent 'the public acknowledgement of the mutual trust, respect and love of the partner-friends' (1984: 92).

In this chapter, I have criticised liberal abstract individualism while continually trying to develop a positive notion of individuality. I have suggested that liberal feminism, despite positive intentions, cannot construct radical alternative notions of individuality while remaining within a framework that centres on an abstract notion of the individual. I have shown that the struggle to develop creative relationships does not occur in social abstraction. Abstraction excludes the trust, promising, love and fidelity fundamental to reciprocal commitment. Abstraction also filters to the wider context of a community, where women and men are supposedly full and equal citizens in political life, but contradictions exist between the abstract liberal individual and concrete particular persons.

In this chapter clear differences were outlined between liberal individualism, which views the individual as prior to the social nexus, and individuality, which incorporates the potential within individual moral subjects and their capacities as social beings. The problem with much liberal-feminist analysis lies in the attempt to contain both views within the same politics, an unsuccessful integration. We must seek to develop further a theory of individuality which recognises 'the individual character of our social nature and the social nature of our individuality' (Eisenstein, 1981: 191), or the essential relatedness of moral identities.

NOTES

1 The reason I emphasise liberal feminism in this chapter is because of its broad general influence on social thought and practice from the beginning of the organised Women's Liberation Movement. This emphasis in no way understates the important of socialist feminism or radical feminism. Socialist and communitarian ideas are implicit in the formulation of many of my alternatives. See Jaggar (1983) for a thorough comparison of liberal, marxist, radical and socialist feminism.

2 Taking into account certain economic changes from the seventeenth century on helps us understand some of the anomalies. From the eighteenth century property-ownership was a major criterion for citizenship. By the nineteenth century even propertyless men were seen as at least able to govern within families, hence, by extension, assumed to have capacities requisite for citizenship. In the nineteenth and twentieth centuries, men organised into trade associations and women lost control of some of their traditional areas like medicine, midwifery and dairying.

3 As Rousseau states, 'The problem is to find a form of association which will defend and protect with the whole common force the person and goods of each associate...uniting himself withall,' (1973: 174). On Rousseau's account, private interests must be sacrificed to the public good. As Gatens points out, this is because, 'The rights of the individual, for Rousseau, are not always consistent with the necessary social pragmatism involved in the public ethic' (1986: 13), rendering it problematic for instance to be a good citizen, and a good parent.

6 Moral development

In the four preceding chapters, I have argued that entrenched conceptions of moral dualism, nature, reason and individualism inhibit an adequate philosophical acceptance of women as moral subjects. I have also depicted various alternatives, in order to make a viable philosophical case for women's acceptance as full moral subjects. But there is more ground to be covered in order to establish the case. In this chapter, I look at current prominent cognitive moral development theories which advocate ideals of moral maturity. I scrutinise what perceptions of cognitive capacity are seen as prerequisites for moral judgement, what cognitive skills are most frequently defined as the tools of the 'moral artisan', and what the nature of moral judgement is presumed to consist in. I focus on the writings of two cognitive moral psychologists, Kohlberg and Gilligan. The discussion of their views is divided into four sections.

First, I summarise Kohlberg's theories from 1958 on, which have received much critical treatment in feminist literature. While Kohlberg's theory is primarily descriptive and makes limited epistemological claims, there is a fine line between description and normative evaluation. I question the philosophical adequacy of Kohlberg's theories, and particularly their practical application to women. As we shall see, in Kohlberg's terms, the defining trait of 'goodness' for women marks them as morally deficient beings. I question whether action deemed immature from Kohlberg's perspective is a result of natural incapacity, a lack of opportunity to develop epistemic responsibility in the traditional form, or the outcome of a different mental construction of moral problems.

In the second section, I probe the validity of asserting a possible differential morality for men and women. I focus on Gilligan's argument, as expressed in *In a Different Voice* (1983). I draw on literature that argues that women's concept of a moral self relies heavily on strong relational bonds that emanate from volitional responsibility to others. I argue that observable differences between people result from socialisation, life-styles and life opportunities, and do not arise from essential moral differences.

The third section addresses major debates that incorporate and extend the arguments of Gilligan. These debates pivot around contrasting notions of the self as primarily an autonomous bearer of individual rights, or as an interdependent self closely connected with others. The different priorities that correspond to these definitions of self are marked. In one instance, the injunction to respect the rights of others is based on a morality of justice that requires a formal, abstract mode of thought. Another alternative places the imperative on care and responds to contextual, narrative modes of understanding. According to Kohlberg's analysis, the absence of a transition from a contextual to an abstract mode signals a failure to progress. I suggest social and philosophical mechanisms that contribute to this, and criticise further the imputation of moral inferiority to emotionally, or contextually, based modes of thought and action. Fourthly, I critically analyse Gilligan's vision of maturity, and offer an alternative approach.

COGNITIVE MORAL DEVELOPMENT

The cognitive developmental approach postulates cognitive transformations in self-conception, arising from successive modes of role-taking which lead to a conception of justice as a mature moral judgement. Kohlberg is the leading contemporary moral developmentalist. Kohlberg acknowledges that cognitive psychologists understate morality's ethical aspect in favour of its behavioural one. In trying to overcome this fault, Kohlberg takes his theory of cognition to be a theory of 'genetic epistemology' which holds 'that an ultimately adequate psychological theory...and an ultimately adequate philosophical explanation...are one and the same theory extended in different directions' (1971: 154). He argues that 'insight into the "is" (the development of knowledge and morality), and insight into the "ought" (epistemology and moral norms and criteria) must have some relationship' (1971: 154).

Kohlberg's empirical studies are based on an acceptance of universal ontogenetic trends which trace the development of individual beings, and maintains that ethical principles are the culmination of sequential moral development. An initial longitudinal study consisted of 84 boys aged two to sixteen (1958). With colleagues, he then studied the process of maturation of character and moral judgement in 76 boys aged ten to sixteen, testing them at three-year intervals until aged 22 to 28 years. He asked the boys to respond to hypothetical moral dilemmas, the 'Heinz dilemma' being the most well known (see Kohlberg and Turiel, 1971). Heinz's wife was dying, and the chemist had overpriced the essential drug. Heinz could not pay, and thus stole it. Based on the boys' responses to this, that is, what they thought Heinz should do (Kohlberg and Gilligan, 1971: 1,072, 1073), six stages were defined, with orientations toward first, punishment and obedience; second, instrumental relativism; third, interpersonal concordance; fourth, law and order; fifth, social-contract legalism; and sixth, universal ethical principles. Recent empirical evidence has led Kohlberg to collapse stages five and six, or at least to withdraw his claim to have confirmed the existence of stage six, as none of his longitudinal subjects in the USA, the UK, Mexico, Turkey, Taiwan, or Israel had attained it (Kohlberg, 1981b; 1984). Nevertheless, he maintains stage six as a vital theoretical construct.

Kohlberg claims to have elucidated universal principles of morality and justice. His stages imply an invariant, universal sequence, with each stage entailing a new logical approach. The most advanced stage corresponds to judgements of consistency, which formalists since Kant argue is a necessary condition of universality, so that moral principles that satisfy this condition are binding on everyone in any situation. Kohlberg analyses the morality of intention or the different perspectives of cognition rather than action itself (1971: 189).

To consider intentions is an important part of role-taking within moral dilemmas and of the development of one's sense of justice. Role-taking, or identification, involves the capacity to understand conflicts from other people's point of view, and ensures a focus on welfare consequences, empathy, and justice—an application 'of the imperative to acknowledge every potential person as a person' (1971: 192). Yet, for Kohlberg, an emphasis on interpersonal relations of mutuality only represents his stage three morality. Justice is defined, rather, as the resolution of conflict 'between competing claims of men' (1971: 192), integrated by rules and roles. He claims with Rawls (1971: 3, 5, 11) that social institutions are organised around principles of justice, equality and reciprocity. Kohlberg supports Piaget's claim that justice is an ideal equilibrium which balances the scales as the 'imminent condition of social relationships' (Piaget, 1948).

Kohlberg's moral stages

Stages three and six are the most pertinent stages for the purpose of my argument. The latter represents Kohlberg's highest stage, the former represents capacities Kohlberg suggests are common to the institution of the family, and thus feature in women's lives. Kohlberg maintains that, characteristically, 'a stage three conception of justice is integrated with a conception of a good interpersonal relationship. The socio-moral order is conceived of as primarily composed of dyadic relations of mutual role-taking, mutual affection, gratitude, and concern for one another's approval' (1971a: 198). Kohlberg raises the issue of whether role-taking in this stage can assume the impartiality he sees as essential. I argue that inherent in this notion of impartiality is the impossibility of genuine role-taking, of really understanding the particular personal dimension of moral dilemmas, a skill more women seem to develop. It is not that women are unable to differentiate the process of identification with the subject of Kohlberg's dilemmas from the abstract notions that decide what is right or wrong, but that genuine identification with others regards abstraction as being inappropriate to real crises. Substantive argument follows that the stage three analysis of women's lives as an inferior model of morality is untenable. The moral judgement typical of a caring, sensitive mother may be less abstract than that of an efficient, rational bureaucrat, but it is not inferior. Furthermore, any conclusion that women are limited to a stage three level, is as much due to Kohlberg's failure to categorise women's responses correctly as it is due to his sexist 'moral turpitude'.

It is in stage six that Kohlberg asserts the principles of justice and respect for persons prevail. These principles incorporate a right to equal consideration, and some notion of treating persons as valuable ends. Few would quibble with this latter stress. I have documented problems arising when 'the specification that treatment of humans as "ends in themselves" is to be defined in terms of rights or claims' (1971: 212). While I have argued that rights and duties are related, Kohlberg's perspective on justice pays less attention to virtue or obligations to specific persons than it does to individualistic rights.

What is entailed in Kohlberg's claims of a progressive movement through morally inferior to superior forms of moral judgement? When Kohlberg uses the term 'inferior' it is in the sense that the stage is to be superceded, and thus pre-dates the emergence of subsequent stages. A thorough analysis of the 'inferiority' of stage three in contrast to stage six is beyond our immediate scope, but it would be interesting to examine whether women capable of formal operational thought in the Piagetian sense still maintain a stage three moral perspective (Kohlberg and Gilligan, 1971: 1,072). If this can be demonstrated, the conclusions would necessitate explanations of the sociological mechanisms that suppress transition to higher stages of moral judgement. In addition, one could reassess answers given by women to Kohlberg and remove the situational-contextual-relational components that cause Kohlberg to automatically assign a stage three classification. If one could show formal operational thinking within typical 'feminine paradigms', then one could demonstrate that Kohlberg's claim of moral inferiority is merely an experimental artefact.

Kohlberg's claims of superiority for the stages are not gradations of the moral worth of individuals, but claims for a hierarchy in forms of moral judgement. He has modified this claim, stating they are a measure of justice reasoning, rather than of moral maturity (1984). He defines standards of moral adequacy by the formal criteria of 'impartiality, ideality, universalizability, pre-emptiveness' (1971: 215) rather than by content. Kohlberg stresses that his meta-ethical conception of the higher stage as more moral is not a normative ethical principle generating moral judgements (1971: 217). That is, a stage six ethic cannot readily prompt a theory of the good or normative outlines of virtue, although questions of justice may lend themselves to precise definition (Kohlberg, 1982: 516). Hence, while it claims to describe what it means to judge morally, it cannot answer questions like, why be moral? or what good is justice? Many fundamental questions of life are probably insoluble, which is why they are fundamental; we grapple with them, never completely answering them. Nevertheless, it does appear grossly inadequate to define justice reasoning without some attempt to answer why we should be moral or just.

Recalling Kohlberg's hesitancy in categorising people at stage six, much of the credibility of stage theories of morality hinges on adequacy claims of the sort Kohlberg makes but fails to establish (Flanagan, 1982: 508). That is, his universal ethical principle orientation lacks the ethical foundation that its prescriptive nature demands (Gibbs, 1977; 1979). Kohlberg's defense of the higher stages require a thorough-going stage six principled argument (Cohen, 1980: 74). Tensions between possible different conceptions of justice remain unresolved. The content of terms such as 'giving each one's due' is not fully explicated, the emphasis being on increasing the abstraction of principles impartially applied to all. The 'cognitive good' is assumed to be a movement from particularity toward abstraction. The relationship between one's capacity for sophisticated moral reasoning, the principles of justice themselves, and one's actions as a moral person remains unclear.

What defining features of the self does Kohlberg stress? He sees human agency primarily in terms of logical competence, or ideal models of moral rationalism. Without the incorporation of dialogue, emotional expressivity, mutual respect, moral evaluation and contextual particularity into ideals of the self, rational cognition is given the central position, according to a 'will of rational competence', (Puka, 1982: 471). To the accusation that this ignores the personal context of moral dilemmas, Kohlberg counters that reasoning about justice is reasoning about social relations of reciprocity, equality and role-changing among actors, albeit at a formal, structural level. That is, it resembles a rational reconstruction of the dilemma, which is reliant on logical consistency and problem-solving effectiveness, with emotional distancing accepted as appropriate. This underplays or obscures the context in which human drama occurs.

Personal dimensions of the moral self seem to be missing. Ethical action is informed by reason but moral reasoning is informed by previous experience. Habermas, in attempting to incorporate this relationship between reason and experience into an ego-identity that is less constrained than a model of abstract autonomy, proposes a seventh stage. This involves a hermeneutical approach to interpretations, 'drawn into the discursive formation of will' (1979: 93).

Although I cannot develop this seventh stage here, it is important to be aware of alternative views that indicate the importance of language, interpretative devices, social interaction and cultural tradition as ways of explaining moral behaviour. Underlying the confrontation between Kohlberg's position and an alternative position like Habermas' are rival approaches to epistemology and ontology, one concerned with data and a view of persons as 'objects of science', the other concerned with interpretation predicted on a concept of persons as self-interpreting beings. I accord the latter emphasis a central role, for being more appropriate for understanding human action as well as intention.

Form and content

The rival approaches again emerge within the form–content relation of Kohlberg's stages. I am not critical of formal abstraction as an activity basic to linguistic and reasoning competence, but of an abstract formalism typified by the separation of form from content. For example, in relation to adolescents, 'The stages tell us how the child thinks concerning good and bad, truth, love, sex, and so forth. They do not tell us what he thinks about, whether he is preoccupied with morality or sex or achievement' (Kohlberg and Gilligan, 1971: 1,076). Clearly, some idea of descriptive components is important in establishing what universality, if any, holds for the processes of thought. But a major problem with formal moral theory is a *content* problem in that the principles have dubious use without some specification of its substantive content. For example, in an attempt to relate personally to an adolescent, knowing *how* the individual thought would be of little or no use without some knowledge of *what* the individual thought about. Admittedly, stage theorists would counter my argument by denying the intention to relate personally, but I maintain that a formal knowledge of someone is deficient without particularised knowledge of the person in question.

I argue, along with others, that one brings 'substantive (sometimes defensible, sometime not) background knowledge and values to the moral reasoning situation' (Flanagan and Adler, 1983: 582). In the Heinz dilemma, the principled approach, in presupposing an acceptance of the primacy of human life, can be seen to provide content and direction to formal rules. Yet, the hypothetical nature of Kohlberg's dilemmas, combined with a formal structural methodology, can mislead us into presuming that the general principle embodies a true morality which is uncomplicatedly aligned with abstraction and impartiality. In these terms, moral progression is aided by further cognitive stimulation, not by explicit teaching of values or virtues. With my stress on practical wisdom rather than formal cognition, learning good habits can be regarded as providing an appropriate moral basis for later stages when rules are followed or rejected because of the justification that they are seen to have or lack (R.S. Peters, 1971: 258).

An overvaluation of formalism, coinciding with an undervaluation of content, disguises the ethics of ambiguity, or the 'grey' areas of life, where formal principles act as guidelines only. It also under-emphasises the importance of crises, problems, confusions, doubts and questions that initiate cognitive change (Braun and Baribeau, 1978: 296). Formal duty might decree that a woman should care for her aging father, but memories of abuse might undermine this formal obligation. There are combinations of desires, goals, feelings and frustrations underlying the moral activity of men and women. The failure to provide explanations that consider such motivations presents a partial picture of moral development.[1] To understand a particular person's moral character, we need to try to understand both the underlying form and the content.

It is not that impartiality and abstract rationality do not have a significant place in moral judgement, but that the tendency to dictate what everyone in the same situation ought to do says nothing about the particular person in question. De Beauvoir writes that we affirm our humanity through situations that, while particular, are universal, hence 'we find in concrete form the conflicts which we have described abstractly' (1980: 145). This affirmation explicitly repudiates all forms of abstraction that prefer formalism to the human dimension, or that have no realisable human form. There are situations where the abstract predominates over the concrete, form over context, impartiality over particularity and vice-versa. A narrow or wide focus affects the balance. The wider the system administered to, the less contextual specific interpretations can be. The emphasis of women's moral agency reflects their historical involvement in small groups. In terms of larger organisational structures, some injection of utility and formal appropriateness is necessary. Yet, the more the distance between a formal role and its specific application, the more likely it is to generate contextual reasons for non-application. These points are rarely addressed in formal moral development theory.

My concern is to emphasise the way formal, unconditional absolutes stand in tension with the way morality figures in our lives, because such absolutes foreclose connections between moral reasoning, moral action and individual life-plans. Morality affects us at a personal, experiential level. As self-interpretive beings, we attach different meanings to experiences. Moral action is influenced by a host of motivations that affect our self-understanding, our interpretation of situations and the ultimate outcome of moral judgement, of which we can only speculate on the possibilities. Taylor calls this the 'significance feature' of moral agency (1985a: 202). This is not a theoretical construct only, but a practical dimension of our social nature in that we come to understandings about the significance of things with others.

An appreciation of the interpretive, contextual basis of moral judgement does not invite moral relativism, but it is predicated on some mutual appreciation about meanings. The more intimate a relationship between people, the broader their range of shared understandings, the more similar are the meanings and priorities they attach to significant features of life. Emotions affecting relationships are not readily converted to rational outlines. Indeed, the fact that emotions have not always been addressed by philosophers relates not only to their uncertain effect on rational choice, but also to their ambiguity. The mental construction of love, jealousy or friendship varies according to our different self-understandings, the different meanings we attach to emotional states and whom the emotions are directed towards—spouse, lover, friend, colleague, child or stranger. Often we do not understand our own emotional state. The interpretive self again comes to the fore. To comprehend the significance factor in people's lives, engaged processes are necessary. Dialogue often clarifies and transforms emotions (Taylor, 1985a: 191).

To summarise this section, I have indicated problems when the relations abstract–concrete, impartiality–particularity, formalism–contextualism are conceived as polarities, rather than as different dimensions of the same event. When faced with the dilemma of context, Kohlberg, in following Hare (1952), distinguishes between moral rules, such as 'Do not kill' and 'Love your neighbour', and moral principles which involve a choice. Kohlberg then argues 'that judgements made in the light of moral principles are contextually relative in the sense that they can be sensitive to features of a particular situation in a manner that judgements made in light of moral rules cannot' (1982: 520). He attacks the criticism that principled moral judgement is so abstract that it ignores context. He defends devices like Rawls' original position, claiming that even a 'veil of ignorance' over the moral judge still leaves sensitivity to situational contexts. I claim the judge here is still perceived as impartial, and disengaged from the anguish of the dilemma.

In the following section, I defend this claim and provide evidence of feminists who, in reacting against the limitations of formalism, posit alternatives that concentrate on context. Despite the tensions implicit between formalism and contextualism, an acceptance of the contextual need not lead to philosophical relativism. It is possible to start with principles (even formal ones) and allow for context and the particular. This provides a balanced basis for a theory and practice of moral identity. To this end, it is not an argument that allows for male abstraction and female contextualism. It is an affirmation that moral identity needs to synthesise formal and relational criteria to formulate adequate moral judgements.

Current debates concerning women and morality tend towards extremes. Earlier chapters have explained the stance that declares women's inferior capability of active moral agency as a result of defects in nature or nurture. A more recent argument asserts that, rather than being at a lesser level of moral development, women have a distinctive thought style, grounded in different modes of experience and interpretation, based on an ethic of care and responsibility. This emphasis celebrates women's difference from men instead of regarding such differences as a constraint. This celebratory stance suggests that women's moral consciousness should be judged by its differences from men's consciousness rather than by notions of abstract rationality, impartiality and the ability to formulate formal principles of justice. We examine now Gilligan's exploration into the possible existence and validity of a differential morality between men and women. The purpose of this is not so much to affirm ineluctable gender differences, but to explain why differences may occur and to emphasise the integrity of the characteristics portrayed as 'different'.

Individuation and early relationships

The background to this difference concerns the typical development of an individuated infant self. Within a patriarchal framework, the persistence of primary identification with the mother ensures an initial sense of unity for the infant. This must be attenuated to develop an individuated sense of self. Psychoanalytic theories traditionally emphasise this process as a *separation*. I maintain that an awareness of self and of other develops as an *interdependent* process.

This process can be explained in terms of the parent-infant tie, and the different way these experiences are internalised. Reasonable conclusions can be drawn from Chodorowian hypotheses. These indicate that gender identity is axiomatic to personality formation and usually irreversibly established by the age of three. In the case of girls, activities seen to incorporate female roles are immediately visible in daily life with people like the prime caretaker, midwives, clinic nurses, baby-sitters, kindergarten and junior-school teachers. Usually, the development of girls' selfhood is embedded in and influenced by a continuing relationship with the mother, marked by affective relations. Consequently, girls generally develop with a basis for 'empathy' built into their primary definition of self in a way that boys do not (1978: 167). Women are thus more likely to relocate themselves in similar primary parent–child or intimate relations (1978: 87–88).

In contrast to this, 'evidence suggests that insofar as a mother treats her son differently, it is usually by emphasising his masculinity in opposition to herself' (Chodorow, 1979: 48). In order to become male, he must assert himself as not-female. Given the frequent and long daily absence of the typical breadwinner father, a boy may physically identify with his father, or other salient males, but comes to define himself primarily in terms of a radical denial of any similarity with his mother. This often coincides with women pushing sons towards differentiation. As his nurturant needs and capacities are curtailed, a boy develops a sense of self that largely assumes the denial of the need for others. Fathers tend to appear as a person of significance in the child's life once core identity has been established.

Despite social changes, such as sole-parent families, increased participation of fathers, equal shared parenting and parenting by non-biological parents, the dominant mode of western parenting is what Balbus termed 'mother-monopolised child rearing'. We await further research to ascertain what effects these changes may be having. Nevertheless, within the more traditional families, women continue to be perceived as naturally available as extensions-of-others, whose sole reason for existence is to gratify others' needs (Chodorow, 1980: 7). The interests of women and those in their care have been considered synonymous, 'moral goodness' being measured accordingly. Indeed, 'this giving of nurturance is so evidently essential to mothering that we are tempted to make nurturance and mother synonymous' (Benjamin, 1980: 144).

The typical masculine expression of this symbolism in scientific terms and relational experiences, conflates objectivity and autonomy, contributing to a desire to master and to dominate, rather than to understand. While, clearly, it is not a new idea that the rationalist, scientific world-view may be dangerous, the feminist contribution makes explicit 'masculine individuation' which leans towards 'rational violence'. The psychoanalytic findings of Chodorow, Dinnerstein and Benjamin, are linked to the exploration of western science and philosophy by Harding, Fox Keller and Flax, and support the work on moral maturation by Gilligan. All these theorists show that there is a differentiation between men and women in the structures of knowing and being that arise from fundamental differences in the early creation of female and male selves. Traditional male separateness, contrasted with female tendencies toward connectedness, characterise both theories of knowledge and personal relations.

If we assume the general tendency for masculinity to be defined through separation and threatened by intimacy, and femininity to be defined through attachment and threatened by separation, this descriptive difference becomes a developmental liability when maturity is defined as severe individuation. While the major revolt against this concept of moral maturity has come from women, an increasing number of men perceive the danger of preferring separateness over connection to others, an autonomous life of work rather than the interdependence of love and care (Gilligan, 1983: 17). Let us now explore the possible different construction of the moral problem by women.

Women, self and morality

These ideas on individuation provide background to Gilligan's notions of women's selfhood and moral identity. Gilligan's work (1983) is a direct attack on the work of her former colleague, Kohlberg, and was prompted by the conspicuous exclusion of women from models of human growth in psychological research. She rejects the assumption of sexual neutrality in scientific objectivity, recognising that categories of knowledge frequently reflect evaluative bias. Male life has been adopted as normative. Gilligan cites Freud (from 1905), Erikson (1950) and Kohlberg (1958 on). In these works, any differences females may exhibit appear as a developmental failure. She cites observations from children's play by Piaget (1932), Mead (1934), Kohlberg (1969) and Leaver (1976). The suggestion is that either girls and boys progress through youth with different interpersonal orientations, based on a different range of social experiences, or that because of these orientations, different experiences occur. In acknowledging differences, Gilligan repudiates inferences of the necessarily problematic nature of women's development as inferior to or deviant from norms that are derived from masculine standards. Gilligan's interest lies in the interaction of experience and thought and the dialogue to which it gives rise. In listening to what people say about themselves, what is significant to them and what connection to others is made, the self is revealed as an interpretive, signifying being. She discovered in interviews a 'different voice' characterised thematically, and rarely documented.

From the outset, it should be appreciated that the association of this 'voice' with women is an empirical observation. Contrasts between male and female voices highlight a distinction between two modes of thought and focus a problem of interpretation rather than represent a generalisation about either sex (Gilligan, 1983: 2). Her findings relate to a general tendency of women to use a different moral perspective. This tendency is discovered through an exploration of the differences that arise in social contexts where combinations of status, power and the consequences of sexuality and reproduction shape the experience of relations. Three different studies used similar questions about conceptions of self and morality and the experience of conflict and choice.[2] The interviewer explored the language and logic of the answers given, attempting to clarify responses.

Gilligan's moral stages

As with traditional moral development theory, Gilligan makes use of the idea of moral stages. She explores the idea that the conflict between self and other constitutes the central moral problem for women. She selects abortion as an appropriate example of this since the choice to abort or not is generally the woman's. Gilligan's focus is on the relation between judgement and action and its effect on others. Gilligan argues that women's construction of moral dilemmas reveals the existence of a 'distinct moral language', distinguished by references to selfishness and responsibility. Gilligan discerns three sequential stages of moral development based largely on an analysis of moral language like should, ought, better, right, good, bad, and shifts in moral thought. These stages consist of first, self-survival; second, maternal morality; and third, an interconnection of other and self. She places emphasis also on the transitional stages, moving from an early articulation of responsibility to a scrutiny of the logic of self-sacrifice.

In the first stage, she perceives an initial concern with self-survival allied with constraints of feeling powerless, disconnected and lonely. Basic survival is the prime concern. The first transition signals a movement away from feeling overwhelmed by the self-centredness this invokes. In the instance of women contemplating abortion, pregnancy obviously affirms feelings of connection and a capacity to assume a mature female role. A certain social status, validated by the personal adoption of consensual judgements on feminine goodness, is conferred on pregnant women—except in cases of teenage pregnancy or, in some circles, pregnancy out of wedlock. Within the first transition there is an early awareness that responsibility should extend beyond the self.

This awareness leads to a second stage, a re-examination of the concept of responsibility as the possibility of a concern for oneself as well as for others. For the individual involved, the logic of this position appears confused. The association of moral goodness with care of the dependant and unequal remains paramount. Yet, the individual remains embedded in the psychology of dependence. At this stage, self-assertion is still feared for its potential to hurt others. This is captured by Kohlberg's stage three where the need for approval is combined with the desire to care for others. Confused in a see-saw of passive dependence and active care, Gilligan describes women as 'suspended in a paralysis of initiative' (1983: 82), exacerbated by the emotional vulnerability that care for others engenders. Limitations of this position relate to the restrictive identification of goodness with self-sacrifice. Women have been convinced of the moral value of self-sacrificial behaviour, but in precluding a fair share of benefits, self-sacrifice often functions oppressively and renders women vulnerable to exploitation. It thus differs from unselfishness, which requires giving everyone's interests proper weight (Tormey, 1976).

With the second transition, there is an attempt to clarify 'the confusion between self-sacrifice and care inherent in the convention of feminine goodness' (1983: 74). It is the first time, for the person in question, that concern with what others think is juxtaposed with a new inner, independent judgement. The relationship between self and others and the logic of self-sacrifice is reconsidered. Lost (or never claimed) judgemental initiative needs to be learnt. There is an acceptance that it is moral to include personal needs within one's judgement. Gilligan claims that this acceptance involves a shift from 'goodness' to 'truth'—seemingly a strange term to use. What Gilligan means is that the morality of action can now be assessed in terms of personal intention and calculated consequences, not on the basis of appearance or others' impressions. It encompasses the desire to be 'good' both by being responsible to others and by adopting a self-responsibility which ensures one is honest to oneself. Within this transition, a rejection of female self-abnegation coincides with an injunction against hurting that is elevated to a moral principle, and is based on the moral equality of self and other. When the 'universal injunction' (1983: 90) to care becomes part of a self-chosen principle, moral obligation enhances both self and others. This does not enunciate 'a new morality, but a morality disentangled from the constraints that formerly confused its perception and impeded its articulation' (1983: 95).

The third stage entails a cognitive reconstruction permitting a new appreciation of the constitution of care, a reconciliation of seemingly disparate concepts of selfishness and responsibility through a transformed understanding of relationships. The priority in moral choice shifts from a concern with survival techniques to concern for others and then to an inclusion of the self. This emergent self expands the concept of goodness to encompass self-worth. There remains a conflict of priorities, but by recognising the costs of passivity there is a new willingness to express responsibility for judgements and to accept responsibility for choices made. Morality is now defined 'in a way that combines the recognition of interconnection between self and others with an awareness of the self as the arbiter of moral judgement and choice' (1983: 96). An acknowledgement of this perspective implies for both sexes the *intersubjective basis of morality* or an affirmation of the connection between self and other.

MORAL CHOICE: CONFLICTS BETWEEN RIGHTS, RESPONSIBILITIES AND RELATIONSHIPS

My aim, now, is to critically examine the links Gilligan makes between moral choice, priorities placed on responsibilities and rights, and how one's relationships affect these priorities. At the root of moral decision-making is the exercise of choice, and the willingness to accept responsibility for it. Uncertain of their personal strength, many women are unwilling to participate in major decision-making, being accustomed to defer to men's judgement and wanting to avoid confrontation. Other women perceive themselves as having no real choice, and thus excuse themselves from the responsibility that decision-making entails. Gilligan insists on the necessity of identifying situations where women 'have the power to choose and thus are willing to speak in their own voice' (1983: 70) and hence focuses on the contemplation of an abortion. Because Gilligan derives so many of her conclusions from this experience, the fact that the majority of women have not faced this dilemma is a serious shortcoming in Gilligan's work. She neither dwells on the responsibility men have for birth control nor the possibility of abortion being a joint decision, nor the exploitative relationships many women find themselves in (O'Loughlin, 1983: 570).

There are various appropriate approaches to moral problems, but I have maintained that some choices are certainly better than others, and some ways of thinking more conducive to better solutions than others. To concentrate solely on underlying logic or the actual moral choice often results in a subjective 'best fit' morality. Both Kohlberg and Gilligan are at times guilty of this. Such an emphasis fails to appreciate the relation of moral understanding and evaluation to choice, and to the possibility that there are good, inappropriate, immoral and a host of other choices.

Let us examine, then, Gilligan's claim that different developmental constructs emerge from different life experiences and influence the precise nature of choice. She suggests that the study of women's lives reveals that moral problems arising from conflicting responsibilities require contextual, narrative modes of thought rather than formal, abstract ones (1983: 19). The contrast between a *rights* conception of morality geared to arriving at a just resolution on which rational persons would agree, and a *responsibility* conception is stark.

Morality of responsibility and relationships

The responsibility dimension of Gilligan's argument hinges on her claim that women tend to interpret moral dilemmas in terms of their experience of relationships. She contrasts two articulate eleven year-olds faced with Kohlberg's Heinz dilemma. The boy sees the dilemma in terms of rules and logic, the girl in terms of narrative and connections. She contrasts responses of eight year-olds deciding when and which friends to play with. The boy resolves his conflict through a hierarchical ordering between desire and duty. The girl concentrates on the network of relations and who may be excluded by alternative decisions. What emerges are a logic of justice and hierarchy contrasted with the seeds of insight central to an ethic of care. The contrasting images of self are a demarcated self defined through separation from others and a self delineated through connection, assessed through activities of care.

The findings invite us to explore how different conceptions of morality produce differences in self-identity and in the moral injunction itself. For example, whereas responsibility for Gilligan's eleven year-old boy 'means not doing what he wants because he is thinking of others' (1983: 38), for the girl 'it means doing what others are counting on her to do regardless of what she herself wants' (1983: 38). The seeming lack of a precise individuation in some girls has been attributed by Freud to narcissism and a failure of 'object' relationships. Gilligan's point, in line with other object relation theorists, is that the activity of women signals a new responsiveness to the self. Reversing usual modes of interpretation, the general absence of violence and aggression in women's fantasies and reality reveals even rules-based competition as threatening to the web of connection and as viable only where relationships are readily displaced (Pollak and Gilligan, 1982). This psychic structuring of self around affiliations, rather than resembling an inadequate sense of self, contains the potential for a more co-operative mode of life.

Yet, we need to avoid any romanticisation of women's experience. Jealousy, bickering and conflict occur in most relationships at some stage. We also need to defend relationally oriented men. The images of hierarchy, assertion, success, dominance and achievement, contrasted with an image of a network, where responses to others involve connections, are caricatures. Many of us oscillate between the two or try to combine them. Any presentation of these images as inevitably tied to gender leads to distortions in accurate representation (see Gilligan, 1983: subjects 15, 32, 63). It ignores two realities. First, Gilligan's analysis seems to ignore women who frequently use abstract principles, talk of duty, rights, obligations, universal values, and appeal to reason, as either a prime mode of judgement or a judgement influenced strongly by some synthesis of abstraction and particularity. Second, while men have been guilty of 'false individuation' (Hampshire, 1978), where the complexities and nuances of ethical life are reduced to discrete actions, many men also espouse an ethic of responsibility, where a sense of obligation may originate through situational ethics and where moral judgement is clearly dependent on emotional ties with others.

Two empirical studies highlight this. An examination of the moral character of 1960s male activists revealed that, while classifiable as 'postconventional' on Kohlberg's scale, they exhibited all the virtues of responsibility, sympathy and caring, considered by some to be incompatible with masculinity (Keniston, 1968). Departing also from a Chodorowian characterisation, these men maintained warm affiliations with their mothers, which they acknowledged as a positive contribution to their identity. Another study on 'postconventional' Russian dissidents identified a three-fold typology, an 'abstract rationalist', 'heroic romantic' and 'carnivalesque historicist' (Zahaykevich, 1982). These last two, in avoiding abstract rationality, emphasised community, relationships and personal solidarity as the bases of morality and political action. All the dissidents were committed to nonviolent resistance. Women's experience does not always lead to a non-hierarchical vision of human connection, and inequality and hierarchy are not always inherent in men's experiences.

Maternalism and context

Nevertheless, relational connections, a contextual basis of moral judgement and a maternal morality recur in Gilligan's work. That is, the moral judgement of women is distinguished by repeated reference to an insistance on the particular, in situations which engage their compassion. In Gilligan's second stage of maturity, she states that women's sense of responsibility is fused with a 'maternal morality that seeks to ensure care for the dependent and unequal' (1983: 74). It is useful to assess this idea of moral good in relation to other ideas. Ruddick, for example, building on Habermas' conception of human interest, claims that thought arises from social practice. She argues that a mother's thought is directed toward 'certain questions rather than others' (1982: 77). This 'thought' includes intellectual capacities, judgements, metaphysical attitudes and values. The 'interest' concerned with shaping an 'acceptable child' varies according to the relevant subculture and social ideology.

Maternal practice is a response of a particular person in a particular socio-historic setting through which a conceptual scheme, such as Gilligan's 'logic of connections', is required to order, evaluate and express practices. It is this unity of reflection, judgement and emotion, which Ruddick terms 'maternal thinking'. What distinguishes maternal thinking from scientific thinking and from any instrumentalism is a metaphysical attitude Ruddick calls 'holding' which is governed by the priority of conserving the fragile. It results in 'distinctive ways of seeing and being in the world' (1982: 80) that assume the priority of personhood.

At the foundation of maternal thought is the capacity for what Weil (1977) calls 'attention' and 'the virtue of love'. Attention can be seen as an intellectual capacity which, as Murdoch says, is connected to a special 'knowledge of the individual' (1971: 28). Attention, in this manner, shows how people 'can be looked at and loved without being seized and used, without being appropriated into the greedy organism of the self' (1971: 65). Neither Weil nor Murdoch is a mother. Although maternal thought generally arises out of the realities of child-care, the biological aspects are less significant. Healthcare workers develop modes of relating to others that are unique in being other-centred, concerned with doing good and preventing harm. This bears no direct resemblance to the specific context of 'maternal morality'. Yet, the attentive preserving and holding clearly overlaps. Compassion 'involves a regard for the good of other persons' (Blum, 1980: 507) whatever the context.

Elshtain, in challenging the 'matriphobia' in some feminist literature, extends the political implications of maternal thinking for the transformation of thought in the public world. She reaffirms the moral primacy of the family and argues that the family need be neither the reactionary, repressive institution of leftist critics, nor the idealistic haven of the right (1982a). She stresses the long-term ties with specific others, the need to belong, an obligation to kin, a commitment to love and attentiveness. The link with Ruddick's conclusions lies in Elshtain's argument that the private experiential basis of women's lives as mothers provides the moral imperative to resist the liberal-individualist, power-based abstractionism (1981: 326–327) discussed in this and the previous two chapters.

Dietz counter argues that the uniqueness of women's experience is best located in history, organisational styles, and distinctive modes of political discourse—but not in the mother's role (1985: 34). I agree that when actions have developed as responses to subjugation, any uncritical appropriation does not challenge this subjugation. Also, the widespread reality of child abuse in western culture cannot be ignored. Yet, in maintaining that reproductive considerations have been central to women's history, there is evidence of the prevalence of a 'maternal morality', but it is part of the moral construction of anyone engaged in the regular care of others. I am arguing that it is a *human* capacity that develops through practice. There is a danger in authors like Gilligan, Ruddick, Miller and Elshtain to elevate care as the superior virtue and then, given its current concentration in women, to assume it provides evidence of an essential feminine moral difference. I am contending that what has been referred to as a maternal morality needs to be evaluated highly as a human virtue, open to all.

Conflict between rights and responsibilities

Within Gilligan's framework, the conflicts most women face are focused within the interaction between rights and responsibilities. She contrasts a typical 'male voice' which stresses self-interest, and a typical 'female voice' which stresses processes of attachment to people who create and maintain community. To substantiate her claim, Gilligan provides examples of men's tendency to assess themselves in terms of individual achievement, particularly in the public workforce, and to tie involvement with others to a limitation of identity, rather than to its realisation. In contrast, women generally fuse identity with intimacy, or at least connection to others. She maintains that these perspectives reflect two different moral ideologies.

The morality of *rights* is predicated on equality and fairness. It is geared to arriving at rational, just resolutions, and hence is concerned with balancing claims. It respects absolute principles of equal respect, truth and fairness and its prime moral injunction is to respect the rights of others. What Gilligan suggests is that the moral imperative for men often coincides with respect for the rights of others with particular emphasis given to non-interference by others. The emotional distance in the 'male voice' is justified by this formalised ethic of rights. What is at stake is the balance of claims to rights. Self-assertion is seen to represent moral strength.

In contrast, the principle of connection invokes a morality tied to the experiential basis of relationships. From the awareness of the 'psychological logic of relationships' (1983: 73) there stems an ethic of *responsibility*. This 'contrasts with the formal logic of fairness that informs the justice approach' (1983: 73) and with an individualistic ethic in that its guiding principle is the attachment to others. This challenges emotional separation and necessitates emotional attachment. Morality is perceived, not as balancing claims, but as a problem of inclusion of those requiring care, and hence as a conflict of responsibility. The moral imperative involves considerations of equity and differences in need, requiring contextual, narrative modes of thought. Even abortion can be recast as an issue of responsibility for the welfare of the foetus and of the woman, rather than the conflict between a right to life or a right to choose (Farrell Smith, 1984: 265; Gilligan, 1987: 23).

It is helpful to situate this discussion within the controversy in moral philosophy between rights and responsibilities and a theory of rights and moral good. Duties and obligations are the formal requirements that accrue to the moral individual with rights. A moral social being has commitments both to self and to others. The precise resolution of whether rights impose correlative responsibilities is not easily reached. Furthermore, it is possible to have a right without exercising it, to have a right without knowing one can claim it, or to have a right denied. The question of rights is particularly pertinent to oppressed groups. Nevertheless, a right does entail an obligation, even in a minimal sense, to respect that right in other persons. This responsibility to respect the rights of others has been conspicuously absent in many relationships and political contexts.

What distinguishes rights and obligations is the issue of choice. Assuming basic freedom and opportunities, rights imply an individual choice, whereas an obligation is binding.[3] The nature of this duty is morally defensible on communitarian grounds. The premise behind the assertion of rights is that of self-respect and the equal right to respect. The converse of this is that the denial or suppression of rights undermines self-respect. In a traditional construction of a theory of right and a theory of good, the former concerns itself with basic rules for adjudicating conflict premised on an acceptance of rights. A theory of the good has by definition an evaluative component built in. In the context of my argument, this includes constituents of good moral being, the basis for loyal friendship, responsible parenthood and enhancing the quality of life. Viewed this way, both rights and responsibilities affirm self-respect and the respect of others.

Justice, rights and community claims

The controversy between rights and responsibilities is similar to the controversy between justice and the good, so I want to defend two claims. First, once rights and responsibilities are seen to be hand in glove, rights can be construed as less individualistic than is customary. Secondly, just as rights and responsibilities are important dimensions of morality, principles and virtues are essential to justice. Indeed, justice is an active virtue in that it renders moral agency self-critical and self-reflective in terms of continually reassessing how to act justly in accordance with principle.

First, a right extends in principle to all, based on an equality of respect. Traditionally, an emphasis on rights is less inclined toward communitarian ethics, precisely because it asserts the primacy of individual rights. This is particularly evident when a rights emphasis is divorced from mutual obligations. The right to freedom for two people living together is a good example. Individual formal rights require a dissolution of 'natural bonds', ignoring family ties to prioritise individual claims, whereas an emphasis on responsibility merges these claims into the overall relationship, counterbalancing the right to freedom with the responsibility to reciprocate. I am not suggesting that a responsibility orientation, as Gilligan construes it, is necessarily more conducive to an assessment of the good, but it is clearly oriented toward determining the needs of people. When responsibilities and rights are considered in conjunction, much of the tension between individual rights and care of others, typically construed as an opposition of selfishness and altruism, is dissipated.

A person who sees moral dilemmas solely in terms of responsibility to others remains blinded in an ideal of selflessness. The awareness of personal rights challenges this morality of self-abnegation by asserting the underlying premise of justice, namely, the basic equality of self and other. Yet while this person might acknowledge self-interest as legitimate, self-assertion might threaten their dependency situations—perhaps financial dependence on a spouse, or the need to care for an aged parent. What this problem exposes is that 'rights language offers a rich vernacular for the claims an individual may make on or against the collectivity, but it is relatively impoverished as a means of expressing individuals' need for the collectivity' (Ignatieff, 1984: 13). By itself, rights language incorporates ideals of fraternity only as mutual respect for each others' rights which defines our common identity—yet, we are more than rights-bearing creatures, and respect for a person extends beyond rights. Thus, it is important to ensure that rights language is neither abstract nor decontextualised, but placed within community needs, in the context of responsibilities towards one's self and others.

This balance between personal interests and communal needs means that moral judgements should be concerned with the contextual appropriateness of applying principles to particular, concrete situations. Exaggeration is conspicuous in Gilligan's (1979) assertion that the morality of rights is necessarily concerned with the individual. Rather, 'rights and duties are concerned precisely with social relatedness, and the very reciprocity of a right and a duty captures that concern' (Broughton, 1983: 611). The incorporation of a communitarian ethics into one's morality ensures a contextual basis for the relation between principled rights and responsibilities.

Moral judgement, thus, entails an integration of rights and responsibilities. This does not reflect a complementarity of the sexes. The consequence of disregarding rights in favour of responsibility alone fails to appreciate the way rights can be reinterpreted. When the tendency towards individualism is abandoned, a compatibility between the constructs is evident. Gilligan suggests changes for men arise from the revitalised experience of self and other. A more contextual frame of reference makes equality more relative and the new equity leads to an ethic of generosity. For women, the principle of care is modified with the recognition of the need for personal integrity so that claims for equality concern obligations to oneself as well as to others.

Justice

I have argued that this view of rights and responsibilities, self and others can sit comfortably within a modified pursuit of justice. Pateman believes that 'love and justice are antagonistic virtues' (1980: 24) in that the demands made by justice and intimate relations are different and opposed. Both respond to different aspects of the human condition. Requisite to justice is the treatment of others according to merit or desert established by formalised logic, but, as I demonstrate shortly, not necessarily by impersonal standards. Love relations cling to the unique individual involved who, as parent, child, lover or friend, is non-transferable.

Rawls claims we need to establish principles of justice precisely because we cannot know individuals well enough for love to serve alone. Presumably, with close friends, we aim to know each other well enough for something other than formal justice to come into play, something more akin to common, mutual goals, interests and needs. Rather than discarding justice as an abstract goal, it is more feasible to realise the constraints of a conception of justice shaped without regard for contingencies or particularities, and to work towards eliminating such constraints. We have noted that a morality of justice, tied to a formal logic of equality, may conflict with particular demands of relationships (Schrag, 1976). Yet, perhaps this tension need not be great. The strict distinction fails to see that, 'while justice requires abstraction, it is intended as the abstract form that caring takes when respect is maintained and responsibility assumed' (Broughton, 1983: 614) for people whom we do not know personally. It is unrealistic to imagine that all social interaction is based on concrete, affectionate ties.

With an increasing interplay between the public and private realms, a heightened sensitivity to the relevant overlap is necessary. That is, justice, love and the responsibilities that accompany it need not be entirely in conflict. Just relations can be loving and responsible, such as when parents do not show favouritism; or, in other situations, just relations can concern formal requirements of equality and impartiality, yet retain a strong sense of responsibility, such as with employment procedures in the public sphere, or with different amounts of pocket money according to age and household duties in the private sphere. While the family may be unsuited to the exercise of formal claims of justice, it plays an important role in providing a framework where a sense of justice can develop and where just habits may be learnt. This presupposes the abolition of institutionalised injustices such as a rigid gender division of labour. Justice, although primarily a 'public virtue, must not only exist in the private world of the family but must necessarily exist there if it is to exist in the broader public sphere' (Kearns, 183: 36). A blend of justice with principles of care and responsibilities may make this feasible.

VISIONS OF MATURITY

In concluding this chapter, I assess Gilligan's 'different voices'. Gilligan makes no claims to be positing ideals for moral philosophy, but her ideals are clearly claims of moral being. These claims refer to sequences in human development, of attachment and separation, intimacy and identity, love and work, mutuality and individuation. Gilligan argues that the 'different voices' relate to gender identity and express different priorities. In restoring the 'missing text', or 'the silence of women in the narrative of adult development' (1983: 156), Gilligan aims to broaden the understanding of moral development by the inclusion of perspectives of both sexes. She argues that both perspectives need to converge in a representation of maturity.

In accepting that transitional crises affect people differently, Gilligan suggests that for women this process toward maturity occurs through their comprehension of the logic of relationships. Admittedly, she calls into question the traditional equation of care with self-sacrifice, but she does not really tell us what crucial determining factors influence this change from self-sacrifice to acceptance of the need for rights within context, explaining it only in terms of a reconstructed cognition based on a re-evaluation of the self and other relations.

Yet, is an 'absolute of care' (1983: 166) sufficient to spur women toward maturity and to lead to the actual, self-assertive claim for equality embodied in the concept of rights? Consistent with Gilligan's argument is the general practice of women who, being aware of the need for equality of respect as a basis to rights, will not jeopardise their priority of care if the practical claim to rights is being frustrated. This occurs even when there is a strong subjective acceptance of one's formal rights. Gilligan rarely mentions constraints of femininity, or positive facilitators to maturity such as the acceptance by both parties of equality and an equal opportunity for claiming and developing rights.

In describing men's process to maturity, Gilligan again fails to explain what type of experiences men will need to face before becoming aware of their active responsibility for assuming care. This explanation would be necessary to alleviate the indifference of a morality of non-interference based on their claim to rights without corresponding responsibilities. It is unrealistic, and unfair to men, to imply that they have all been in relationships where they dominated claims to rights, or where destructive violence was a feature. The experiences that may demonstrate differences between other and self need to be clearly explicated. Unless this is done, it is not clear why the 'absolutes of truth and fairness' (1983: 166) inherent in the concepts of equality and reciprocity, should be suddenly exposed to men as inadequate.

Moral voices

In hearing two distinct voices, Gilligan maintains that for both sexes, integration, complementarity, two contexts for decision-making, new understandings and dialogue provide for better insights (1983: 100, 166, 174). I argue that the convergence of justice and care Gilligan points toward is more problematical than she indicates. I draw on Gilligan's 1987 qualifications and other theorists who extend her ideas and highlight three facets of her conclusions. First, I critically examine her orientation differences and assess whether they maintain dichotomous, stereotypical views of women and men. Second, I clarify the relationship between the two perspectives. Third, I examine the nature of 'the dialectic that creates the tension of human development' (1983: 156), advocating a synthesis of moral voices.

Orientation differences

Gilligan maintains that there are 'two disparate modes of experience that are in the end connected' (1983: 174). These are identified by cognitive modality, theme and self-identity and are associated with gender. They are 'cross-cutting perspectives' (1987: 25), or different ways of organising the basic elements of moral judgement. An awareness by both sexes of the rich variety of moral experience exposes the 'contextually relative' (1983: 166) dimensions of moral judgement. To clarify, this form of relativism is not reducible to mere individual preference, but has meaning in relation to moral contexts and shared moral principles. Let us look at this contextual relativism and then at the orientation differences.

Murphy and Gilligan, in attempting to deal with relativist dilemmas, posit a two-category typology which contrasts a 'post-conventional formal' mature cognition with a 'post-conventional contextual' maturity. The first supposedly resolves relativist dilemmas by constructing a formal logical system derived from concepts such as social contract, or natural rights, but virtually eliminates any variances different contexts might imply. In contrast, they suggest that the reasoning of the second category emanates 'from an understanding of the contextual relativism of moral judgement and the ineluctable uncertainty of moral choice' (1980: 83). Its articulation, as Gilligan (1983) presents it, is manifest in an ethic of responsibility, focusing on the consequences of choice. The criterion for the adequacy of moral principles is altered from that of objective truth to that of 'best fit', which is established within the context of the dilemma in question. This permits alternative formulations for different dilemmas, in the context of uncertainty and ambiguity where, rather than decisive solutions, emphasis on a notion of 'it depends' permits adaptive moral judgements.

Murphy and Gilligan suggest that notions of fairness and reciprocity underlying formal moral principles constitute one context in which to resolve moral dilemmas, particularly of a hypothetical nature, but the confrontation with *actual* dilemmas, such as the inability to communicate with a lover, a lawyer's unwitting prosecution of an innocent man, the reaction to a spouse's infidelity, a couple's choice of an abortion and the difficulty of truth and forgiveness, initiates different types of moral questioning conducive to a reconstructed moral understanding. Similarly, Held, in arguing for an understanding of sincere moral experience, is critical of veils of ignorance, utilitarian spectators or other constructions of impartiality bound to formalist frameworks. I endorse her view 'that the considered judgement arrived at through real experience instead of through disembodied reflection may be more important, serious and reliable for moral theory than its ideal counterpart' (1984: 48). This is because it incorporates a synthesis between principle and context.

Yet, do Gilligan's work on 'different voices' and Gilligan and Murphy's proposition of a 'best fit' morality adequately deal with Held's 'considered judgement'? While Gilligan's position is a vast improvement on a non-detached notion of morality, there are stark shortcomings. That is, if it appears that the actual relational contents are not as important as the way in which such concreteness is considered, then, content itself becomes a form of interpretation (Broughton, 1983: 625). This is a critical point. Gilligan tries to overcome problems inherent in structural approaches, which tend to abstract from reality, by placing prime focus on the experiential basis of morality with all the concreteness, content, practicality and personal action this entails.

164

Paradoxically, Gilligan thus fails in an area I have stressed is crucial, namely, the connection between traditionally accepted opposites, in this case between content and form, the concrete and the abstract, experience and concept, function and structure, action and thought. The possibility of transformed relations lessens. Any gravitation toward a psychology of personality traits, rather than a theory of moral development, exacerbates this danger. Otherwise, the notion of 'connected versus separated voices' too easily assumes the status of a personality distinction, rather than an evaluative ethical position.

This has important implications for any conclusions as to the validity of a differential morality, particularly in terms of whether it is cognitive skills, developed through social practices, or moral skills which are being highlighted. Clearly, a healthy scepticism of scoring ranges (Colby et al., 1983) and an attempt to classify moral judgement are needed in order to incorporate fully the complexity of human experience. What is troubling in the instance under discussion is not so much the doubt 'that dialectical, context-sensitive morality is superior to context-insensitive morality or pure formalistic morality' (Flanagan, 1983: 511), but any tendency for it to be associated with the voice of female morality. The question is one of appropriateness within given contexts.

How, then, can sensitivity to appropriateness avoid emotivism which explicitly links morality with merely subjective preferences? This is important because of the widespread contemporary conjunction of the moral with the private which is, ironically, part of the twentieth-century publicisation of private life. Alternative, sensitive responses to identical circumstances do not necessitate a relativist position. That is, in positing an 'ethics of ambiguity', it is unnecessary to leap from the assertion of the uncertainty and ambiguity of morality to a renunciation of moral judgement. I am advocating a reciprocal relationship between moral principles and contextual adaptability.

Stocker's example of duty and friendship clarifies this. He argues that sensitivity and contextualism 'are as needed for duty as for friendship' (1987: 60) and that 'friendship gives rise to special duties' (1987: 65). If some see a problem with a duty of affection, Stocker reminds us that 'we do criticise ourselves for not showing affection' (1987: 66), and a good friend is careful not to violate duties of friendship. Nevertheless, as we all know with strained relations, 'relating to people as friends differs from relating to them on principle, from duty' (1987: 67). He also points out that responsibility claims can be hierarchically ranked: we do have different responsibilities toward different friends according to our evaluation and prizing of such friendships.

Clearly, different moral inquiries and practices require different moral approaches, so that 'the contexts in which experience is obtained may make a difference' (Held, 1987: 113). One would expect that the person who has spent adult life predominantly in a parenting role will experience different dilemmas from the person who has been the sole breadwinner, but whether they interpret the same dilemma differently is another issue. Gilligan largely ignores other important processes by which explanations come to be socially constructed, such as age, class and race (Addelson, 1987: 105). Little research has documented class and ethnic differences in gender identity, particularly extending Chodorow, Dinnerstein, Rich and Gilligan.

One view that does confront racial differences suggests that 'people (men?) of African descent and (Western?) women appear to have similar ontologies, epistemologies, and ethics' (Harding, 1987: 299). This view suggests further that black women's and men's contextualisation of morality and evaluation of social ties posits a cultural alternative to Gilligan's model. The alternative lies in a collective social conscience, manifest in a concern for reciprocity, commitment to kin and community, a firm sense of responsibility for others and limited access to rights. Close-knit working-class communities are traditionally bound together strongly by a variety of shared purposes, histories, interests, life situations. Urban redevelopment is a major contributor to the rapid disintegration of the communal identity which provided communities with purpose, despite mass unemployment, poverty and inadequate housing (Wiener, 1980). Clearly, the notion of bonds and connectedness extend beyond the supposed exclusivity of a 'woman's voice'. Furthermore, with socio-historical changes, the notion of identity itself is continually called into question. Changes in the role of family structures and in attitudes to men and women generally will invariably alter the basic premises and conditions on which theories of feminine moral identity have been constructed.

An overriding emphasis on context does not solve the puzzle as to whether we start with the different orientations that we use for different moral practices, or whether we use different moral approaches for different moral inquiries. Gilligan seems to want to say both, as I do, but the implications for the alternatives differ. The former question lends itself to an explanation of gender difference and differential socialisation, the latter to an acceptance of the variegated nature of human complexity. A problem with this occurs only when one view maintains gender division, and the other is seen to transcend it. It is difficult to avoid accusations of traditionalism where there are hints of the normative construct of these voices. The feminist critique against the 'male voice' is clear and widely accepted, but some women still have problems with a critique of the 'female voice' given the historical novelty of its re-evaluation. The need to delineate women's experience in their own terms is crucial. Yet it is important to assess the degree to which experience is both genuinely self-defined and ideal. Gilligan now asserts she has used a 'critical ethical perspective' (Kerber et al., 1986: 327). We now explore this claim.

Relationship between moral voices

Gilligan's recent writings state that the justice and care perspectives cut across dichotomies like thinking–feeling, egoism–altruism, theoretical–practical reasoning, so that all human relationships can be characterised both in terms of equality and attachment (1987: 20). What, then, is her understanding of the convergence in judgement? To explain this, she uses an analogy to the visual arts rabbit-duck figure where you can see the rabbit and then the duck but never simultaneously. She suggests that the focus phenomenon proves 'that people have a tendency to lose sight of one moral perspective in arriving at moral decisions—a liability equally shared by both sexes' (1987: 26). I argue that her analogy is inappropriate for understanding the complexity and intricacies of human moral dilemmas. I substantiate this by demonstrating her failure to really grapple with the relationship between the two perspectives, that important 'middle ground' discussed in chapter two. As a consequence, this precludes a genuine appreciation of the dialectic of human development which I maintain permits multiple versions of moral synthesis, rather than the simple convergence of two voices.

Even if we assume with Gilligan that there are only two voices, as opposed to many voices or voices with various possibilities (Nicholson, 1983: 533), it is crucial to elucidate the relationship between the different voices or the differences among these voices. For example, it is not clear how Gilligan would categorise a woman who spoke (thought and acted) in the 'male voice' and a man who spoke in a 'female voice'. Presumably, it is possible to describe a highly individualistic woman in instances of assertive rights claims as using the 'male voice', and a sensitive, co-operative, communitarian man as using the 'female voice'. The failure to adequately address internal relations seems to resurrect distinctions such as cognition–affect.

Gilligan clarifies the relation more clearly in her later work. Care, construed within a justice framework, is 'the mercy that tempers justice' (1987: 24). This could include special obligations within personal relationships, or altruism freely chosen. Accordingly, a concern for rights, equality and justice may constrain what a compassionate person can do, 'but in no way does it deny the moral importance of compassion' (Hill, 1987: 135). Similarly, justice within a care framework specifies a 'respect for people in their own terms' (Gilligan, 1987: 24). Indeed, caring is not a whimsical notion. It is guided by principles. While the problems involved in contexts that require care, nurture, empathy or sensitive parenting deal with issues 'above and beyond the moral minimums that can be covered by principles concerning rights and obligations, that does not mean that these minimums can be dispensed with' (Held, 1987: 119).

While Gilligan positively acknowledges that compassion tempers justice and that care without justice is inadequate, she sees moral development as 'the integrity of two disparate modes of experience that are in the end connected' (1983: 174). Recalling the focus phenomenon as evidenced in the rabbit-duck figure, she writes that 'what makes seeing both moral perspectives so difficult is precisely that the orientations are not opposites nor mirror images or better and worse representations of a single moral truth. The terms of one perspective do not contain the terms of the other' (1987: 30). I disagree. You can reinterpret perspectives to eliminate possible antagonism, or to be more inclusive. The tension remains so that the principles of justice sit uncomfortably with the urgency to include another, just like a desire to maintain informal attachments and equity necessitates we consider formal principles of justice and equality. The point of actively challenging both categories is precisely to challenge the past intransigence of static categories, and, I believe, to work toward a realistic synthesis. Gilligan maintains that 'one perspective may overshadow or eclipse the other, so that one is brightly illuminated while the other is dimly remembered' (1987: 31). If these perspectives are part of the dialectic of human development the whole point of a dialectical understanding is to work through the struggle between seemingly opposing or overshadowing forces. The resultant synthesis is never a simplistic A + B and every synthesis alters the nature of the next dialectical interaction.

Synthesis of voices

It seems to me that a synthesis of perspectives is essential for an integrated notion of moral identity. While in most instances of formal logic or quantifiable objects, A + B amounts to the same thing as B + A, this does not necessarily hold true in the case of qualitative characteristics. The fact that it does not has important ramifications. For example, the consequences in relationships of anger followed by forgiveness is markedly different from those of forgiveness followed by anger. Gilligan gives the impression that A + B is the same as B + A. Let me explain by taking A to represent Gilligan's 'male voice' and B her 'female voice'.

I argue that the A + B combination places the individual at more of a social advantage than the combination B + A, but that neither is ideal. For a man to have had a strong sense of self-confidence in his claims to rights, to which is added an ethic of care and responsibility, is to ensure that his concept of self remains, if not primary, at least very clear, but now within a more caring and relational framework.

For a woman to have this sense of self arrive after a long history of embeddedness with others does make it a very different notion of the self from that of the male, despite them both being autonomous, caring subjects. Furthermore, the understanding of both rights and responsibilities differ for these individuals (Stocker, 1987: 57). While they co-exist, they differ in definition, in priority and in practice.

Sociologically, we now have examples of increasing numbers of professional, political, managerial and academic women, who have discovered a new sense of autonomy, yet retain a strong interconnective outlook. Yet, it is precisely these women, struggling for success—defined as achievement and public recognition—who still struggle with the potent dilemmas of guilt, self-sacrifice, selfishness and time-juggling when there are children involved, in a way less evident in their male counterparts. Even the legal guarantees of equal treatment are not sufficient either to transcend women's 'difference' or to transform it into their strength (Markus, 1986: 439). A contextual sense of self ensures that in times of crisis, or when significant others leave—such as in a broken relationship, children leaving for school or from home—disruptions have a marked effect not only on practical considerations, but on identity. Removed from her familiar context, the less confident woman often retains few noticeable traces of 'her self'. To use Gilligan's language, when a women has a matured 'female voice' to which the 'male voice' is added, a situation of conflict between self and others may easily result in the familiar practice of women's self-sacrifice, which is complicated by it being construed as 'moral goodness.'

What I am advocating is a synthesis of voices and a notion of identity viewed as a self-in-relations. This synthesises individuality and sociality (Gould, 1978; 1988) in that it takes into account the self, others, the context, and the contextual self. What Gilligan has construed as 'different voices' cannot be simplistically combined in the development of a strong sense of self. As a vision for future relations, I support the emergence of self-in-relations (A $\leftrightarrow$ B) rather than self-and-relations (A + B), or the relational-self (B + A). Where the emphasis is on the last two combinations, it is very difficult for one side of the convergence not to dominate, particularly in moments of conflict. The side with the most 'practice' generally prevails.

The attempt to formulate new visions for the future is frustrated by the difficulty of liberating the imagination. We are so accustomed to thinking in dualistic frameworks that we still approach many of these issues as if traits are essentially masculine or feminine. The failure to identify many character models of the strong, caring person of either sex makes my assertion that a self-in-relations is preferable to the relational-self seem susceptible to the accusation that I am denigrating the 'female voice' in favour of the 'male voice'. This is not so. I see the need to encourage, particularly in our children, the simultaneous emergence of what Gilligan has called the 'female voice' and the 'male voice' while allowing for 'other voices' to emerge. This is very different from a convergence. The hope is that all voices can develop without the negative attributes with which they have been associated. Where there is an emphasis of the self as developing within an intersubjective framework, a clear sense of individuation, conceived in positive terms, and thus free of the negative connotations of emotional distance and separation, can emerge with a concept of a self defined in response to others. This is not possible where children are raised in a context of hostility or violence. With the removal of the negative attributes associated with stereotypical 'voices', we can cease to view them as 'male voices' or as 'female voices'. I assume the *inseparability of the self and context*, and advocate a genuine self-in-relations. This allows a vast range of character traits, differentiated not by gender restrictions, but by a conscious affirmation of the sexual component of one's identity as a moral subject.

In this context, self-in-relations assumes a theoretical and a practical basis. It is an active notion of agent-morality, confirmed by (not defined through) recognition by other subjects. It is my concern that much of the current feminist emphasis on the positive evaluation of the relational-self correctly perceives the dangers of development being reduced to the separate self, but does not pay sufficient attention to the need for a strong concept of selfhood. It is necessary to have a clearly emerging sense of self, before one can be 'morally good' in any situation, whether care for others, or a claim for one's rights. How this strong concept of self differs from the traditional individualistic 'male voice' is that it emphasises an individuated sense of self as connectedness with others, rather than separation from, or domination of, others. There is no contradiction. The fundamental themes acknowledged here are interconnection, mutual recognition and individuality within community. Possible gender differences within this construct affirm the particularity of moral subjects and the multiplicity welcomed in a narrative version of agent-morality.

The key to fostering this multiplicity lies in grasping the potential inherent in the dialectic that sustains the tension of moral development. This makes it exciting to work through different combinations of perspectives. I have maintained repeatedly that an acknowledgement of tension is different from an acceptance of inevitable polarity, conflict or antagonism, in that it necessitates questioning of the relations between contrasts in an attempt to transcend dualism. Coping positively with these tensions contributes to the construction of integrated identities who can confirm both general human dignity and specific individuality (Benhabib, 1987: 169; Meyers, 1987: 146). I have demonstrated the need for a balance, or a synthesis between alternatives, as vital to the poignant complexity of being moral.

NOTES

1   I offer three examples of the absurdity of failing to do so. Sophisticated theologians, capable of principled reasoning of upper stages, espouse a morality of subjection to God's will, and thus are classifiable by Kohlberg at stage four. Second, when choosing partners to live with, we all have a different set of motivations. Generally, one prefers to know personal details, and not just that someone's conceptual sophistication and invocation of principles of justice and welfare are exemplary. Consider a third situation, where employers have a vacancy to fill. Without entering the affirmative action debate, the non-suitability of many female applicants can be viewed by 'impartial spectators' as a straightforward case of inadequate qualification or experience, where women have no right to the job. Without a consideration of possible changes in moral judgement or actual constraints influenced by pregnancies, child-birth, disruption of study and work experience and lack of emotional support, only a partial picture of these women is viewed.

2   The first was a college student study that explored identity in 25 students who took a course on moral and political choice, followed up 5 years later. The second was an abortion decision study which interviewed 29 women aged 15–33 who in their first trimester of pregnancy were considering an abortion. This was followed up a year later. Hypotheses generated by the findings of this research were refined in a third rights and responsibilities study. A sample of 144 people were involved at 9 points in the life cycle, 6–9, 11, 15, 19, 22, 25, 25–27, 35, 45, 60, with 8 males and females at each stage. Two males and females at each age were more intensively interviewed.

3   For example, one could choose not to pursue the right to accumulate property as those in religious orders where a duty to live frugally is accepted. Some might accept the right but balance this with the concomitant obligation to be aware of others in need. Others may pursue the right and refuse to accept that an obligation coincides. Some may deny this is a right at all.

7 Affirmation of difference

In this chapter, I look specifically at the case for asserting that there is some unique female moral stance as it is presented through the example of women's involvement in the peace movement. In focusing on this example, the chapter has a somewhat different character from previous ones which introduced practical examples sparingly and then only to highlight particular theoretical points. The rationale for making a practical example central to this chapter is straightforward: the example in question offers a vivid illustration of the position of certain groups who claim that women have developed a sociologically distinctive morality, enables the previously noted theoretical dilemmas confronting such a position to appear in sharper focus, and, in sum, provides extra support for my attempt to steer a middle course between the extremes of male-oriented philosophy and feminist exclusivism.

PEACE, WAR AND AN EXPLORATION OF DIFFERENCE

The following discussion is divided into two sections. In the first, I examine women's attitudes toward the issues of peace and non-violence. I do not provide a thorough analysis of the growing literature on these issues, but offer a reflective, critical assessment of representative samples of feminist peace discourse. I draw on selections from anthologies and pay particular attention to the objectives, motivations and achievements of women in peace movements. In the second section, I engage in a more analytic treatment of the relation between sexual identity and violence. I refer specifically to the interconnections of masculinity, war and domination. I also try to ascertain why some women are intent on claiming their right to engage in combat.

Women, peace and non-violence

The nature of autonomous women's peace groups offers an apt example of a deliberate attempt by some women to affirm their femaleness. It should be stated from the outset that most women do not take an active part in politics or belong to peace groups, but there is evidence of a marginal statistical tendency for more women to be explicitly pro-peace than men (Goertzel, 1983; Brody, 1984; Burris, 1984; Smith, 1984). This tendency does not belie the fact that some women are active in modern terrorist groups such as the Red Brigades, Black September, the Irish Republican Army and the Bader Meinhoff, or that women with power, like Meir, Ghandi or Thatcher, may exhibit a ruthlessness which is no different from that exhibited by many men with power. Additionally, women are participants as well as victims in physical and verbal violence and aggression. Nevertheless, exceptions do not understate the general tendency for most westerners to accept that 'to be peaceful' is a characteristic trait that most women either develop or possess naturally.[1]

Four major motivations recur in women's writings concerning their involvement in the peace movement: a fear of the nuclear threat, a concern to emphasise how an abstract threat may turn into a concrete possibility, a personal responsibility and an assumed instinctual or spiritual orientation to the preservation and nurture of life. First, the fear expressed concerning the accumulation and escalation of nuclear arms, the reluctance of wide-scale disarmament, and the threat of war is articulated by many women as a private anxiety that assumes terrifying proportions in their nightmares. Experiencing radioactive fallout, radiation malaise, decay, terror, or annihilation as a dream is vastly different from envisaging it in abstract. It resembles a film being screened for oneself. Many women note that men laugh at their dreams. In the words of one woman, it is not that men do not fear a nuclear holocaust, but that they do not describe the feeling of panic that women talk about (Cook and Kirk, 1983: 18). We are accustomed to differentiate ourselves from our dreams by testing the reality of the world we have woken up into against the dream world we have left. 'Dreams about nuclear war are different in this respect from other dreams. There is no waking up from this nightmare' (Cook and Kirk, 1983: 21).

For many women, this fear acts as the catalyst for the transition from private anxiety to a move, albeit tentative, to collective, public commitment which is often characterised by the media as sincere but naive and emotional. To counter such a characterisation, these 'excited, wild women' claim the second motivation, that thinking about cruise missiles in the abstract language of political debate, where death is discussed in facts and figures, is easier than thinking about one person's death from radiation sickness. That is, these women are also motivated by a concern that an abstract threat may become a concrete possibility. Accordingly, they refuse to discuss the issue of nuclear arms in solely abstract terms, but, rather, insist on confronting its particular consequences too. This is the difference between contemplating the Heinz dilemma and facing your own mother dying. This antipathy to conceiving of the nuclear issue in wholly abstract terms coincides with a refusal to be distanced from

173

others, precisely, as argued in earlier chapters, because the abstraction from shared feelings with others provides a psychological basis for domination and violence. This abstract basis justifies the theoretical rightness of goals even if the practical translation has deleterious effects on the lives of many human beings. In the instance of war, such an attitude sees only military dominance and can create an indifference not only to the burning of a village, but also to the raping of its women and girls.

Abstraction and objectification are necessary components of violent social acts. Seeing oneself as essentially separate from another 'entity' permits one to do to that entity what one would not do to oneself. Conversely, empathy with others means feeling with them to such a degree that hurting them entails damaging oneself. Empathy involves a full acceptance of what it means to be a self-in-relations. A knowledge-based sensitivity derives largely from experience. Consequently, many people cannot recognise in another person feelings they have not experienced themselves (Dilthey, 1976: 212). The tendency to rationalise or excuse unacceptable levels of human suffering results from an abstract perspective that cannot incorporate empathy. An appraisal of this tendency makes many women, and an increasing number of men, wary of accepting the credibility of a wholly abstract analysis of militarism.

In continuing this line of discussion, other women suggest that fear of an anonymous, militaristic threat diverts attention from familiar instances of domestic violence, incest, rape and sexual harassment (Some London Revolutionary Feminists, 1983: 20). Their claim is that attention should not be redirected from personal, concrete oppression to what they see as an abstract notion of 'the rest of the world', for they maintain that this diminishes the forcefulness of the 'daily war' waged on women. Current suffering seems more immediate than 'pending doom'. The acknowledgement of current suffering can, however, coincide with fear of potential suffering. The threat of nuclear war is not highlighted by women in peace movements as an external abstract issue, distinct from a person's material position, but is an extension of concrete circumstances and, for many, its logical conclusion. I return to this shortly.

Thirdly, the women in question feel anger at the anticipation of possible violence, and the need to respond personally to threats of destruction. Again, counter to the criticism that such a response detracts from immediate concerns, these feelings of anger emanate from a context of experience and urge women to confront each other with consequences of daily existence, particularly the responsibilities which, for many, derive from their roles as life-givers and sustainers. This concern directly acknowledges the connection between care of humans and care of the planet.

It is difficult analytically to distinguish this morality of responsibility, explained in the previous chapter, from a fourth motivation, namely, the priority many women give to nurture. Within the women's peace movement, two major forms of this priority are a joy in the creativity of life and the specific nurture of children. Those emphasising the former priority affirm unequivocally the instinctual or spiritual basis of their conviction that nothing in the world is more important than peace. The imperative for political action is rooted in the significance granted to all life-affirming behaviour. Personal commitment to this relies on inner energy cultivated through harmony with life. This often involves dipping into the nonverbal, but fertile, part of ourselves in order to name the unnamable and delving into one's spirit (Bishop, 1982: 161; Rich, 1980a).

Advocates of the second variation on this priority of nurture maintain that when one is involved with children, the sense of personal responsibility is heightened as is the urgency of the struggle for peace which is transformed from an optional right to an obligation. One woman felt an added urgency for peace after having a child. 'My immediate, instinctive reaction to nuclear war is in my capacity as a mother...another dimension had been added to my caring' (Jones, 1983: 65, 67). The vulnerability and dependency of babies is thus extended into a political consciousness, based on a combination of newly discovered rights and responsibilities.

For women involved in the peace movement, there is a common embrace of symbolic representations. The chief symbol is the 'weaving of webs'. Links in a web are fragile, but the more threads it is composed of, the greater its strength. A frequent occurrence at places like Three Mile Island, Greenham Common and Pine Gap is the symbolic gesture of spinning and weaving coloured yarns and ribbons, and placing photographs of children, friends and lovers in the web. The image of birth and hope exposes the opposition between life-creating and life-destroying work. The spinning, weaving, tying, knotting and repairing, contrasts to the ripping, tearing and destroying in violence and warfare, where there is an indiscriminate destruction of links (McAllister, 1982: 289). The patterns that emerge symbolise the interconnectedness of life, the delicate balance of dependency between living beings. The celebration is frequently turned into dance, drama or art forms, emphasising connections, spirals and tapestries.

All the above motivations for women in the peace movement—an emphasis on fear, the concrete, personal responsibility and nurture—relate to the claim explored in earlier chapters that women's identity is frequently grounded in serving others. This basis of selfhood often incorporates negative dimensions like indefinite ego-boundaries, or excessive self-sacrifice, but it also encourages empathy, co-operation and arbitration skills. The development of these strengths within situations of inequality or unreflective femininity renders the assertion of uniqueness problematical, requiring further critical analysis.

Feminism and peace movements

A useful focus for this analysis lies in assessing the relationship between women's involvement in the peace movement and the connection of this involvement with feminism. Various paradigms could be outlined, but I contrast those women who rely uncritically on traditional feminine roles and those who are explicitly feminist. The traditionalists define special roles for women based on reproductive potential. They draw an intrinsic relation between a natural life-giving and preservational role, and the abhorrence of destruction. Explicitly feminist groups fall into two main camps. One group views both the peace and women's movements as different but analogous. That is, they view sexism as a system of injustice, in which violence is one dimension. A second group asserts this more forcibly. They claim that sexism is not merely a particular form of violence, but that it lies at the basis of all violence. The extreme radical position asserts that if this is so, then the violence behind nuclear weaponry and military artillery stand as the ultimate manifestation of patriarchal control, rendering all men responsible. Within this second group, a causal relationship between feminism and women's involvement in the peace movement is clear. Reasons behind autonomous action differ for those advocating traditionalist values of femininity and feminists opposing patriarchal values. We pursue these reasons further.

First, coincidence of an involvement in peace groups with the embrace of traditional femininity relates primarily to emotional responses to similar issues. The common bond is the 'deep fear for our children's futures hanging in a mushroom cloud above our heads' (Jones, 1983: 4). This bond is forged through the involvement of mothers, grandmothers, midwives, teachers, religious people, or anyone concerned with nurturing. Practical constraints of time and energy, and the presence of young, demanding children are features of these groups. I have critically appraised the assumed female naturalness of empathy, caring and co-operation that these groups stress elsewhere. Within these groups, such characteristics are generally embraced simply because of their intrinsic value to nurturing. This perspective is neither necessarily feminist nor political, but stems from the stark realisation that life is threatened. Indeed, some of the groups involved deliberately avoid associating with feminism for fear of losing their broadly based appeal.

Another group, which abhors the idea of a broad base and which identifies strongly with exclusivist feminist principles, offers an extreme example of the embrace of traditionalist feminine characteristics. One writer representative of this view urges us not to call peaceful qualities 'human ones'. 'To grant them to all human beings loses the point', says Gearhart (1982: 271), maintaining further that to insist on the benefit of men in becoming nurturing and empathetic is valid only in a context where patriarchy insists that women who climb its hierarchical ladder become as ruthlessly violent as its male predecessors. This logic is difficult to follow. Admittedly, a formidable objection to any assertion of female supremacy, in terms of natural peacefulness, lies with women who have gained power and equal status in the male hierarchy through consciously adopting ruthless, competitive, or forceful behaviour patterns. Both politically conservative and politically radical traditionalists maintain that women, through their 'special nature', do not naturally engage in such practices. Yet, the problem with such an assertion of female supremacy is that its allusions to 'female nature' coincide with the persistence of patriarchal norms, hence should be appraised critically. Moreover, if typically feminine values are virtuous, then it seems they should be commendable for all who practice them, including men. Yet consider the consequences of the following statements, 'Women want...no more sons. We will not spend 20 years of our lives raising a potential rapist, a potential batterer, a potential BIG man...The proportion of men must be reduced to and maintained at approximately 10% of the human race' (Gearhart, 1982: 282, 271). Such a position is ludicrous unless one wants seriously to contemplate mass abortion of males, male infanticide or female cloning.

This exclusivist female position substitutes women's solidarity for radical feminist analysis. Clearly the mother and child icon pulls heart strings. The image of the perennial 'Earth Mother', a fecund conciliator, is one the media likes to exploit. Any maternal image or apparent passivity on the part of women appears appropriate to such imagery. From this perspective traditional structures are left intact. Yet, another view that might simply disregard the experiential aspects of mothering as necessarily reactionary alienates the majority of women who consciously choose to bear and care for children. Again, I reiterate, when the processes of critique are kept alive, so that there is a reformulation of positive attributes, what emerges are not merely revamped, outmoded concepts, but transformed, dynamic ones, constantly subject to self-reflection, change and diverse interpretations. This means that the mothering image can be imbued with new possibilities, liberated from past restrictions.

In the groups discussed above, it is not accurate to state that there is no critical analysis of femininity, but certainly women's relationship to peace is perceived by these groups as more 'natural' than men's. Yet both ideals of maleness and femaleness have developed desirable and undesirable character traits many of which are derived from perceptions of 'nature'. Just as the feminist demand is made of men to justify their privileged positions, rationales must be provided for women's actions, including any justification of separatism (Thiele, 1985: 15). Yet, within the extremist position, the major explanation given of female uniqueness is that the feminine propensity toward peacefulness provides a focus to channel emotions and life-affirming attributes. It becomes difficult to avoid concluding that all women are naturally peaceful. By this logic, aggressive women can be tolerated more than gentle, caring men, precisely because they are women. This is not a fair comment. I have argued repeatedly that the vision of mature moral identities acknowledges that good, moral characteristics belong to both women and men, whose differences will enhance the richness of life.

Eco-feminism

A more tenable feminist position is presented with 'eco-feminism', a term coined by French writer d'Eaubonne in 1974 to represent women's potential for bringing about an ecological revolution (Green Agenda, 1987: 22). The ecological dimension stresses the need for harmony with nature, that self-reliance and the quality (rather than the quantity) of life are important, that small is beautiful (rather than large being powerful), and that non-violent, diverse approaches are more conducive to improving the quality of life than is aggressive conformity. In seeking to develop harmonious, reciprocal relations with nature, this position's ecological emphasis is similar to that exemplified in green politics. Whereas the peace groups mentioned earlier had tenuous links with feminism, this is a specifically feminist analysis.

The central eco-feminist claim is that there is a clear relation between ecological equilibrium, nuclear disarmament, peace and certain feminist goals. Expressed differently, connections can be drawn between pollution and pornography, militarism and rape, cruise missiles and aggressive competition. For example, the eco-feminist protest at radioactivity given off by the inadequate disposal of nuclear waste is directed toward its association with nuclear warfare, its potential to destroy the soil and water and its association with birth defects, miscarriages, leukemia and cancer. The key to understanding this relation between ecology, feminism and a striving toward peace is through a feminist critique of violence and domination, and through understanding the importance of connections. I take up the issue of domination shortly, in the context of a feminist understanding of war. At this stage I explore the general feminist resistance to violence, not only to women's bodies, but to all living things, as part of a valuing of connectedness. As a point of clarification, many men espouse an ecological sensitivity and a strong resistance to violence. The aim of this analysis is to penetrate the specific feminist motivation that might make an anlysis by women different from an analysis by men.

Eco-feminists identify the prime source of difference as originating within the gender structure. They believe that while society remains deeply sexist, no peace movement can gain substantial results. Eco-feminists maintain that a driving force behind war and the nuclear build-up is a concept of self based not just on domination, but specifically on sexual domination. As outlined, popular masculine notions of aggression, dominance and non-dependence have fed themselves on an arrogant mastery of nature and women, and over women perceived as natural beings. The domination of nature, thus, is linked to the destructiveness inherent in rigid gender divisions. To some extent these divisions rely on women permitting the caring qualities associated with femaleness to be considered natural. In reinforcing the association of women with nature, women's vulnerability to domination increases. I am not suggesting that women participate willingly in their own oppression, although, in some circumstances, powerlessness provides no conspicuous options such as for victims of domestic violence (Burley, 1982). When women become aware of others dominating them, the tolerance of oppression becomes more difficult despite the frequent lack of immediate options. Yet, the struggles people face in being wrapped in interlocking structures of domination are powerful. Breaking the mesh, such as with a woman's decision to leave a violent partner, is difficult, complicated and emotionally draining.

In order to deal with such structures of domination, eco-feminism links feminism, ecology and peace as interrelated facets of a struggle toward an ideal of human community with moral concerns. In an eco-feminist enterprise, the moral concern is directly tied to the elimination of domination and to the centrality of reproduction so that an appreciation of human capacity, rooted in the experience of birth 'helps us to keep before our mind's eye the living reality of singularities, differences, and individualities rather than a human mass as objects of possible control or manipulation' (Elshtain, 1985: 53). The emphasis on reproduction avoids metaphorical imputations on 'Mother Nature' that were invoked in both the conservative and radical exclusivist traditionalist positions discussed earlier. In these positions, the emphasis is on natural purpose and function. An eco-feminist emphasis values the rhythms and processes of life, as being intrinsic to human potential, and is thus relevant to those who are not parents themselves. The stress is on positive growth in contrast with objectification, and on connections in contrast with discrete happenings. The following personal statement is a poignant recognition of this stress. 'The seed of my own eco-feminist consciousness was planted at the burial of a small daughter. Her birth and death opened me to the metabolism of nature and the sense of my own life in its never ending cycle of reciprocity and exchange' (Salleh, 1985: 8). In this context, analyses of reproduction provide the means to expose complex pathological dimensions of mothering that tend to coincide with patriarchy. Again, in extracting the negative dimensions of such pathology, and in critically re-evaluating what remains, a new sense of empowerment for women engaged in such processes is encouraged as the basis for inner strength and personal integrity.

Now, while the gender differentiation in reproductive experiences is culturally universal, the hostility to nature is not (Plumwood, 1986: 130). In subsistence and agricultural communities that depend on nature for survival or a livelihood, natural forces are revered, or minimally, respected. I have explained the western hostility in terms of the stereotypical male drive to produce culture or objective knowledge and to dominate whatever is other—women, children, nature, ideas—either as an attempt to compensate for the creative potential of women, or as an urge toward domination. The result is a tendency toward objectification, and dehumanisation, both components of psychic violence and precursors of physical violence. This objectification, or splitting of the subject and object, comes 'less naturally' when a subject is engaged in the process of nurture of others, where a subject is participating in the growth processes of fellow subjects. The sensibility required for this growth is a harmonious, non-alienated mode of being. While a nurturing sensibility may be more frequently found in women, it is not, as I have repeatedly argued, intrinsically female. Rather, differences in early experiences contribute to different notions of moral identity.

We are talking about a mode of being where there is an effort to transcend instrumental relationships between self, others and nature and where the parts of the relationship 'are symbolised as different, but not opposed elements of a shared community' (Balbus, 1982: 354). When objectification and domination cease to pervert the struggle for recognition, whether this is erotic, dialogic, or concerned to affirm self-identity, then there is a repudiation of a 'them and us' or 'self and other' mentality, and a new vision of non-exploitative interaction emerges. Differences between women and men are not translated into a hierarchical dualism, but can coexist fruitfully with common concerns and sensibilities. For women in particular, this means refusing to be objects of purely sexual or emotional service and to instigate an expression of their own selfhood, in order to pursue meaningful recognition. For men, the process involves reconciling autonomy with intimacy. For both, it involves rejecting conflictual self–other relations, in favour of interdependence. This understanding of relationships translates readily into holistic approaches to nature.

Non-violence

This interdependence is not an easy goal, hence we must spell out the struggles involved in moving towards it. The context for contemporary eco-feminism is a milieu where language includes references to radiation kill-ratios, nuclear proliferation and first-strike capability. As Luther King expresses it, the choices are not between non-violence and violence, but between 'non-violence and non-existence' (Cook and Kirk, 1983: 76). A key organisational concept in eco-feminism is the principle of non-violence. This principle encourages traits similar to those fostered in the women's liberation movement, namely decentralised, nonhierarchical organisation, initiative, interdependence, co-operation, dialogue, mutual support, respect and care. Its specific aim is for improved relationships. The focus for change is tripartite: on individuals, on personal and intimate relations, and on new forms of social community and economic sustainability.

Aside from it organisational benefits, the principle of non-violence provides strategies that make sense of a personal rage directed at the non-fulfilment of human potential or at the exploitation of the natural environment. Let me explain. This rage does not incorporate violence, for there is a deliberate attempt in this perspective to combine legitimate rage with compassion. Confrontation without recourse to violence and aggression assumes that non-violence is at least as accessible a part of human nature as violence has been assumed to be. The emotive basis of the confrontation is undeniable. For example, in the face of media sensationalism, to focus attention solely on the emotional display of women lying in the middle of a railway track, misses the political motivation behind the act, or the underlying reason for it, such as to block a train carrying nuclear waste. Yet, the claim by some extreme feminists that even gentle men are more likely to provoke violence precisely because they are male invokes invalid naturalistic arguments and stifles possibilities of challenging polarised beliefs and practices. Non-violence is an important principle within all holistic practices.

Empowerment
The holistic dimension of an eco-feminist perspective represents a 'politics of connectedness', where actions of any sort affect the continuum of objectification or growth. This connectedness can be understood through the concept of empowerment, the idea of personal strength facilitated through interaction with others. There is a clear difference between power over another and personal power. The former is open to abuse and emanates from an impetus to control knowledge, possessions or persons. In contrast, the realisation of personal power challenges these traditional powers and prompts a general re-evaluation of personal capacities for creating and choosing alternatives that neither oppress others, nor are oppressive in themselves.

There are two obvious reasons why the idea of empowerment is important to feminist theory. First, while not all women are powerless and some women also manipulate and exploit others, many women have experienced daily harassment, abuse and destructiveness where, as victims, they respond to situations rather than define them. Taking control, defining goals and personal boundaries is novel to many women. Just as in individual psychotherapy, internalisation of 'the problem' gives the patient the basis from which to work through a solution, when women realise that part of 'their problem' may lie in their 'self'—in a confused, ill-defined or frustrated self-understanding—the foundation is laid for change. Furthermore, self-empowerment provides a basis from which to challenge those accustomed to having power over others, so that it becomes easier to refuse to co-operate in hierarchical structures of domination and submission. As Gandhi wrote, 'The first principle of non-violent action is that of non-co-operation with everything humiliating' (Shivers, 1982: 188). He writes further, 'if women would realise the strength of non-violence, they would not consent to be called the weaker sex' (1982: 186). For women to capitalise on their moral power and act in defiance of their historical portrayal as victims of male domination is to claim, with legitimacy, active self-determination based on personal empowerment.

The second reason why the idea of empowerment is important to feminist theory is that it appears to conflict with traditional notions of passive, weak femininity. The biblical claim, 'Blessed are the peace-makers' (Matthew, 5: 9), has assumed all sorts of passive connotations, but should be seen as an active principle that necessitates a 'working for peace', a deliberate giving of the self that defies the self-denigration traditionally associated with women. Herein lies part of the problem. Women often believe in their worth to everyone but themselves. The problem lies in the typical equation of female moral power with self-sacrifice adopted by women who see their worth as lying solely in their role as mothers and/or wives. Not all self-sacrifice is dutiful, guilt-appeasing, manipulative, flattering or favour-seeking but it is frequently reducible to these when it lacks the sense of self-worth I am referring to. Change requires an 'unlearning of powerlessness', and taking anger seriously, so that the working through of strong emotions can free us to confront, to expose, and to grow.

This realisation of personal strength with others lays a basis for harmonious existence on more than a private level. Arendt, in questioning the historical consensus that violence is merely the most flagrant manifestation of power, criticises concepts of collective violence or the reduction of politics to domination. Arendt defines power as the human ability to act in concert with others and to begin afresh. Violence not only nullifies this type of power, but guarantees an additional loss—that of the space authentic empowerment requires to flourish. Yet, when citizens act together to break repetitive cycles of violent behaviour, either people's spirits are crushed, as in demonstrations against repressive regimes, or they are empowered. According to Arendt, effective political being is sustained through co-operation among political beings who can trust in the strength of their capacities. For many women, an important prerequisite to participating in co-operative endeavours involves a rejection of self-sacrifice in favour of self-love, a rejection of dominance in favour of active peace. Eco-feminism provides a clear framework in which such empowerment can occur.

The problem in translating this type of personal and communal empowerment into a political arena is due partly to intransigent notions of power, persistently defined in terms of domination or superiority. This problem is forcefully evident in the relationship between political power and gendered power, particularly in the way in which masculinity, military capacity and civic personality coexist. By 'civic personality' I mean what philosophy traditionally views as the 'good citizen'. It is relatively straightforward to demonstrate that power has been embedded in the typical masculine undertakings intrinsic to war, such as aggression, conquest and domination. In demonstrating this, it is understandable why some feminists might disregard the idea of political power entirely. If it can be demonstrated further that such power is not merely a form of masculine power, but is more insidiously immersed in our ideals of civic personality, then the task is to expose and denounce such ideals of power, while simultaneously isolating the dimensions of civic ideals that have or have not been affected by such tendencies.

After the preceding analysis of women's involvement in peace movements, an exploration into ideals of war may appear strange. It is not. Questions about masculinity, war and domination connect with central ideals of the philosophical tradition, such as moral being, selfhood, autonomy, treatment of other individuals, concern with universal moral principles and the insistence on transcending private interests. Lloyd argues that any 'claim that citizenship has been hitherto masculine only because of a perverse desire to exclude women from status and power, while war is somehow masculine on a deeper level, overlooks these conceptual connections, and fails to confront the full dimensions of the maleness of western political ideals' (1986: 64). In exploring these connections, albeit briefly, it will become clear that concepts of selfhood are intermeshed with expectations of military defence and citizenship. To explain the symbolic representation behind these ideals, I examine what is meant by the 'manliness of war' and then what is at stake with the admittance of women to combat positions.

The manliness of war

The links between military participation, ideals of masculinity and citizenship are not accidental, particularly when consolidated into public ideals. Hartsock shows the influence of the notion of 'eros' in perceptions of war as a 'manly pursuit' (1984). She defines the range of eros broadly to include the erotic fusion, sensuality, and creativity of the spirit. She suggests that there is a masculine eroticism which forms a part of military valour and it is defined predominantly as competition for dominance. Similarly, in ancient Greek texts, political power is directly associated with masculinity, particularly in the personage of the warrior-hero. To the Homeric warriors, in the *Illiad*, heroism on the battlefield is the supremely masculine role.[2] It leads to the enjoyment of public esteem, and, through this, to ideas of immortality. The emphasis on public reputation means that to 'lose face' is tantamount to losing one's moral identity, where loss is defined as a capitulation to bodily or emotional concerns, or is defined as 'acting like a woman'. When there is a striving to rise above what women symbolically represent as particular natural entities, in favour of the glories of spirit, reason, or universal concerns, there is a tendency not only to reject a female principle or force, but to reject women themselves.

To cite an example of such a rejection, we recall Plato's works where spiritual activity is valued, and the body is seen to inhibit it. Diotima, in teaching Socrates the art of love, informs him that the object of love is the birth of beauty in body or soul. Those pregnant in body, achieve an immortality through their offspring, 'but souls which are pregnant—for there certainly are men who are more creative in their souls than in their bodies—conceive that which is proper for the soul to conceive' (1955: *Symposium*, 264), namely wisdom and virtue. To Plato, fecundity and the state of 'being pregnant' are insignificant, compared to the mental activity of men's achievement of wisdom or immortality. A 'good woman' can share immortality in a limited sense by surrendering sons to 'significant deaths' on the battlefield. This represents a higher mode of giving birth.

A historical jump to Rousseau provides a good illustration of the demand that citizens suppress the particularities of personal life. He provides an account of what it means to be a citizen. 'A Spartan mother had five sons with the army. A Helot arrived; trembling she asked his news, "Your five sons are slain." "Vile slave, was that what I asked thee?" "We have won the victory." She hastened to the temple to render thanks to the gods. That was a citizen' (1977: 8). It is her interest in the progress of battle that signals her virtue as a citizen, not any personal concern. Rousseau does not endorse this chilling suppression of natural emotion. His version of a good society requires close associations between nature and motherhood. This demands women's exclusion from the public realm in order to protect it from uncontrolled passion and to protect those 'female natural feelings' from the corruptions of public life. Femininity is thus constituted by being contained, excluded from the public, the very realm wherein our Homeric hero gained recognition. Despite its horrors, women do support the warriorhood of their fathers, brothers, lovers, sons and friends.

How does war offer the prospect of achieving 'true selfhood'? Kant talks of war as having something 'sublime' about it. For him, the sense of the sublime highlights what differentiates humans from mere nature. The perceived superiority of reason over imagination comes again to the fore. 'The sublime is what pleases immediately through its opposition to the interest of sense' (1951: 107). Contemplation of the sublime is almost likened to moral consciousness. Kant's association of war with the sublime links it with the consciousness of universality and autonomous selfhood. In answering the question as to what people admire, Kant defines the soldier as 'a man who shrinks from nothing, who fears nothing' yet who exhibits 'all the virtues of peace, gentleness, compassion' (1951: 102). It is not that Kant endorses war, but he makes it clear that it elicits the mature stages of reason's development, particularly by evoking the capacity to transcend nature. Attempts to transcend nature, through conquering it, lead to the domination of whatever is defined as nature—women, physical environments or instinctive passion.

That power and sexuality are frequently intertwined is incontestable. Returning to Hartsock's central notion of the eros of the masculine citizen, it is noteworthy that she suggests that typical erotic fusion takes the form of the search for the conquest of the other's will. The conquest involves some subjugation of sensuality to rationality. This subjugation does not underestimate the importance of sensual pleasure or spontaneous inclinations to hedonism, but tends to place even these inclinations under the rubric of a calculating mentality. Additionally, while such a mentality does not directly devalue the children born to women and the processes necessary for their nurture, it grants public esteem to what can be 'born' to minds uncontaminated by physical necessities. Intrinsic to the conquest of the will and the calculating mentality is a 'rational violence' (Benjamin, 1980: 167), whereby self-boundaries are established by negating the other. The rational character of this violence relates to calculative control by the violator who employs, through whatever means, the will of the violated. In personal relationships this not only repudiates dependency and intimacy, but also avoids any consequences of isolation, through retaining possession of another as an object.

In the political community this conquest is embodied in the role of 'hero warrior', one of the few unique roles to men in modern society. With this role, a military and nuclear mentality is contiguous with a persisting patriarchal consciousness. The critical determining feature of this consciousness is a dualistic representation of the world which lends itself readily to oppositional approaches and a personal detachment from the full range of human emotions. Both patriarchy and military pursuits use violence (psychological or physical) and assert the need to control. Parallels can be drawn between domestic violence, rape, pornography, incest, sexist discrimination and misogyny, and the more public manifestations of militarism, economic imperialism and the nuclear build-up, in terms of either violence or the urge to dominate. I want to make a distinction between a justified defence force that has a prime preservatory purpose, and a militarism and nuclearism that surge for ever increasing supremacy, through the possession of more powerful weapons. I shall explain how the latter frequently influences the former.

The systematic dehumanisation of people is one such instance. A preoccupation with size, power, control and achievement is often not concerned whether one humiliates or degrades another in the process of achieving desired goals. The common root between sexism and militarism is a dualistic conception of the 'Other', be it women, land, ideas, tribal or foreign enemies. In stories about basic training and combat, men frequently admit that a major purpose of basic training 'is to dehumanise a male to the point where he will kill on demand' (Michalowski, 1982: 327). Misogynist obscenities are used to intensify violent sensations in training fighters, to reinforce the coincidence of violence and virility. Consider the following remark about a man who had contributed to the pregnancy of several women: 'That guy doesn't shoot any blanks' (Kokopeli and Lakey, 1982: 233). When aggressive dominance is equated with masculinity, sexuality is linked with military function. Psychological control is achieved by threatening sexual identity. Any sign of weakness or submission is seen to be 'like a woman' and as a capitulation from the masculine cause. The most extreme association of violence and masculine virility is gang rape in war, where the last man to rape a woman shoots her—rape being an assertion of perverse power (Brownmiller, 1975). A militarist mentality posits the choices as coercive force and public success or cowardice and failure. Conflict-resolution skills, like compromise, empathy and reciprocal bargaining, are interpreted as 'soft'. Attempts to explain this mentality as intrinsic to the 'manliness of war' go deeper than a mere assertion that it is manly to defend the weak. It affirms the combatant as becoming a 'real man' as a fulfilment of citizenship rights.

Women in combat

Within such a context, what lies behind women's involvement in the military? We need to draw together moral intention and moral action. This moral scrutiny is like the central paradox of deterrence, where one cannot 'refuse to decouple the morality of a threat from the morality of the action threatened' (Okin, 1983: 17). We have argued above that in many political milieus, an involvement in (or willingness to be engaged in) military pursuits has been an integral part of active citizenship. Most feminists would agree that the wider demands of equal citizenship should demand no special exemptions from civil duties for women, and no special privileges of civil rights reserved exclusively for men. In regard to the question of admitting women into combat, complications arise with this response to equality precisely because of the assumed contribution of 'natural' aggression by the male combatant. We approach this question from two slants, from the perspective of an emphasis on equal rights and from that of an assertion of the pacifying effect of women. My purpose is to understand further the intermeshing of gender, selfhood and citizenship.

Equal right to combat
The idea that political equality for women should include the right and duty to bear arms appears puzzling to some for it sits incongruously with traditional ideas and ideals of femininity—ideals of women as passively dependant on male protection and lacking the character traits of courage and persistence (Lloyd, 1986: 64). This seeming incongruence must be discussed alongside the dangers of uncritically demanding equality with men while not scrutinising the nature of the equality being striven for. Indeed, the emphasis on equality under current discussion may be a misplaced emphasis—just as most women would suggest that the decision concerning an abortion should not be an equal one between women and men. Hence, we are addressing the issue of equality, the focus of equality and the question of individual rights. If particular character traits required for the military can be shown to be morally objectionable, then access in itself may be questionable.

A counter argument to the equal right to combat could point out that the type of female authority feminists are striving for as a character ideal is not likely to emerge just from granting women formal equality of rights, and especially not from granting them the right to participate in combat. If equality simply means sameness, then this lacks reflection on what one is demanding equality of. Take the example of senior executive positions. Equal opportunity for some women may mean the same opportunity as men to receive senior positions, for others having equal access, or even the right to decline high-stress positions. Flexibility absorbs the possibility of different priorities into equal opportunities, instead of an insistence on sameness. The question concerns both equality and rights. Just as most citizens do not desire the equal right to terrorise or to torture, and most people would refute the validity of calling these 'rights', we need to question whether all the 'rights' men have had access to are morally desirable rights, or rights conducive to human flourishing. Hence, the argument that the military is irremediably sexist and misogynist may show that women soldiers might be morally harmed in an institution that replicates gender hierarchy, and hence that efforts to struggle for an equal right to combat may not be fruitful. The suggestion that this conclusion adopts a defeatist position regarding military sexism may reflect realism and not undue pessimism.

Yet the dismissal of women's right to fight, by claiming that those who want to fight are merely 'masculinist exceptions' who threaten the symbolic association of women with creation and preservation, is a product of a tradition that, in its exclusion of women from full citizenship rights, necessarily casts them as exceptions. The unreflective praise of such exceptions ignores the historical constitution of femininity which has been defined through exclusion and in opposition to masculinity.

Hence, the struggle for the right to participate in combat and command troops has symbolic significance for women, who have been seen as being in need of men's protection. Attempts in 'dividing the protector from protected, defender from defended is a linchpin of masculinist as well as military ideology' (Ruddick, 1983a: 472). Furthermore, excuses that women in the military are too weak, too psychologically volatile or too much trouble to men are inadequate. Nevertheless, the difficulties of reconciling feminist goals with militarist aims appear extensive. The distinction made earlier between the military as a defence unit, and militarism as a movement motivated by an urge to control is important. While I justify the preservatory motivations, I reject the surge for domination. Nevertheless, what is seen by some feminists as the importance of establishing the right to engage in combat has led to a focus on feminist goals *within* the military establishment, rather than on the option of simply withdrawing in protest against its assumed masculinist ideology.

There is particular symbolic significance in demonstrating women's ability in an institution where masculine ideology has been crystalised because it challenges a philosophical claim for full equality, citizenship and self-respect. These claims focus on the relation between moral integrity, equality and rights. As noted, there is a philosophical distinction between moral rights and obligations. A right must be extendable at least in principle to all. The possession of rights in most cases precedes reference to the duties such possession might entail, even if dutiful entailments are part of the larger context in which rights-talk finds its place. The point is that, with respect to rights, responsibility is expected of their possessors only if the rights are exercised. It is through exercise that duties and obligations arise. But here the exercise of rights remains optional, that is, one can choose not to act upon rights to which one is fully entitled without moral approbation. There is, by way of contrast, no such option with moral obligations, which are imperative and binding on moral agents. Not to fulfil one's moral obligations is to fail in one's duty as a moral being. Given this distinction between rights and obligations, an emphasis on rights in the context of our present discussion means that 'a right to fight does not itself entail the duty to serve...A feminist may claim the right for women to participate in combat but believe that it is almost always wrong for anyone of either sex to take up arms' (Ruddick, 1983a: 472). Ruddick's point is that a moral decision to renounce weapons depends on the prior right to take up arms.

But what, we could ask, is the point of possessing a right one may never want to pursue, or that one may deliberately reject? The important answer is that the denial of the initial right leaves one powerless and, in this instance, suggests a further example where rights of citizenship have not always been extended to women. On the other hand, to have a right presupposes equal status and a respect for an individual's choice in taking up or rejecting the right. In short, one's integrity as a moral identity is at stake here. The distinctions between defence and militarism, rights and obligations have practical implications. In the case of defending one's country, as distinct from superpower strivings, for women to claim the right to combat means they too have a responsibility to participate in defence. I consider that the most significant counter-argument to granting the right of women to combat and military participation is the one concerning the probability that women will be induced to accept the most negative definitions of ideal masculinity, that is, definitions of brute strength, aggression, abstract objectification and, ultimately, masculine ideals of citizenship. If this is the consequence of an equal right to combat, it fails to evaluate morally the nature of this right, and what consequences flow from adopting such 'equality'.

Pacifying effect of women
A second response to the question of admitting women into combat declares that it is not outrageous to suggest that by drafting women 'in the interests of peace' both feminists and antimilitarists could be satisfied. That is, this position contends that the presence of women within the military is likely to have a pacifying effect. This contention brings into focus once again the issue of women's putative 'special nature'. Peacefulness is assumed to be a feminine attribute, whereas warriorhood is in most cultures explicitly connected to masculinity and to ideal notions of being. Young soldiers, wanting to avoid accusations of feminisation, often welcome war as a rite of passage to prove their 'machismo' and adulthood. Given the strong masculinist ideology within the military, is it possible that women's presence may alter the values that help to direct military strategy?

Both men and women generally tend to believe that women are more peaceful than men. As I have repeatedly argued, this association between women and peace should not be construed as evidence of an essential female nature. Rather, many of women's salient 'differences' indicate cognitive styles that derive from women's social location. I have demonstrated why women tend to develop preservative love as a practical, caring valuing of persons, particularly when, as mothers, women have been engaged in conserving the fragile, reconciling differences, and maintaining harmony. This attitude involves a respect for conditions conducive to growth and a notion that domination acts contrary to such conditions. Viewed by Murdoch's 'eye of love' (1971: 95, 99), military fantasies of violent control and domination are repulsive, for the fulfilment of such fantasies endangers what caring people seek to preserve. Yet while preservation and humility are valuable in themselves, sentimentalising such traits ignores their historical constitution, that is, the extent to which they have developed in response to women's exclusion from public life. The suggestion that these traits could be given a new and positive expression within military ranks is questionable, not least because of their evolution within a situation of exclusion and inequality.

We need to keep questioning the nature of the differences women might be expected to introduce within the military. For example, peaceful women might have different conceptions of 'what it means to "win" a battle, what counts as an "acceptable" loss, what makes for a "just war"' (Ruddick, 1983a: 478). Yet one wonders what would be the motivation for 'peaceful women' to join. Furthermore, documentaries that include personal accounts of participation in war provide evidence that some men are affected profoundly by the callousness of wartime destructiveness, in a similar way to that in which it is assumed that most women would be affected.

Perhaps the crucial factor here for both men and women is the extent to which the interconnection or interdependence of people is seen to be at the root of moral life and to provide its basic framework. For, if a moral framework of interdependence is widely accepted so that it is appreciated that all humans require recognition by others as persons, we might anticipate a considerable tempering of the tendency to objectify people as less than fully human which so often allows blithe justifications of war. The problem is that the importance of interdependence can be asserted in partial or distorted ways that fail to extend recognition to everyone. It can appear, for instance, in exclusivist, parochial or chauvinistic guises where it is associated with specific nationalist movements, cultural identities, political causes and the like. In these situations, the mutual recognition of persons as persons applies only to those who belong to the same cause, and it is easy to consider outsiders as deficient in basic humanity, or as a threat to some cherished identity, and to objectify them accordingly.

With this objectification, a dissociation from the moral significance of violent actions, such as is required in the military, permits a compartmentalisation of certain aspects of morality and behaviour, so that one can act without questioning what one is doing, or for what purpose. There is a connection between abstract approaches to people as objects and a capacity to engage uncritically in military involvement. A loyalty to abstract causes permits a generalised hatred for an enemy, envisaged in abstract form simply as 'the enemy'. This abstract conceptualisation lessens the moral impact of the consequences of acts of hostility. The easier it is to distance oneself from the personal consequences of destruction, the easier it is to engage in destructive activities. If this is so then those attracted into the military forces would be those who readily project themselves beyond the realm of particularities, and can engage without excessive inner disturbance in practices requiring aggression, conquest, domination and destruction.

Indeed, Ministries of Defence and army medical personnel have been reluctant to acknowledge the reality of combat related 'Post Traumatic Stress Disorder'. Soldiers suffering from trauma experience combat fatigue, nightmares, sleep disorders, rage, guilt, shell shock and flashbacks tied in with images of their experiences, particularly with the processes of killing and the visual impact of dead and mutilated bodies. Memories of a rifle noise or an explosion can be triggered by a car backfiring, leading to an immediate distressing response. The cult of army machismo, with its intense peer pressure to suppress any admission of emotional sensitivity has, until recently, stifled community awareness of the human tragedy in many soldiers' lives.

I argue that it is not likely women could act as a force for peace within the military for two major reasons. First, it is more likely that the type of women attracted to the military would be those prepared to perpetuate its ideology and practices rather than to act as a critical or a subversive force. That is, their general motivations are probably not dissimilar to the men who join or are conscripted, but the explicit reasons why women might pursue military prestige may differ. Certainly, a female ruthlessness that suppresses the emotive personal dimensions is essential to military success. The desire for such success might be an overreaction to accepted notions of submissive femininity. The traditional male posture is disposed to objectify the other, whereas the traditional female posture disposes women to accept objectification (Benjamin, 1980: 167). A rejection of submission may unwittingly translate into objectification which is interpreted as protectiveness. Protectiveness may be welcomed readily into public institutions concerned with welfare, health, or education, for instance. In the case of defence forces, however, while they are protective, they must be prepared to attack. Any pacifying force that may exist in either women or men is rendered negligible.

Second, the assertion of women's pacifying tendencies raises the problem of reinforcing gender stereotypes. This type of feminist theorising may aptly be situated 'inside the broader frames of beautiful souls and just warriors as features of inherited discourse' (Elshtain, 1985: 47). The problem with this inheritance is that the 'beautiful soul' position celebrates an ontologically given feminine principle: affiliant, nurturing and peaceful. An extreme feminist

191

appropriation of this principle sees men not merely as 'just warriors', but as aggressive beasts. Both the principle and the appropriation of the principle are blatantly inaccurate. They incorporate a dual essentialism, and ignore the balance I have stressed is crucial in articulating the dimensions of *both* femininity and masculinity which either distorts or enhances humanity. Furthermore, the implications of such an appropriation deepens prevailing segregations by enjoining women to associate in separate communities based on the values they embrace, free from callous, disconnected males. Just as all women do not necessarily conform to the naturalistic assumptions made about them, likewise not all soldiers are necessarily heartlessly aggressive. If we imagine our husbands, lovers, fathers, brothers, sons or male friends in situations of forced conscription or emergency defence, many of us believe they would humanise their opponents, would be repulsed by much of the killings, would see in concrete form the physical and potential psychic damage of violence, and would do everything possible to preserve their comrades. The poetic writings of Owen are a perfect example of this type of empathy. His poem *Insensibility* is a passionate diatribe against those who 'By choice...made themselves immune/ To pity and whatever mourns in man' (1971: 38).

In this chapter, I have looked at a practical example of some women's claims to difference, namely their active pursuit of peace. I have also looked at some women's rejection of this pursuit in favour of an equal right to combat. Clearly, not all women are peaceful and not all men are dominating. Nevertheless, I maintain that the most significant contribution of this affirmation of difference lies in the potential of 'thinking about peace maternally' (Ruddick, 1987: 248). This affirmation is not the exclusive prerogative of women, but its uniqueness lies in the predominance of it in the lives of women who care for children. As such, men who contribute in a meaningful manner to the care of others can learn from this affirmation of difference and, to a large degree, replicate it themselves. I do not want to romanticise mothering, or the fact that the constraints of poverty, racism or abuse act as forces of violence in many women's lives. Rather, I want to conclude by drawing on the strengths of maternal peace.

As Ruddick (1987) points out, children are vulnerable and this vulnerability tends to elicit either aggression or care. Because the deliberate damaging of children counts as personal failure in contradicting the protection and nurturance that defines maternal work (1987: 249), mothers tend to avoid protracted violence toward their children. Furthermore, wanting the love of their children, they know the 'cost of dominating is paid in the fear and hatred of the dominated' (1987: 254). Mothers' own position in relation to conflict often shifts from powerlessness in relation to their partners and society generally, to power in relation to their children who exploit their emotional vulnerability by alternately accepting powerlessness by being submissive, or by asserting power and behaving unco-operatively.

While mothers generally strive to keep the peace by removing causes for battle, like a disputed marble, or an uneven distribution of chocolate, and by teaching principles of self-respect, honesty and equity, fighting is also an important part of mothers' lives. They fight on behalf of their children against neighbours, teachers and health workers and they teach children to defend themselves. Mothers' peace-making is not concerned with abstract causes but is 'embedded in particular passions for particular children and for the particular people and groups of people on whom those children depend' (Ruddick, 1987: 250). It is firmly situated within specific communities, with shifting differentials of power. What it has to teach us is that 'peace is a way of living in which participants counting on connection demand a great deal of each other' (1987: 253). This task of actively working for peace through one's interactions is radical in its unique base, its challenge to the idea that peace is passive and violence is acceptable, and in its applicability to all children, women and men who seek harmoniously to affirm their moral identities.

NOTES

1 I want to stress that this is particularly a Western occurrence. Lowe (1986) writes how in the language of an ethnic group living in the hinterland of Mindoro in the Philippines, the Hanunoo people there have no words for war, aggression, hatred and anger. 'You could slap their faces and they would not respond'. Marcos' economic patronage to favoured cronies resulted in an invasion of industrialists and miners who stole their land, depriving them of their livelihood. The Hanunoo now know the meaning of the words war, aggression, hatred and anger.

2 The *Illiad* gives an account of Alexandros, son of Priam, King of Troy, who took Helen of Sparta back to Troy as his wife. The princes of Greece took ships manned by fighters with a view to force the return of Helen. The Greeks remained before Troy for nine years, storming, plundering and eventually destroying Troy, according to 'the will of the gods'. The text is full of the language of slaughter of brothers, fathers, sons, quarrels, duels, truces, courage, strength and spirit.

Conclusion:
Women, men and
moral identity

To conclude, I want to summarise my argument by answering three questions. First, what difference should one expect in the moral philosophy practiced by women?[1] Secondly, does feminist moral philosophy enlighten us on the nature of moral identity generally, or only on that of women's specific identity? Thirdly, what does it mean to be a moral subject and to affirm one's moral identity?

To answer the first question, it seems undoubtedly true that in the relevant literature the tone and content of the writings does reiterate 'the voice Gilligan heard, made reflective and philosophical' (Baier, 1985: 53). Feminist philosophers, concerned to articulate ideals of moral identity are positing new visions of moral maturity based on re-evaluated character traits. Yet it is probably also true to say that what is needed is a central concept around which to structure a comprehensive moral theory which, as Baier suggests, 'might accommodate these moral insights women tend to have more readily than men...(and yet be) acceptable both to reflective women and to reflective men' (1985: 56). This suggestion invites two further responses. Some feminist philosophers might not accept that women want a moral theory that accommodates both men and women, a point I disagree with and take up in answering questions two and three. Others might also argue that Gilligan's ethic of care and responsibility acts as an adequate concept to which emergent literature can respond.

For example, Baier hypothesises that a theory most expressive of women's insights and concerns would centre on an 'ethic of love' combined with men's preoccupation with 'obligations' and that the connecting concept could be 'appropriate trust'. This concept does mediate between reason and feeling and is concerned primarily with relations, co-operation, recognition of duties and moral virtues. It resembles Blum's notion of 'true compassion' which he argues spurs us 'to a deeper understanding...than rationality alone could ensure' (1980: 516). Yet, with Baier's 'trust', I sense a 'Gilligan convergence', premised on gender traits not open to radical change. While it is an important response of current theory to reinstate women's unique contribution into the larger body of moral theory, I see dangers in convergence solutions, or solutions that appear as such. A converging concept seems to merge the best qualities of traditional femininity with the best of traditional masculinity and then call the result 'human'. This lacks a critical questioning of sexual difference and of ambiguity and cannot stand as a viable alternative. To me, the crucial distinguishing feature of feminist moral philosophy is that it explains the uniqueness of *being woman* or of *being man* as well as of *being human*. Thus I use the idea of *self-in-relations* as the most adequate concept to elucidate the moral identity of women and of men.

This answers my second question as to whether feminist moral theory enlightens us on the nature of moral identity generally or only on that of women's specifically. In terms of a comprehensive moral theory of identity, I assume the basic similarity between men and women. An articulation of our *commonality* as moral subjects needs, thus, to cover the experiences of *both* women and men. It seems to me to make sense theoretically, logically and strategically to delineate clearly the potential of human identity and then to examine what difference the differences really make. To this end, I take seriously the contingent *differences* of our moral identity, without polarising these differences or ethical ideals along gender lines.

My method for doing this is as a dialectician, to point to syntheses that overcome the one-sidedness of various views. The resolution of moral dilemmas arising from conflicts between nature and purpose, reason and passion, individuality and sociality, rights and responsibilities, care and justice is complex; humans are complex; deciding how to make satisfactory decisions is complex. Rather than pessimistically concluding that conflict and antagonism are inevitable responses to such complexities, arising tensions should be weighed so that choices can balance respect for self-autonomy with respect for the autonomy of others.

To extend the above examples, when nature and purpose lose their static connotations, they both can be reinterpreted to build on the natural characteristics women and men share, like rationality, emotionality, intention and agency while leaving enough scope for the individual interpretation of how a rational, emotional, motivated agent purposefully responds. Similarly, our reason not only informs our passions and vice-versa but they mutually enhance each other. Individuality is confirmed through sociality, and sociality is not just the sum of its parts but is constituted through the distinctiveness of particular individuals. If we have the right to individual claims for justice and equality we have the responsibility to ensure these claims consider the social requirements of attachments to others and equity.

The attempt to find a manageable, *personal and political synthesis* requires a sensitivity to contextual detail. This is not a relativism that has significance only in relation to context or to individual preference, but it involves a struggle with the uncertainties about understanding and interpreting complex principles and their possible ramifications given each new context. Working toward a synthesis acts to break the hegemony of traditional thought structures and the gender-differentiated practices that rely on dualistic assumptions, by acknowledging new moral tensions, new combinations of possible solutions and new forms of subjectivity. This provides a framework for an emancipatory ethic that is holistic in dealing with general identity and sex-specific dimensions of identity.

What, then, does it mean to embrace this emancipatory ethic? What does it mean to be a moral subject and to affirm one's identity? The simple answer is that there *are* alternatives to ideas of the self that are suppressive, limiting, indecisive or defined by others, even if the struggles involved in achieving satisfactory alternatives are manifold. I posit the alternative notion of modern identity as a self-interpreting being who poses the question, 'how can I know myself?' in a way that avoids scientific objectivism and yet moves beyond subjectivism. That is, it provides ample scope for variances in moral identity, without indiscriminately letting everything in. While being open-ended, it is also evaluative. The self-knowledge of this moral agent is a knowledge grounded in ethical principles and everyday context, that draws on shared values as well as personal experience and individual meanings, and yet seeks to avoid a conflict between individuality and community by trying to ascertain, with others, what common purposes might aid the mutual development of human potential.

The key to affirming this notion of moral identity lies in arduous but worthwhile *dialogue* to determine *shared values, common purposes* and the conditions whereby *human potential* might be realised. Then we can increase the appreciation of our *commonality with others* and our *differences from others*. I argue that the central concept in this idea of moral identity is that of *self-in-relations*. This narrative sense of self confirms individuality and the social basis of our selfhood through the intermeshing of personal histories. To acknowledge that our moral identity is intrinsically connected to the inhibition or growth of significant others is to place identity within a dynamic position. Where there is the desire for identity to flourish, the self is given the impetus to wrestle with tensions inhibiting self-growth. While there is a responsibility both to self and to others, the moral filter is the person's sense of identity, for to violate personal identity undermines self-respect (Taylor, 1976: 289–296; Meyers, 1987: 151).

Thus, in developing our own individuality we must respect the individuality of others and resolve moral dilemmas in a way that minimises hurt. Reciprocity ensures such a respect. With reciprocal relations, it is not just individual selves considering each other, but a true interconnection between self and other, mutually reinforcing each other. Such a context encourages healthy, flourishing relationships, and permits a balance of roles between acting and supporting, recognising other moral selves, and being recognised as a moral identity. I have suggested ways in which women and men as moral subjects can share the balance of such a mutual recognition. To build on the shared components of moral identity and to help others explore exciting, plural modes of being encourages the growth of distinctive qualities and addresses the whole of moral identity.

NOTES

1 Baier (1985) cites as examples Elizabeth Anscombe's work on intention, Sissela Bok's work on lying and secrecy, Claudia Card on mercy, Cora Diamond on animals, Marilyn Fyre, Philippa Foot on moral virtue, Virginia Held, Alison Jaggar, Sabina Lovibond, Ruth Barcan Marcus on moral dilemmas, Mary Midgley, Iris Murdoch, Gabrielle Taylor on pride, love and integrity, Jenny Teichman on illegitimacy, and Susan Wolf.

Bibliography

Addelson, Kathryn Pyne (1987) 'Moral Passages' in Kittay and Meyers (eds), *Women and Moral Theory* New Jersey: Rowman and Littlefield

Adorno, Theodor et al. (1950) *The Authoritarian Personality* New York: Harper and Row Publishers

Adorno, Theodor et al., and Max Horkheimer (1979) *Dialectic of Enlightment*, trans. J. Cumming, London: Verso

Allen, Christine Garside (1976) 'Sex Identity and Personal Identity' in King-Farlow and Shea (eds) *Values and the Quality of Life* New York: Science History Publications

—— (1979) 'Can a Woman Be Good in the Same Way as a Man?' in Osborne (ed.) *Woman in Western Thought* New York: Random House

Aquinas, Thomas (1963–1975) *Summa Theologiae*, 60 Vols., trans. Dominican Fathers, Blackfriars ed., London: Eyre and Spottiswoode

Arblaster, Anthony (1985) *The Rise and Decline of Western Liberalism* London: Basil Blackwell

Ardener, Shirley (ed.) (1975) *Perceiving Women* London: Malaby Press

Arendt, Hannah (1974) *The Human Condition* Chicago: The University of Chicago Press

Aristotle (1972) *The Politics*, trans. T.A. Sinclair, London: Penguin Books

—— (1977) *The Nicomachean Ethics*, trans. J.A.K. Thomson, London: Penguin Books

—— (1979) *De Generatione Animalium* in Osborne (ed.) *Woman in Western Thought* New York: Random House

Augros, Robert and Stanciu, George (1987) *The New Biology. Discovering the Wisdom in Nature* Boston: New Scientific Library

Augustine, St (1887) *Select Library of Nicene Fathers,* trans. A.W. Haddan and W.G.T. Shedd, London: Buffalo

Baier, Annette C. (1985) 'What do Women Want in a Moral Theory?' *Noûs,* Vol. XIX, No. 1, pp. 53–63

Balbus, Isaac D. (1982) *Marxism and Domination, A Neo-Hegelian, Feminist, Psychoanalytic Theory of Sexual, Political and Technological Liberation* Princeton: Princeton University Press

Baldock, Cora V. and Cass Bettina (eds) (1983) *Women, Social Welfare and the State* Sydney: George Allen and Unwin

Banks, Olive (1982) *Faces of Feminism, A Study of Feminism as a Social Movement* Oxford: Martin Robertson

Barrett, Michèle (1980) *Women's Oppression Today, Problems in Marxist Feminist Analysis* London: Verso

Bartky, Sandra Lee (1981) 'Toward a Phenomenology of Feminist Consciousness' in Vetterling-Braggin et al., (eds) *Feminism and Philosophy* New Jersey: Littlefield, Adams and Co.

Bedau, Hugo Adam (1968) 'The Right to Life', *Monist*, 52, pp. 550–572

Benhabib, Seyla (1987) 'The Generalized and the Concrete Other: The Kohlberg-Gilligan Controversy and Feminist Theory' in Kittay and Meyers (eds) *Women and Moral Theory* New Jersey: Rowman and Littlefield

Benjamin, Jessica (1978) 'Authority and the Family Revisited: or A world without Fathers?', *New German Critique*, Vol. 13, pp. 35–57

—— (1980) 'The Bonds of Love: Rational Violence and Erotic Domination', *Feminist Studies*, 6, No. 11, pp. 144–174

—— (1981) *Internalisation and Instrumental Culture: A Reinterpretation of Psychoanalysis and Social Theory* Michigan: University Microfilms International

Berger, Peter L. and Luckmann, Thomas (1976) *The Social Construction of Reality. A Treatise in the Sociology of Knowledge* London: Penguin Books

Berger, Pamela (1985) *The Goddess Obscured: Transformation of the Grain Protectress from Goddess to Saint* Boston: Beacon

Berlin, Isaiah (1969) *Four Essays on Liberty* Oxford: Oxford University Press

Bernstein, Richard J. (1983) *Beyond Objectivism and Relativism: Science, Hermeneutics, and Praxis* Oxford: Basil Blackwell

Bible (1971) *Revised Standard Version* Oxford: Oxford University Press

Birke, Lynda (1986) *Women, Feminism and Biology* Sussex: Wheatsheaf Books

Bishop, Margaret (1982) 'Feminist Spirituality and Nonviolence in McAllister (ed.) *Reweaving the Web of Life* Philadelphia: New Society Publishers

Blum, Lawrence (1980) 'Compassion' in Rorty (ed.) *Explaining Emotions* Berkeley: University of California Press.

—— (1982) 'Kant's and Hegel's Moral Rationalism: A Feminist Perspective', *Canadian Journal of Philosophy*, Vol. XII, No. 2, pp. 287–302

Bologh, Roslyn Wallach (1984) 'Feminist Social Theorizing and Moral Reasoning: On Difference and Dialectic', in Randall Collins (ed.) *Sociological Theory, 1984* San Francisco: Jossey-Bass Publishers pp. 373–393

Braidotti, Rosi (1986) 'Ethics revisited: Women and/in philosophy' in Pateman and Gross (eds) *Feminist Challenges* Sydney: Allen & Unwin

Braun, C.M.J. and Baribeau, J.M.C. (1978) 'Subjective Idealism in Kohlberg's Theory of Moral Development: A Critical Analysis', *Human Development*, 21, pp. 289–301

Breakwell, Glynis M. (1979) 'Woman: Group and Identity?' *Women's Studies International Quarterly*, Vol. 2, pp. 9–17

Brennan, Teresa and Pateman, Carole (1979) 'Mere Auxiliaries to the Commonwealth: Women and the Origins of Liberalism', *Political Studies*, Vol. 27, No. 2, pp. 183–200.

Brody, Charles (1984) 'Differences by Sex in Support for Nuclear Power', *Social Forces*, Vol. 63, No. 1

Broughton, John M. (1983) 'Women's Rationality and Men's Virtues: A Critique of Gender Dualism in Gilligan's Theory of Moral Development', *Social Research*, Vol. 50, No. 3, pp. 597–642

Brownmiller, Susan (1975) *Against our will: men, women and rape* New York: Simon and Schuster

Brubaker, Rogers (1984) *The Limits of Rationality, An Essay on the Social and Moral Thought of Max Weber* London: George Allen and Unwin

Burley, Jennifer (1982) *Stop Press* Victoria: Greenhouse Publications

Burris, Val (1984) 'The Meaning of the Gender Gap: A Comment on Goertzel', *Journal of Political and Military Sociology*, Vol. 12

Caldecott, Leonie and Leland, Stephanie (eds) (1983) *Reclaim the Earth* London: The Women's Press

Caplan, Arthur L. (ed.) (1978) *The Sociobiology Debate* New York: Harper and Row

Capra, Fritjof (1982) *The Turning Point: Science, Society and the Rising Culture* London: Wildwood

Chesler, Phyllis (1980) *About Men* Toronto: Bantam Books

Chodorow, Nancy (1971) 'Being and Doing: A Cross-cultural Examination of the Socialisation of Males and Females' in Gornick and Moran (eds) *Woman in Sexist Society* New York: Basic Books, Inc., Publishers

—— (1978) *The Reproduction of Mothering, Psychoanalysis and the Sociology of Gender* Berkeley: University of California Press

—— (1979) 'Family Structure and Female Personality' in Rosaldo and Lamphere (eds) *Woman, Culture and Society* Stanford California: Stanford University Press

—— (1980) 'Gender, Relations, and Difference in Psychoanalytic Perspective' in Eisenstein and Jardine (eds) *The Future of Difference* Boston: G.K. Hall

Chodorow, Nancy and Contratto, Susan (1982) 'The Fantasy of the Perfect Mother' in Thorne (ed.) *Rethinking the Family* New York: Longman

Cixous, Hélène (1984) 'Sorties' in Marks and de Courtivron (eds) *New French Feminisms* New York: Schocken Books

Clark, Lorenne (1976) 'The Rights of Women: The Theory and Practice of the Ideology of Male Supremacy' in Shea and King-Farlow (eds) *Contemporary Issues in Political Philosophy* New York: Science History Publications

Clark, Lorenne M.G. and Lange, Lynda (eds) (1979) *The Sexism of Social and Political Theory: Women and Reproduction from Plato to Nietzsche* Toronto: University of Toronto Press

Clavir, Judith (1979) 'Choosing Either/or: A Critique of Metaphysical Feminism', *Feminist Studies*, 5, No. 2 pp. 402–410.

Clément, Catherine (1984) 'Enslaved Enclave' in Marks and de Courtivron (eds) *New French Feminisms* New York: Schocken Books

Code, Lorraine (1981) 'Is the Sex of the Knower Epistemologically Significant?', *Metaphilosophy*, Vol. 12, Nos. 3 and 4, pp. 267–276

—— (1983) 'Responsibility and the Epistemic Community: Woman's Place', *Social Research*, Vol. 50, No. 3, pp. 537–555

—— (1984) 'Toward a 'Responsibilist' Epistemology', *Philosophy and Phenomenological Research*, Vol. XLV, No. 1, pp. 29–50

—— (1986) 'Simple Equality Is Not Enough', *Australian Journal of Philosophy*, Vol. 64, pp. 48–65

Cohen, Alan (1980) 'Stages and Stability: The Moral Developmental Approach to Political Order' in Wilson and Schochet (eds) *Moral Development and Politics* New York: Praeger

Colby, Anne et al. (1983) *The Measurement of Moral Development: Standard Issue Scoring Manual* Cambridge: Cambridge University Press

Coltheart, Lenore (1986) 'Desire, consent and liberal theory' in Pateman and Gross (eds) *Feminist Challenges* Sydney: Allen & Unwin

McLaughlin, Eleanor Commo (1974) 'Equality of souls, Inequality of sexes: Woman in Medieval Theology' in Ruether (ed.), *Religion and Sexism* New York: Simon and Schuster

Comte, Auguste (1974) *The Positive Philosophy*, Intro. Abraham Blumberg, trans. Harriet Martineau, New York: HMS Press

Cook, Alice and Kirk, Gwyn (1983) *Greenham Women Everywhere, Dreams, Ideas and Actions From the Women's Peace Movement* London: Pluto Press

Cott, Nancy (1977) *The Bonds of Motherhood* New Haven: Yale University Press

Daly, Mary (1973) *Beyond God the Father: Toward a Philosophy of Women's Liberation* Boston: Beacon Press

—— (1978) *Gyn/Ecology—The Metaethics of Radical Feminism* Boston: Beacon Press

de Beauvoir, Simone (1975) *The Second Sex*, trans. and ed. H.M. Parshley, England: Penguin Books

—— (1980) *The Ethics of Ambiguity*, trans. B. Frechtman, New Jersey: Citadel Press

De Groot, J.J.M. (1910) *The Religious System of China* Leyden: E.J. Brill

De Lubac, Henri S.J. (1971) *The Eternal Feminine, A Study on the Poem by Teilhard de Chardin*, trans. René Hague, London: Collins

Derrida, Jacques (1979) *Spurs: Nietzsche's Styles* Chicago: University of Chicago Press

Descartes, René (1960) *Descartes, Spinoza, Leibniz, The Rationalists*, trans. John Veitch, New York: Dolphin Books

Dewey, John (1938) *Logic: The Theory of Inquiry* New York: Holt

Dietz, Mary G. (1985) 'Citizenship with a Feminist Face. The Problem with Maternal Thinking', *Political Theory*, Vol. 13, No. 1, pp. 19–37

Dilthey, Wilhelm (1976) *Selected Writings*, ed. H.P. Rickman, Cambridge: Cambridge University Press

Dinnerstein, Dorothy (1976) *The Mermaid and the Minotaur, Sexual Arrangements and Human Malaise* New York: Harper and Row

Di Stefano, Christine (1983) 'Masculinity as Ideology in Political Theory: Hobbesian Man Considered', *Women's Studies International Forum*, Vol. 6, No. 6, pp. 633–644

Douglas, Mary (1978) *Purity and Danger. An Analysis of the Concepts of Pollution and Taboo* London: Routledge and Kegan

Dowrick, Stephanie and Grundberg, Sibyl (eds) (1980) *Why Children?* London: The Women's Press Ltd.

Duncan, Graeme (ed.) (1983) *Democratic Theory and Practice* Cambridge: Cambridge University Press

Dworkin, Ronald (1978) 'Liberalism' in Hampshire ed., *Public and Private Morality* Cambridge: Cambridge University Press

Easton, Susan (1984) 'Functionalism and Feminism in Hegel's Political Thought', *Radical Philosophy*, 38, pp. 2–8

Eichler, Margrit (1980) *The Double Standard, A Feminist Critique of Feminist Social Science* London: Croom Helm

Eisenstein, Hester (1984) *Contemporary Feminist Thought* London: Unwin Paperbacks

Eisenstein, Hester, and Jardine, Alice (eds) (1980) *The Future of Difference* Boston: G.K. Hall

Eisenstein, Zillah (ed.) (1979) *Capitalist Patriarchy and the Case for Socialist Feminism* New York: Monthly Review Press

—— (ed.) (1981) *The Radical Future of Liberal Feminism* New York: Longman

Elshtain, Jean Bethke (1975) 'The Feminist Movement and the Question of Equality', *Polity*, Vol. 7, No. 4, pp. 452–478

—— (1978) 'Liberal Heresies: Existentialism and Repressive Feminism' in McGrath (ed.), *Liberalism and the Modern Polity* New York: Marcel Dekker Inc.

—— (1981) *Public Man, Private Woman, Women in Social and Political Thought* Oxford: Martin Robertson

—— (1982a) 'Feminism, Family and Community', *Dissent*, 29, 4, pp. 442–449

—— (ed.) (1982b) *The Family in Political Thought* Sussex: The Harvester Press

—— (1982c) 'Feminist Discourse and Its Discontents: Language, Power, and Meaning' in Keohane et al. (eds) *Feminist Theory, A Critique of Ideology* Chicago: The University of Chicago Press

—— (1985) 'Reflections on War and Political Discourse. Realism, Just War, and Feminism in a Nuclear Age', *Political Theory*, Vol. 13, No. 1, pp. 39–57

Engels, Friedrich (1940) *The Origin of the Family, Private Property and the State* Moscow: Foreign Languages Publishing House

English, Jane (ed.) (1977) *Sex Equality* New Jersey: Englewood Cliffs

Erikson, Lois V. (1980) 'The Case Study Method in the Evaluation of Developmental Programs', in Lisa Kuhmerker et al. (ed.), *Evaluating Moral Development* New York: Character Research Press

Feinberg, Joel (1970) 'The Nature and Value of Rights', *Journal of Value Inquiry*, 4, pp. 243–257

Ferguson, Ann (1981) 'Androgyny As an Ideal for Human Development' in Vetterling-Braggin et al. (eds) *Feminism and Philosophy* New Jersey: Littlefield, Adams and Co.

Feuerbach, Ludwig (1957) *The Essence of Christianity*, trans. George Eliot, Intro. Karl Barth, foreword H. Richard Niebuhr New York: Harper Torch Books

Feyerabend, Paul (1975) *Against Method: Outline of an Anarchistic Theory of Knowledge* London: N.L.B.

Firestone, Shulamith (1970) *The Dialectic of Sex: The Case for Feminist Revolution* New York: Bantam Books

Fishman, Joshua A. (ed.) (1972) *Readings in the Sociology of Language*, 3rd ed., The Hague: Mouton & Co.

Flanagan, Owen J. (1982) 'Virtue, Sex and Gender: Some Philosophical Reflections on the Moral Psychology Debate', *Ethics*, Vol. 92, pp. 499–512

Flanagan, Owen J. and Adler, J.E. (1983) 'Impartiality and Particularity', *Social Research*, Vol. 50, No. 3, pp. 576–595

Flax, Jane, (1976) 'Do Feminists Need Marxism?', *Quest* Vol. 3, No. 1

—— (1978) 'Critical Theory as a Vocation', *Politics and Society*, Vol. 8, No. 2, pp. 201–223

—— (1981) 'Psychoanalysis and the Philosophy of Science: Critique or Resistance', *The Journal of Philosophy*, Vol. 78, pp. 561–569

—— (1983) 'Political Philosophy and the Patriarchal Unconscious: A

Psychoanalytic Perspective on Epistemology and Metaphysics' in Harding and Hintikka (eds) *Discovering Reality* Dordrecht: D. Reidel Publishing Co.

Foreman, Ann (1977) *Femininity as Alienation: Women and the Family in Marxism and Psychoanalysis* London: Pluto Press

Foucault, Michel (1977) *Language, Counter—Memory, Practice*, (ed.) Donald F. Bouchard, trans. D.F. Bouchard and Sherry Simon, New York: Cornell University Press

Franzway, Suzanne (1986) 'With problems of their own: Femocrats and the Welfare State, *Australian Feminist Studies*, No. 3, pp. 45–57

Friedl, Ernestine (1975) *Women and Men, An Anthropologist's View* New York: Holt, Rinehart and Winston

Friedman, Marilyn (1987) 'Care and Context in Moral Reasoning' in Kittay and Meyers (eds) *Women and Moral Theory* New Jersey: Rowman and Littlefield

Fuchs, Jo-Ann Pilardi (1983) 'On the War Path and Beyond: Hegel, Freud and Feminist Theory', *Women's Studies International Forum*, Vol. 6, No. 6, pp. 565–572

Gadamer, Hans-Georg (1975) *Truth and Method*, trans. G. Barden and J. Cumming, London: Sheed and Ward

—— (1981) *Reason in the Age of Science*, trans. Frederick G. Lawrence, Cambridge Massachusetts: The MIT Press

Garside, Christine (1972) 'Women and Persons', in Margaret Andersen (ed) *Mother was not a Person* Montreal: Content Publishing and Black Rose Books

Gatens, Moira (1985) 'Philosophy of the Body', *Philosophy—Women's Conference*, Sydney

—— (1986a) 'Feminism, philosophy and riddles without answers' in Pateman and Gross (eds) *Feminist Challenges* Sydney: Allen & Unwin

—— (1986) 'Rousseau and Wollstonecraft: Nature vs Reason', *Australasian Journal of Philosophy*, Vol. 64, pp. 1–15

Gearhart, Sally Miller (1982) 'The Future—If There is One—Is Female' in McAllister (ed.) *Reweaving the web of Life* Philadelphia: New Society Publishers

Gibbs, John (1977) 'Kohlberg's Stages of Moral Judgement: A Constructive Critique', *Harvard Educational Review*, 47, pp. 42–61

—— (1979) 'Kohlberg's Moral Stage Theory: A Piagetian Revision', *Human Development*, 22, pp. 89–112

Gibson, Mary (1977) 'Rationality', *Philosophy and Public Affairs*, Vol. 6, No. 3, pp. 193–225

Gilligan, Carol (1977) 'In a Different Voice: Women's Conceptions of the Self and of Morality', *Harvard Educational Review*, 47, pp. 481–517

—— (1979) 'Woman's Place in Man's Life Cycle', *Harvard Educational Review*, 49, pp. 431–446

—— (1983) *In a Different Voice, Psychological Theory and Women's Development* Cambridge: Harvard University Press

—— (1984) 'The Conquistador and the Dark Continent: Reflections on the Psychology of Love', *Daedalus*, Summer

—— (1987) 'Moral Orientation and Moral Development' in Kittay and Meyers (eds) *Women and Moral Theory* New Jersey: Rowman and Littlefield

Gilligan, Carol and Langdale, S. (1981) 'The Contribution of Women's

Thought to Developmental Theory: The Elimination of Sex-Bias in Moral Development Research', *National Institute of Education Interim Report*, pp. 83–93

Glass, James (1978) 'Rationality and Mind: Distortion and Mystification in Political Analysis' in McGrath (ed.), *Liberalism and the Modern Polity* New York: Marcel Dekker Inc.

Glennon, Lynda M. (1979) *Women and Dualism, A Sociology of Knowledge Analysis* New York: Longman

Goertzel, T.G. (1983) 'The Gender Gap: Sex, Family Income and Political Opinions in the Early 1980s', *Journal of Political and Military Sociology*, Vol. 11, No. 2

Goldberg, Steven (1974) *The Inevitability of Patriarchy*, 2nd ed., New York: William Morrow and Co

Gornick, Vivian and Moran, Barbara K. (1971) *Woman in Sexist Society. Studies in Power and Powerlessness* New York: Basic Books, Inc., Publishers

Gould, Carol (1976) 'The Woman Question: Philosophy of Liberation and the Liberation of Philosophy' in Gould and Wartofsky (eds) *Women and Philosophy* New York: G.P. Putman's Sons

—— (1978) *Marx's Social Ontology, Individuality and Community in Marx's Theory of Social Reality* Cambridge Massachusetts: M.I.T. Press

—— (1983) 'Beyond Causality in the Social Sciences: Reciprocity as a Model of Non-exploitative Social Relations,' in R.S. Cohen and M.W. Wartofsky (eds) *Epistemology, Methodology and the Social Sciences* D. Reidel Publishing Co, pp. 53–88

—— (ed.) (1984) *Beyond Domination, New Perspectives on Women and Philosophy* New Jersey: Rowman and Allanheld

—— (1988) *Rethinking Democracy, Freedom and Social Co-operation in Politics, Economy and Society* Cambridge: Cambridge University Press

Gould, Carol and Wartofsky, W. Marx (eds) (1976) *Women and Philosophy, Toward a Theory of Liberation* New York: G.P. Putman's Sons

Graves, Robert (1978) *New Larousse Encyclopedia of Mythology* London: Hamlyn

Green, Philip (1982) *The Pursuit of Inequality* Oxford: Martin Robertson

Green, Karen (1986) 'Rawls, Women and the Priority of Liberty', *Australasian Journal of Philosophy*, Vol. 64, pp. 26–36

Green Agenda (1987) *New Internationalist*, pp. 22–23

Greer, Germaine (1970) *The Female Eunuch* London: MacGibbon and Kee

Griffin, Susan (1980) *Woman and Nature, The Roaring Inside Her* New York: Harper, Colophen Books

Grigson, Geoffrey (1976) *The Goddess of Love: The birth, triumph, death and return of Aphrodite* London: Constable & Co.

Gross, Elizabeth (1986a) 'Philosophy, Subjectivity and the body: Kristeva and Irigaray' in Pateman and Gross (eds) *Feminist Challenges* Sydney: Allen & Unwin

—— (1986b) 'Conclusion: What is feminist theory?' in Pateman and Gross (eds) *Feminist Challenges* Sydney: Allen & Unwin

Haan, Norma (1978) 'Two Moralities in Action Contexts', *Journal of Personality and Social Psychology*, 36, pp. 286–305

Habermas, Jürgen (1971) *Knowledge and Human Interests*, trans. J.J. Shapiro, Boston: Beacon Press

—— (1977) 'Hannah Arendt's Communications Concept of Power', *Social Research*, Vol. 44, No. 1

—— (1977) *Toward a Rational Society, Student Protest, Science and Politics*, trans. J.J. Shapiro, London: Heinemann

—— (1979) *Communication and the Evolution of Society*, trans. Thomas McCarthy, London: Heinemann

Hampshire, Stuart (ed.) (1978) *Public and Private Morality* Cambridge: Cambridge University Press

Haraway, Donna (1978) 'Animal Sociology and a Natural Economy of the Body Politic', *Signs*, 4, pp. 21–60

—— (1987) 'A Manifesto for Cyborgs: Science, Technology and Socialist Feminism in the 1980s', *Australian Feminist Studies*, No. 4, pp. 1–42

Harding, Sandra (1979) 'The Social function of the Empiricist Conception of Mind', *Metaphilosophy*, Vol. 10, No. 1, pp. 38–47

—— (1983) 'Why Has the Sex/Gender System Become Visible Only Now?' in Harding and Hintikka (eds) *Discovering Reality* Dordrecht: D. Reidel Publishing Co.

—— (1984) 'Is Gender a Variable in Conceptions of Rationality? A Survey of Issues' in Gould (ed.) *Beyond Domination* New Jersey: Rowman and Allanheld

—— (1986) *The Science Question in Feminism* New York: Cornell University Press

—— (1987) 'The Curious Coincidence of Feminine and African Moralities: Challenges for Feminist Theory' in Kittay and Meyers (eds) *Women and Moral Theory* New Jersey: Rowman and Littlefield

Harding, Sandra and Hintikka, Merrill B. (eds) (1983) *Discovering Reality, Feminist Perspectives on Epistemology, Metaphysics, Methodology, and Philosophy of Science* Dordrecht: D. Reidel Publishing Co.

Hare, Richard M. (1952) *The Language of Morals* Oxford: Clarendon Press

Hartmann, Heidi (1979) 'The Unhappy Marriage of Marxism and Feminism: Towards a More Progressive Union', *Capital and Class*, No. 8

Hartsock, Nancy C.M. (1983) *Money, Sex and Power. Toward a Feminist Historical Materialism* New York: Longman

—— (1983b) 'The Feminist Standpoint: Developing the Ground for a Specifically Feminist Historical Materialism' in Harding and Hintikka (eds) *Discovering Reality* Dordrecht: D. Reidel Publishing Co.

—— (1984) 'Prologue to a Feminist Critique of War and Politics' in Stiehm (ed.) *Women's Views of the Political Worlds of Men* New York: Transnational Publishers, Inc.

Hegel, Georg W.F. (1973) *Philosophy of Right*, trans. T.M. Knox, Oxford: Oxford University Press

—— (1979) *Phenomenology of Spirit*, trans. A.V. Miller, Oxford: Clarendon Press

Held, Virginia (1973) 'Reasonable Progress and Self-Respect', *Monist*, 57, pp. 12–27

—— (1984) *Rights and Goods: Justifying Social Action* New York: Free Press

—— (1987) 'Feminism and Moral Theory' in Kittay and Meyers (eds) *Woman and Moral Theory* New Jersey: Rowman and Littlefield

Hill, Thomas (1977) 'Servility and Self-Respect' in English (ed.) *Sex Equality* New Jersey: Englewood Cliffs

—— (1987) 'The Importance of Autonomy' in Kittay and Meyers (eds) *Women and Moral Theory* New Jersey: Rowman and Littlefield

Hobbes, Thomas (1974) *Leviathan* London: Penguin Books

Hollis, Martin and Nell, Edward (1975) *Rational Economic Man* New York: Cambridge University Press

Holmstrom, Nancy (1982) 'Do Women have a Distinct Nature?' *The Philosophical Forum*, Vol. 14, No. 1, pp. 25–42

Homer, *Illiad*, trans. according to the Greek, George Chapman, London: Simpkin, Marshall, Hamilton, Kent and Co. Ltd., N.D.

Horkheimer, Max (1947) *Eclipse of Reason* New York: Oxford University Press

—— (1959) 'Authoritarianism and the Family', in R.N. Anshen (ed.) *The Family: Its Function and Destiny* New York: Harper and Row Publishers

Hubbard, Ruth and Lowe, Marian (ed.) (1979) *Genes and Gender: Pitfalls in Research on Sex and Gender* New York: Gordian Press

Hughes, Patricia (1982) 'Fighting the Good Fight: Separation or Integration?' in Miles and Finn (eds) *Feminism in Canada* Montreal: Black Rose Books

Hume, David (1888) *A Treatise of Human Nature*, (ed.) L.A. Selby-Bigge Oxford: The Clarendon Press

Ignatieff, Michael (1984) *The Needs of Strangers* London: Chatto and Windus

Irigaray, Luce (1977) 'Women's Exile', *Ideology and Consciousness*, Vol. 7

Jaggar, Alison (1973–74) 'On Sexual Equality', *Ethics*, Vol. 84, pp. 275–291

—— (1983) *Feminist Politics and Human Nature* Sussex: The Harvester Press

—— (1984) 'Human Biology in Feminist Theory: Sexual Equality Reconsidered' in Gould (ed.) *Beyond Domination* New Jersey: Rowman and Allanheld

Janeway, Elizabeth (1971) *Man's World, Woman's Place: A Study in Social Mythology* New York: Dell Publishing

Jay, Nancy (1981) 'Gender and Dichotomy', *Feminist Studies*, 7, No. 1, pp. 38–56

Jonas, Hans (1984) *The Imperative of Responsibility. In Search of an Ethics for the Technological Age* Chicago: The University of Chicago Press

Jones, Lynne (ed.) (1983) *Keeping the Peace, A Women's Peace Handbook* London: The Women's Press

Kaberry, Phyllis M. (1939) *Aboriginal Woman, Sacred and Profane* New York: Blackstone

Kant, Immanuel (1951) *Critique of Judgement*, trans. J.H. Bernard, New York: Hafner Press

—— (1964) *Groundwork of The Metaphysics of Morals*, trans. H.J. Paton, New York: Harper Torch books

Kanter, Rosabeth Moss (1977) *Men and Women of the Corporation* New York: Basic Books Inc. Publishers

Kearns, Deborah (1983) 'A Theory of Justice—and Love; Rawls on the Family, *Politics* Vol. 18, No. 2, pp. 36–42

Keat, Russell (1983) 'Masculinity in Philosophy', *Radical Philosophy*, No. 31, pp. 15–20

Keller, Evelyn Fox (1982) 'Feminism and Science', *Signs*, 7, No. 3, pp. 589–602

—— (1983) *A Feeling for the Organism; The Life and Work of Barbara McClintock* New York: W.H. Freeman

—— (1985) *Reflections on Gender and Science* New Haven: Yale University Press

Keniston, K. (1968) *Young Radicals* New York: Harcourt, Brace and World

Keohane, Nannerl O., Rosaldo, Michelle Z., Gelpi, Barbara C. (eds) (1982) *Feminist Theory, A Critique of Ideology* Chicago: The University of Chicago Press

Kerber, Linda et al. (1986) 'On *In a Different Voice*: An Interdisciplinary Forum', *Signs*, Vol. 11, No. 2

King-Farlow, John and Shea, William R. (eds) (1976) *Values and the Quality of Life* New York: Science History Publications

Kittay, Eva Feder and Meyers, Diana T. (eds) (1987) *Women and Moral Theory* New Jersey: Rowman and Littlefield

Klein, Renate Duelli (1983) 'The 'Men-Problem' in Women's Studies: The Expert, The Ignoramus and the Poor Dear', *Women's Studies International Forum*, Vol. 6, No. 4, pp. 413–421

Koedt, Anne, Levine, Ellen, Rapone, Anita (eds) (1973) *Radical Feminism* New York: Quadrangle

Kohlberg, Lawrence (1958) *The Development of Modes of Moral Thinking, Choice in the Years 2–16*, Ph.D. diss., University of Chicago

—— (1971)'From Is to Ought: How to Commit the Naturalistic Fallacy and Get Away With It in the Study of Moral Development' in Mischel (ed.) *Cognitive Development and Epistemology* New York: Academic Press

—— (1973) 'The Claim to Moral Adequacy of the Highest Stage of Moral Judgement', *Journal of Philosophy*, 70, pp. 630–645

—— (1981a) *The Meaning and Measurement of Moral Development* Worcester Mass: Clark University Press

—— (1981b) *The Philosophy of Moral Development: Moral Stages and the Idea of Justice* New York: Harper and Row

—— (1982) 'A Reply to Owen Flanagan and Some Comments on the Puka-Goodpaster Exchange', *Ethics*, Vol. 92, pp. 513–532

—— (1984) '*The Psychology of Moral Development*' San Francisco: Harper and Row

Kohlberg, Lawrence and Kramer, E. (1969) 'Continuities and Discontinuities in Childhood and Adult Moral Development', *Human Development*, 12, pp. 93–120

Kohlberg, Lawrence and Turiel, E. (1971) 'Moral Development and Moral Education', in G. Lesser (ed.) *Psychology and Educational Practice* Chicago: Scott, Foresman

Kohlberg, Lawrence and Gilligan, Carol (1971) 'The Adolescent as a Philosopher: The Discovery of the Self in a Postconventional World', *Daedalus*, 1070, pp. 1051–1086

Kokopeli, Bruce and Lakey, George (1982) 'More Power Than We Want: Masculine Sexuality and Violence' in McAllister (ed.) *Reweaving the Web of Life* Philadelphia: New Society Publishers

Korsmeyer, Carolyn (1976) 'Reason and Morals in the Early Feminist Movement: Mary Wollstonecraft' in Gould and Wartofsky (eds) *Women and Philosophy* New York: G.P. Putman's Sons

Kristeva, Julia (1984) 'Woman Can Never Be Defined' in Marks and de Courtivron (eds) *New French Feminisms* New York: Schocken Books

Lambert, Helen H. (1978) 'Biology and Equality: A Perspective on Sex Differences', *Signs* 4, pp. 97–117

Lange, Lynda (1976) 'Reproduction in Democratic Theory' in Shea and King-Farlow (eds) *Contemporary Issues in Political Philosophy* New York: Science History Publications

—— (1981) 'Rousseau and Modern Feminism', *Social Theory and Practice*, Vol. 7, No. 3, pp. 245–277

Lee, Patrick C. and Stewart, Robert Sussman (eds) (1976) *Sex Differences, Cultural and Developmental Dimensions* New York: Urizen Books

Lerner, Gerda (1979) *The Majority Finds Its Past: Placing Women in History* New York: Oxford University Press

Lloyd, G.E.R. (1966) *Polarity and Analogy: Two Types of Argumentation in Early Greek Thought* Cambridge: Cambridge University Press

Lloyd, Genevieve (1979) 'The Man of Reason', *Metaphilosophy*, Vol. 10, No. 1, pp. 18–37

—— (1983a) 'Masters, Slaves and Others', *Radical Philosophy*, No. 31, pp. 2–9

—— (1983b) 'Public Reason and Private Passion', *Politics*, Vol. 18, No. 2, pp. 27–35

—— (1983c) 'Reason, Gender, and Morality in the History of Philosophy', *Social Research*, Vol. 50, No. 3, pp. 490–513

—— (1984a) *The Man of Reason, 'Male' and 'Female' in Western Philosophy* London: Methuen

—— (1984b) History of Philosophy and the Critique of Reason', *Critical Philosophy*, Vol. 1, No. 1, pp. 5–23

—— (1986) 'Selfhood, War and Masculinity' in Pateman and Gross, *Feminist Challenges* Sydney: Allen & Unwin

Locke, John (1963) *Two Treatises of Government* Cambridge: Cambridge University Press

Lowe, Marian and Hubbard, Ruth (eds) (1983) *Woman's Nature: Rationalisations of Inequality* New York: Pergamon Press

Lowe, Barry (1986) 'How greed gave a gentle people to anger', *The Weekend Australian Magazine*, 4 Dec., pp. 27–28

Lugones, Marià C. and Spelman, Elizabeth V. (1983) 'Have we got a Theory for you! Feminist Theory, Cultural Imperialism and the Demand for "The Woman's Voice"', *Women's Studies International Forum*, Vol. 6, No. 6, pp. 573–581

Lukes, Steven (1974) *Power: A Radical Analysis* London: MacMillan

—— (1984) *Individualism* Oxford: Basil Blackwell

Maccoby, Eleanor Emmons and Jacklin, Carol Nagy (1974) *The Psychology of Sex Differences* Stanford, California: Stanford University Press

MacIntyre, Alasdair (1982) *After Virtue, a study in moral theory* London: Duckworth

MacKinnon, Catherine A. (1982) 'Feminism, Marxism, Method and the State: An Agenda for Theory', *Signs* 7, pp. 515–544

Macpherson, C.B. (1973) *Democratic Theory, Essays in Retrieval* Oxford: Clarendon Press

Marcuse, Herbert (1972) *One Dimensional Man* London: Abacus

Marks, Elaine and de Courtivron, Isabelle (eds) (1984) *New French Feminisms, An Anthology* New York: Schocken Books

Markson, Elizabeth W. (ed.) (1983) *Older Women. Issues and Prospects* Toronto: Lexington Books

Markus, Maria (1986) 'Women, Success and Civil Society: Submission to, or Subversion of, the Achievement Principle', *Praxis International*, Vol. 5, No. 4, pp. 430–442

Martin, Mike W. (ed.) (1985) *Self-Deception and Self-Understanding: New Essays in Philosophy and Psychology* Kansas: University Press of Kansas

Marx, Karl (1975) *Early Writings*, (ed.) L. Colletti London: Penguin Books

Massey, S.J. (1983) 'Is Self-Respect a Moral or a Psychological Concept?' *Ethics* Vol. 93, pp. 246–261

McAllister, Pam (ed.) (1982) *Reweaving the Web of Life, Feminism and Non Violence* Philadelphia: New Society Publishers

McFadden, Maggie (1984) 'Anatomy of Difference: Toward a Classification of Feminist Theory', *Women's Studies International Forum*, 7, pp. 495–504

McGrath, Michael J. Gargas (ed.) (1978) *Liberalism and the Modern Polity. Essays in Contemporary Political Theory* New York: Marcel Dekker Inc.

McMillan, Carol (1982) *Women, Reason and Nature, Some Philosophical Problems with Feminism* Oxford: Basil Blackwell

Merchant, Carolyn (1980) *The Death of Nature, Women, Ecology, and the Scientific Revolution* San Francisco: Harper and Row Publishers

Meyers, Diana T. (1987) 'The Socialised Individual and Individual Autonomy: An Intersection between Philosophy and Psychology' in Kittay and Meyers (eds) *Women and Moral Theory* New Jersey: Rowman and Littlefield

Michalowski, Helen (1982) 'The Army Will Make a "Man" out of You' in McAllister (ed.) *Reweaving the Web of Life* Philadelphia: New Society Publishers

Midgley, Mary (1981) *Heart and Mind, The Varieties of Moral Experience* Sussex: The Harvester Press

Midgley, Mary and Hughes, Judith (1983) *Women's Choices. Philosophical Problems Facing Feminism* London: Weidenfeld and Nicolson

Miles, Angela and Finn, Geraldine (eds) (1982) *Feminism in Canada: From Pressure to Politics* Montréal: Black Rose Books

Mill, John Stuart (1869) *The Subjection of Women* London: D. Appleton

—— (1963) *A System of Logic, Philosophy of Scientific Method*, (ed.) Ernest Nagel, New York: Hafner

—— (1973) *A Logical Critique of Sociology*, (ed.) Ronald Fletcher, London: Nelson

Mill, John Stuart and Taylor, Harriet (1970) *Essays on Sex Equality*, (ed.) Alice S. Rossi, Chicago: University of Chicago Press

Miller, Jean Baker (1976) *Toward a new Psychology of Women* Boston: Beacon Press

Miller, Jane (1986) *Women Writing about Men* London: Virago

Millett, Kate (1971) *Sexual Politics* New York: Avon Books

Mills, Patricia Jagentowicz (1983) *Woman, Nature and Psyche: The Domination of Nature in the Tradition of Critical Theory*, Unpub. Ph.D. thesis, York University: Toronto, Ontario

Mischel, Theodore (ed.) (1971) *Cognitive Development and Epistemology* New York: Academic Press

Mitchell, Juliet (1973) *Woman's Estate* New York: Vintage Books

Mitchell, Juliet, and Oakley Ann (ed.) (1982) *The Rights and Wrongs of Women* London: MacMillan

Montefiore, Alan (ed.) (1973) *Philosophy and Personal Relations, An Anglo-French Study* London: Routledge and Kegan Paul

Morgan, Robin (ed.) (1970) *Sisterhood is Powerful. An Anthology of Writings from the Women's Liberation Movement* New York: Vintage Books

—— (1977) *Going too Far: The Personal Chronicle of a Feminist* New York: Random House

Murdoch, Iris (1971) *The Sovereignty of Good* New York: Schocken Books

Murphy, John M. and Gilligan, Carol (1980) 'Moral Development in Late Adolescence and Adulthood: A Critique and Reconstruction of Kohlberg's Theory', *Human Development*, 23, pp. 159–170

Nails, Debra (1983) 'Social–Scientific Sexism: Gilligan's Mismeasure of Man', *Social Research*, Vol. 50, No. 3, pp. 643–664

Nicholson, Linda J. (1983) 'Women, Morality, and History,' *Social Research*, Vol. 50, No. 3, pp. 515–535

O'Brien, Mary (1983) *The Politics of Reproduction* Boston: Routledge and Kegan Paul

O'Donnell, Carol and Golder, Nerolie (1986) 'A Comparative Analysis of Equal Pay in the U.S., Britain and Australia', *Australian Feminist Studies*, No. 3, pp. 59–90

O'Faolain, Julia and Martines, Lauro (eds) (1974) *Not in God's Image, Women in History* Glascow: Fontana Collins

Okin, Susan Moller (1979) *Women in Western Political Thought* Princeton: Princeton University Press

—— (1982) 'Women and the Making of the Sentimental Family', *Philosophy and Public Affairs*, Vol. 11, No. 1

—— (1983) 'The Moral Acceptability of Nuclear Deterrence: A Critique', *Politics*, Vol. 18, No. 2, pp. 16–26

O'Loughlin, Mary Ann (1983) 'Responsibility and Moral Maturity in the Control of Fertility—or, A Woman's Place is in the Wrong', *Social Research*, Vol. 50, No. 3, pp. 556–575

Osborne, Martha Lee (ed.) (1979) *Woman in Western Thought* New York: Random House

Owen, Wilfred (1971) *The Collected Poems of Wilfred Owen* (ed.) C. Day Lewis, London: Chatto and Windus

Panichas, George A. (ed.) (1977) *Simone Weil Reader* New York: McKay

Pargetter, Robert and Prior, Elizabeth W. (1986) 'Against the Sexuality of Reason', *Australasian Journal of Philosophy*, Vol. 64, pp. 107–119

Parsons, Talcott (1951) *The Social System* Glencoe Illinois: Free Press

Parsons, Talcott, and Bales, R.F. (1955) *Family, Socialisation and Interaction Process* Glencoe Illinois: Free Press

Parsons, Susan (1986) 'Feminism and Moral Reasoning', *Australasian Journal of Philosophy*, Vol. 64, pp. 75–90

Pateman, Carole (1980) '"The Disorder of Women": Women, Love and the sense of Justice', *Ethics*, 91, pp. 20–34

—— (1983) 'Feminism and Democracy' in Duncan (ed.) *Democratic Theory and Practice* Cambridge: Cambridge University Press

—— (1984) 'The Shame of the Marriage Contract' in Stiehm (ed.) *Women's Views of the Political World of Men* New York: Transnational Publishers, Inc.

—— (1986) 'Introduction: The theoretical subversiveness of feminism' in Pateman and Gross (eds) *Feminist Challenges* Sydney: Allen & Unwin

Pateman, Carole, and Gross Elizabeth (eds) (1986) *Feminist Challenges, Social and Political Theory* Sydney: Allen and Unwin

Peters, R.S. (1971) 'Moral Developments: A Plea for Pluralism' in Mischel (ed.) *Cognitive Development and Epistemology* New York: Academic Press

Piaget, Jean (1948) *The Moral Judgement of the Child* Glencoe Illinois: Free Press

Pierce, Christine (1971) 'Natural Law, Language and Women' in Gornick and Moron (eds) *Woman in Sexist Society* New York: Basic Books, Inc., Publishers

Pierson, Ruth and Prentice, Alison 'Feminism and the Writing and Teaching of History' in Miles and Finn (eds) *Feminism in Canada* Montréal: Black Rose Books

Plato (1955) *Plato Selections*, (ed.) Raphael Demos, New York: Charles Scribner's Sons

—— (1971) *The Republic*, trans. H.D.P. Lee, London: Penguin Books

Pleck, Joseph B (1981) *The Myth of Masculinity* Cambridge Mass: MIT Press

Plumwood, Val (1986) 'Eco-Feminism: An Overview and Discussion of Positions and Arguments', *Australasian Journal of Philosophy*, Vol. 64, pp. 120–138

Pollak, S. and Gilligan, C. (1982) 'Images of Violence in Thematic Apperception Test Stories', *Journal of Personality and Social Psychology*, 42, pp. 159–167

Pomeroy, Sarah B. (1976) *Goddesses, Whores, Wives, and Slaves, Women in Classical Antiquity* New York: Schocken Books

Poole, Ross (1985) 'Morality, Masculinity and the Market', *Radical Philosophy*, pp. 16–23

Prusak, Bernard (1974) 'Woman: Seductive Siren and Source of Sin?' in Ruether (ed.) *Religion and Sexism* New York: Simon and Schuster

Puka, B. (1982) 'An Interdisciplinary Treatment of Kohlberg', *Ethics*, Vol. 92, pp. 468–490

Rawls, John (1971) *A Theory of Justice* Cambridge Mass: Harvard University Press

Raymond, Janice (1985) 'The Visionary Task: Two Sights—Seeing', *Women's Studies International Forum*, Vol 8, No. 1, pp. 85–90

Reiter, Rayna (ed.) (1976) *Towards an Anthropology of Women* New York: Monthly Review Press

Rich, Adrienne (1979) *Of Woman Born, Motherhood as Experience and Institution* London: Virago

—— (1980a) *On Lies, Secrets, Silence, Selected Prose 1966–1978* London: Virago

—— (1980b) 'Compulsory Heterosexuality and Lesbian Existence', *Signs 5*, No. 4, pp. 631–660

Richards, Janet Radcliffe (1982) *The Sceptical Feminist, A Philosophical Enquiry* London: Penguin Books

Rorty, Amèlie Oksenberg (ed.) (1976) *The Identities of Persons* Berkeley: University of California Press

—— (1980) *Explaining Emotions* Berkeley: University of California Press

Rosaldo, Michelle Zimbalist and Lamphere, Louise (eds) (1979) *Woman, Culture and Society* Stanford California: Stanford University Press

Rosaldo, Michelle Zimbalist (1980) 'The Use and Abuse of Anthropology: Reflections on Feminism and Cross-Cultural Understanding,' *Signs*, 5, 3, pp. 389–417

Rose, Hilary (1983) 'Hand, Brain and Heart: A Feminist Epistemology for the Natural Sciences', *Signs* 9, No. 1

Rousseau, Jean-Jacques (1973) *The Social Contract and Discourses* (ed.) G.D.H. Cole, London: J.M. Dent

—— (1977) *Émile*, trans. Barbara Foxley, London: Everyman's Library

Rubin, Gayle (1976) 'The Traffic in Women: Notes on the Political Economy of Sex' in Reiter (ed.) *Towards an Anthropology of Women* New York: Monthly Review Press

Ruddick, Sara (1982) 'Maternal Thinking' in Thorne (ed.) *Rethinking the Family* New York: Longman

—— (1983a) 'Pacifying the Forces: Drafting Women in the Interests of Peace', *Signs*, Vol. 8, No. 3, pp. 471–489

—— (1983b) 'Preservative Love and Military Justice', *Psychology Critique*, 3, pp. 14–23

—— (1987) 'Remarks on the Sexual Politics of Reason' in Kittay and Meyers (eds) *Women and Moral Theory* New Jersey: Rowman and Littlefield

Ruether, Rosemary Radford (ed.) (1974) *Religion and Sexism, Images of Woman in the Jewish and Christian Traditions* New York: Simon and Schuster

—— (1983) *Sexism and God-Talk, Toward a Feminist Theology* Boston: Beacon Press

—— (1984) 'Sexism, Religion and the Social and Spiritual Liberation of Women Today' in Gould (ed.) *Beyond Domination* New Jersey: Rowman and Allanheld

—— (1985) 'Feminist Interpretation: A Method of Correlation' in Letty M. Russell (ed.) *Feminist Interpretation of the Bible*, Oxford: Basil Blackwell, pp. 111–124

Salleh, Ariel Kay (1981) 'Of Portnoy's Complaint and Feminist Problematics: A Reconciliation with Critical Theory', *Australian and New Zealand Journal of Sociology*, Vol. 17, No. 1, pp. 4–13

—— (1985) 'From Feminism to Ecology', *Social Alternatives*, Vol. 4, No. 3, Jan. 1985, pp. 8–12

Sandel, Michael J. (1982) *Liberalism and the Limits of Justice* Cambridge: Cambridge University Press

Sargent Lydia (ed.) (1981) *Women and Revolution* Boston: South End Press

Sartre, Jean-Paul (1973) *Being and Nothingness* New York: Washington Square Press

Scanzoni, Letha and Hardesty, Nancy (1975) *All We're Meant to be, A Biblical Approach to Women's Liberation* Texas: Word Books, Publisher

Schochet, Gordon J. (1975) *Patriarchalism in Political Thought, The Authoritarian Family and Political Speculation and Attitudes Especially in 17th century England* Oxford: Basil Blackwell

Schopenhauer, Arthur (1892) *Studies in Pessimism*, trans. T. Bailey Saunders, 3rd ed., London: Swan Sonnenschein & Co.
—— (1965) *On the Basis of Morality*, trans. E.F.J. Payle, New York: Bobbs Merrill, Library of Liberal Arts
Schrag, Francis (1976) 'Justice and the Family', *Inquiry*, 19, pp. 193–208
Scott, Hilda (1974) *Does Socialism Liberate Women?* Boston: Beacon Press
Sen, Amartya K. (1977) 'Rational Fools: A Critique of the Behavioural Foundations of Economic theory', *Philosophy and Public Affairs*, Vol. 6, No. 4, pp. 317–44
See, Katherine O'Sullivan (1982) 'Feminism and Political Philosophy', *Feminist Studies*, Vol. 8, No. 1, pp. 179–194
Shea, W.R. and King-Farlow J. (eds) (1976) *Contemporary Issues in Political Philosophy* New York: Science History Publications
Shivers, Lynne (1982) 'An Open Letter to Gandhi' in McAllister (ed.) *Reweaving the Web of Life* Philadelphia: New Society Publishers
Shorter, Edward (1975) *The Making of the Modern Family* New York: Basic Books, Inc. Publishers
Smith, Dorothy (1974) 'Women's Perspective as a Radical Critique of Sociology', *Sociological Inquiry*, pp. 44
—— (1979) 'A Sociology for Women', in J. Sherman and E.T. Beck (eds) *The Prism of Sex: Essays in the Sociology of Knowledge*, Madison: University of Wisconsin Press pp. 135–187
Smith, Joan (1983) 'Feminist Analysis of Gender: A Mystique' in Lowe and Hubbard (eds) *Woman's Nature* New York: Pergamon Press
Smith, Janet Farrell (1984) 'Rights-Conflict, Pregnancy and Abortion' in Gould (ed.) *Beyond Domination* New Jersey: Rowman and Allanheld
Smith, T.W. (1984) 'The Polls: Gender and Attitudes Towards Violence', *Public Opinion Quarterly*, Vol. 48
Soble, Alan (1983) 'Feminist Epistemology and Women Scientists', *Metaphilosophy*
Some London Revolutionary Feminists (1983) *Breaking the Peace. A collection of radical feminist papers* London: Only Women Press
Spelman, Elizabeth J. (1977–78) 'On Treating Persons as Persons', *Ethics*, Vol. 88, pp. 150–161
—— (1982) 'Woman as Body: Ancient and Contemporary Views', *Feminist Studies*, Vol. 8, No. 1, pp. 109–131
—— (1983) 'Aristotle and the Politicisation of the Soul' in Harding and Hintikka (eds) *Discovering Reality* Dordrecht: D. Reidel Publishing Co.
Spender, Dale (1981) *Men's Studies modified: the impact of feminism on the academic disciplines* New York: Pergamon Press
—— (1982) *Man Made Language* London: Routledge and Kegan Paul
Starhawk (1979) *The Spiral Dance: A Rebirth of the Ancient Religion of the Great Goddess* San Francisco: Harper and Row
Steedman, Carolyn (1986) *Landscape For a Good Woman, A Story of Two Lives* London: Virago
Stiehm, Judith H. (ed.) (1984) *Women's Views of the Political World of Men* New York: Transnational Publishers, Inc.
Stocker, Michael (1987) 'Duty and Friendship: Toward a Synthesis of Gilligan's Contrastive Moral Concepts' in Kittay and Meyers (eds) *Women and Moral Theory* New Jersey: Rowman and Littlefield

213

Stone, Lawrence (1977) *The Family, Sex and Marriage, 1500–1800* London: Weidenfeld and Nicolson

Stone, Merlin (1978) *When God was a Woman* New York: Harvest

Tapper, Marion (1986) 'Can a Feminist be a Liberal?', *Australasian Journal of Philosophy*, Vol. 64, pp. 37–47

Taylor, Charles (1971) 'What is Involved in a Genetic Psychology?' in Mischel (ed.) *Cognitive Development and Epistemology* New York: Academic Press

—— (1976) 'Responsibility for Self' in Rorty (eds) *The Identities of Persons* Berkeley: University of California Press

—— (1985a) *Human Agency and Language, Philosophical Papers 1* Cambridge: Cambridge University Press

—— (1985b) *Philosophy and the Human Sciences, Philosophical Papers 2* Cambridge: Cambridge University Press

Thiele, Bev (1985) 'Women, Nature and the Peace Movement', *Social Alternatives*, Vol. 4, No. 3, pp. 13–16

Thompson, Janna (1983) 'Women and the High Priests of Reason', *Radical Philosophy*, No. 31, pp. 10–14

—— (1986) 'Women and Political Rationality' in Pateman and Gross (eds) *Feminist Challenges* Sydney: Allen & Unwin

Thorne, Barrie (ed.) (1982) with Yalom, Marilyn *Rethinking the Family, Some feminist questions* New York: Longman

Thornton, Merle (1986) 'Sex equality is not enough for feminism' in Pateman and Gross (eds) *Feminist Challenges* Sydney: Allen & Unwin

Tiger, Lionel (1969) *Men in Groups* New York: Random House

Tiger, Lionel and Fox, Robin (1978) 'The Human Biogram', in Arthur L. Caplan (ed.) *The Sociobiology Debate* New York: Harper and Row, pp. 57–63

Tolson, Andrew (1977) *The Limits of Masculinity* London: Tavistock

Tormey, Judith Farr (1976) 'Exploitation, Oppression and Self-Sacrifice' in Gould and Wortofsky (eds) *Women and Philosophy* New York: G.P. Putman's Sons

Trebilcot, Joyce (1974–75) 'Sex Roles: The Argument from Nature' *Ethics*, Vol. 85, pp. 249–255

Tuana, Nancy (1983) 'Re-fusing Nature/Nurture', *Women's Studies International Forum*, Vol. 6, No. 6 pp. 621–632

Unger, Roberto M. (1976) *Knowledge and Politics* New York: The Free Press

Vetterling-Braggin, Mary, Elliston, Frederick A. and English, Jane (eds) (1981) *Feminism and Philosophy* New Jersey: Littlefield, Adams and Co.

Walker, John C. (1983) 'In a Diffident Voice: Cryptoseparatist Analysis of Female Moral Development', *Social Research*, Vol. 50, No. 3, pp. 665–695

Warner, Lloyd (1937) *A Black Civilisation: A Study of an Australian Tribe* (rev. ed.), New York: Harper and Row

Warner, Marina (1978) *Alone of all Her Sex, The Myth and the Cult of the Virgin Mary* London: Quartet Books

Waterman, A. (1981) 'Individualism and Interdependence', *American Psychologist*, 136, pp. 762–773

Weber, Max (1958) *The Protestant Ethic and the Spirit of Capitalism*, trans. Talcott Parsons, New York: Charles Scribner's Sons

—— (1978) *Economy and Society, An Outline of Interpretive Sociology*, (ed.), Guenther Roth and Claus Wittich, Vol. 1 and 2, Berkeley: University of California Press

Weisstein, Naomi (1977) 'Psychology Constructs the Female' in English ed., *Sex Equality* New Jersey: Englewood Cliffs

Weston, Anthony (1984) 'Toward the Reconstruction of Subjectivism: Love as a Paradigm of Values', *The Journal of Value Inquiry*, Vol. 18, No. 3, pp. 181–194

Whitbeck, Caroline (1976) 'Theories of Sex Difference' in Gould and Wartofsky (eds) *Woman and Philosophy* New York: G.P. Putnam's Sons

—— (1984) 'A Different Reality: Feminist Ontology' in Gould (ed.) *Beyond Domination* New Jersey: Rowman and Allanheld

Wiener, Ron (1980) *The Rape and Plunder of the Shankill, Community Action: the Belfast Experience*, Belfast: Farset Co-operative Press Ltd.

Williams, J. and Giles, H. (1978) 'The Changing Status of Women in Society: an intergroup perspective', in H. Tajfel (ed.) *Differentiation between Social Groups* New York: Academic Press

Wilson, Edward O. (1975) *Sociobiology: The New Synthesis* Cambridge Mass: The Belknap Press of Harvard University Press

Wilson, R.W. and Schochet, G.J. (eds) (1980) *Moral Development and Politics* New York: Praeger

Wolff, Robert Paul (1968) *The Poverty of Liberalism* Boston: Beacon Press

Wolin, Sheldon (1972) 'Political Theory as a Vocation' in M. Fleisher (ed.) *Machiavelli and the Nature of Political Thought* New York: Atheneum

Wollstonecraft, Mary (1967) *A Vindication of the Rights of Woman*, (ed.) Charles W. Hagelman, Jr. New York: N.W. Norton and Co.

Wyatt, Jean (1986) 'Avoiding Self-Definition: In defense of Women's right to merge', *Women's Studies*, Vol. 13, pp. 115–126

Yeatman, Anna (1984) 'Despotism and Civil Society: The Limits of Patriarchal Citizenship' in Stiehm (ed.) *Women's Views of the Political World of Men* New York: Transnational Publishers, Inc.

Young-Bruehl, Elisabeth (1987) 'The Education of Women as Philosophers', *Signs*, Vol. 12, No. 2, pp. 207–221

Zahaykevich, M.K. (1982) *A Study of the Psychological Development of Soviet Human Rights Activists*, unpub. Ph.D. thesis, Teachers College, Columbia University.

Index

opportunity, 4, 60, 126–7, 129,
187–9, right to combat, 187–92;
rights, 126–7
equality, 2, 4, 29, 38, 137, 187–92;
liberal, 132–6
Erikson, Lois V., 152
ethics, 17, 18, 19, 114, 115, 130
exclusion of women, 6, 30–1, 96,
188
exclusivity, female, x, 14
experience: dialogue and, 44–6;
female, 34, 39–43, 63, 155–7;
identity and, 33
expressivism, 30, 41–2

family, 71–2, 103–4, 132, 133,
136, 137, 138
father–child relationship, 79–80,
151
Feinberg, Joel, 18
femaleness, 35, 37–9, 84, 93; and
maleness, 26–8, 29–30
femininity, xiii, 9, 26, 31, 35, 41,
60, 62, 63, 75, 84, 108, 150–1,
188, 195
feminism: and difference, 59–64,
see also difference, 59–64; and
individualism, 120; liberal, xi,
11–12, 38, 121, 131–41;
Marxist, 12; metaphysical, 9, 64;
and nature, 72–3; and peace
movements, 176–8; and
philosophy, chapter 1; radical, 3,
12; and sexual identity concepts,
34; socialist, 67
feminism, eco-, 81–3, 178–83
feminist: epistemology, 13, *see also*
epistemology; ontology, 13, *see
also* ontology; perspective vs
feminist standpoint, 9–11; views
of woman and nature, 73–8
feminists: male, 45; men and, 45
femocrats, 52
Ferguson, Ann, 60
Feuerbach, Ludwig, 58
Feyerabend, Paul, 98
Firestone, Shulamith, 2, 8, 34
Fishman, Joshua A., 44
Flanagan, Owen J., 146, 147, 165
Flax, Jane, 65, 67, 90, 96, 102, 106,
116, 151
Foot, Philippa, 197

formalism and contextualism,
147–9
Foucault, Michel, 15
Frankfurt School, 77, 80, 116–17,
117
Franzway, Suzanne, 52
freedom, 116–17, 128
Freud, Sigmund, 152
Friedan, Marilyn, 105
Fyre, Marilyn, 197

Gadamer, Hans-Georg, 11, 98–9,
114
Gandhi, Mahatma, 182
Gatens, Moira, 3
Gearhart, Sally Miller, 42, 176–7
gendered identities, 108–9
Gibson, Mary, 128–9
Giles, J., 8
Gilligan, Carol, xii, 106, 142–3,
150–70, 194
Glass, James, 61
Glennon, Lynda M., 26, 28, 47, 49,
50, 52
God, 48, 50, 52, 55, 103
goddess, woman as, 74
Goertzel, T.G., 173
Goldberg, Steven, 69
Golder, Nerolie, 60
goodness: feminine, 70–2, 142,
153; the nature of, 18–21, 85–6,
92
goods, basic, 19
Gould, Carol, 4, 22, 24, 63, 89, 96,
114, 115, 131, 169
Greek concept of reason, 92, 93–4,
97, 98
Green, Karen, 135, 136
Green, T.H., 120
Greer, Germaine, 72, 105
Griffin, Susan, 34, 45, 73–5
Grigson, Geoffrey, 74
Gross, Elizabeth, 4, 6, 14, 15, 46, 49
Grundberg, Sibyl, 38
gynocentrism, x, 34–46

Habermas, Jürgen, 22, 44, 130–1,
146–7, 157
Hampshire, Stuart, 156
Haraway, Donna, 69
Harding, Sandra, 8, 9, 11, 15, 68,
70, 79, 86, 108, 151, 166